Meatpackers and Beef Barons

Meatpackers
and Beef Barons

COMPANY TOWN IN A GLOBAL ECONOMY

Carol Andreas

UNIVERSITY PRESS OF COLORADO

Copyright © 1994 by Carol Andreas

Published by the University Press of Colorado, P.O. Box 849, Niwot, Colorado 80544

The University Press of Colorado is a cooperative publishing enterprise supported, in part, by Adams State College, Colorado State University, Fort Lewis College, Mesa State College, Metropolitan State College of Denver, University of Colorado, University of Northern Colorado, University of Southern Colorado, and Western State College of Colorado.

Library of Congress Cataloging-in-Publication Data

Andreas, Carol.
    Meatpackers and beef barons: company town in a global economy / Carol Andreas.
        p.   cm.
    Includes bibliographical references (p.   ) and index.
    ISBN 0-87081-321-8 (alk. paper). — ISBN 0-87081-322-6 (pbk.: alk. paper)
    1. Packing-house workers — Colorado — Greeley.   2. Trade-unions — Packing-house workers — Colorado — Greeley.   3. Packing-houses — Colorado — Greeley.   4. Beef industry — Colorado — Greeley.   5. ConAgra, inc.   I. Title.
HD8039.P152U52 1994
331.88'1649'009788872 — dc20   93-44445
                                                                                                                              CIP

The paper used in this publication meets the minimum requirements of the American National Standard for Information Sciences—Permanence of Paper for Printed Library Materials. ANSI Z39.48–1984

∞

10 9 8 7 6 5 4 3 2 1

Contents

Preface   vii

Introduction: "Easy money!"   1
1. Immigrants Then and Now   9
2. The Making of a Modern-Day Company Town   31
3. Breaking the Union   59
4. Standing Together, Body and Soul   83
5. The 1990s: "You're paid to work, not to think"   109
6. Lessons from a Century of Struggle   133
Epilogue   155

Appendix A   171
Appendix B   185
Notes   191
References   211
Index   217

Preface

We are living in a time when the goal of policy-makers worldwide is to adapt national economies to a world economy dominated by industrial capitalist interests. The first to suffer the consequences of this process have been native and colonized peoples of semi-feudal societies, known euphemistically as the Third World. Others on the periphery of capitalist development, such as working-class citizens of Eastern European countries and what was formerly the Soviet Union, are reeling under the burden of indebtedness incurred by their governments to Western banks. These governments have been weakened further by the need to discipline workers to compete in the world market.

U.S. military institutions play a preeminent role in international politics. This role influences decisions made by government officials everywhere. It does not assure, however, that U.S. workers can escape the hardships of an economic system in which labor is but one more commodity to be bought and sold on the open market. In the United States, increasing numbers of women and men are now competing for jobs with wage-workers in "free-production zones" that have been established to accommodate business enterprises in semi-colonial situations abroad. Many U.S. laborers are themselves immigrants from countries devastated by unfavorable trade relations, the usurpation and despoilation of natural resources, and the dismantling of state-run enterprises. It is projected that by the end of the twentieth century, 80 percent of the U.S. workforce will be immigrants, ethnic minorities, and women.

Transnational corporations are impelled to look for sources of cheap labor in a world labor market. They also seek access to natural resources unfettered by environmental regulations. Corporate leaders are forcing open new markets for products and demanding that production and trade relations be unencumbered by labor movements, tariffs, or other obstacles to the pursuit of profit. The demands of these corporations are constantly in conflict with the needs of workers and their families and with other residents of communities affected by corporate operations. People need stable employment in a healthy environment or access to land and water to produce the necessities of life for their own survival and well-being. Corporations are increasingly a threat to the realization of these basic needs.

Nowhere are the contradictions between the requirements of business and the needs of workers and consumers more evident than in the production of meat. Meat processing is the fourth largest manufacturing industry in the United States. One-third of North American land is used for the grazing of cattle. More than half of the potable water consumed in the United States is used for livestock production, and over one-half of the cropland is devoted to the production of livestock feed.[1] In recent decades, as other U.S. businesses were becoming less competitive internationally, red meat began to grow as an international trade commodity. A decline in the consumption of red meat in the United States has been accompanied by a dramatic expansion of livestock production and trade worldwide. Beef producers, in particular, have called upon local, state, and national governments to ease the strain of competition. They press government entities to subsidize the industry by delegitimizing unions; limiting regulations protecting consumers, workers, and the environment; and providing assistance in the search for cheap labor and new markets. Companies that have been most successful in these efforts have now attained unprecedented power to control access to resources and markets. Social costs to the public are also unprecedented.

Meatpackers and Beef Barons traces the development of the meatpacking industry in Greeley, Colorado. As a case study, Greeley is particularly appropriate because modern "boxed beef"[2] processing began here as a small family business, Monfort of Colorado, and evolved into one of the most lucrative and powerful corporate entities in the world: ConAgra Red Meats, a division of ConAgra, Inc.

This book is not intended to address all the public issues that surround the production of red meat. The focus of *Meatpackers and Beef Barons* is on the restructuring of the production process in the red meat industry and that restructuring's effect on people who work in meatpacking plants and on the communities where they live.

The plight of rural communities, family farmers, and relocated workers affected by plant closures and economic recession in the U.S. heartland has received some attention in the U.S. media and in academia. Yet, little attention has been given to the impact of recent changes in the meatpacking industry on meatpackers themselves. *Meatpackers and Beef Barons* contributes to the growing literature on the social effects of economic and political crises by documenting the hardships and struggles of the workers involved. They, and the communities in which they live, are effectively held hostage by corporate domination. Understanding and addressing these issues is important not only to those who are immediately affected but to everyone who is committed to developing of grassroots democracy in our communities and workplaces.

Initial research for this book was done by a collective composed of myself (a sociologist teaching at the University of Northern Colorado [UNC] in Greeley), Viviano Torres (an employee at the Monfort slaughterhouse in Greeley), Sue Tungate (a UNC sociology graduate), Elaine Schmidt (a part-time librarian at UNC and a long-time community activist in Greeley), Lyn Yarroll (a freelance writer), and Tod Baccigalupi (a former member of the Department of Sociology at UNC who is now at Metropolitan State College in Denver). We met regularly during the 1989–1990 school year, collecting historical material from the Greeley Municipal Museum and other local sources, conducting library research on the meatpacking industry, sharing clippings from current news sources, and beginning to establish contacts among former strikers, strike leaders, workers, and ex-workers. The collective dissolved when the school year was over and several members moved away from Greeley.

Most of the interviews for *Meatpackers and Beef Barons* were carried out during the summer of 1990 and thereafter. Previously unpublished testimony is also used from a 1987 hearing held at Greeley's Our Lady of Peace Church. Robin Litman assisted with the project in July 1990 and July 1991, accompanying me on out-of-town interviews and editing early versions of the manuscript. George Villa and Secundino (Sal) Salazar, both former slaughterhouse employees, were helpful in making contacts with workers, as were a number of students in my classes. We also received valuable information from local union organizers and interviewed officials of the United Food and Commercial Workers union (UFCW) who came to Greeley from Denver and elsewhere. We kept in touch with the Denver-based Work Injured Citizens of Colorado and participated in *Al Frente de Lucha* (at the forefront of the struggle), a Greeley-based community organization that began publishing testimony from Monfort workers in 1990.

We received testimony from nearly one hundred people, most of whom were or had been line workers at the beef slaughterhouse or at the Portion Foods plant in Greeley. The Chinook Fund Boulder/Denver provided funding for the transcription of taped interviews and for travel and copying expenses. Because several previous efforts to conduct research or to write about the Monfort company have elicited hostility or threats against those involved, we conducted our research without publicity and asked participants to keep our conversations confidential. (Employees of Monfort were told that their identity would not be revealed publicly until the manuscript went to press. The opening story in the book's introduction is a composite.)

When enough information had been compiled to begin writing, I solicited comments and assistance from colleagues. They put me in touch with people in Kansas, Nebraska, Iowa, and Missouri who were also engaged in researching meatpacking and meatpackers. Some of us met for the first time at the Midwest Sociological Society meetings in April 1991, where we shared information and ideas at a panel on "Agroindustries' New Homes: The Incorporation of Rural and International Communities into the Changing World Economy." Since then our networking has extended to other states. I owe a great deal to these colleagues, whose contributions are cited throughout this book. I am also grateful to the editors of the University Press of Colorado for their interest in this manuscript, and to the staff of the press for their able assistance in the process of publication.

In addition to those already mentioned, I would like to thank my sons, Joel, Ronald, and Peter, for helpful comments on the manuscript at different stages of production. I would also like to thank UNC professor Ann Garrison, on whom I relied for statistical information about Weld County's economy; Barbara Armour and Marc Major, UNC students who provided encouragement and assistance in the spring and summer of 1991; Mary Virnoche (currently a graduate student at the University of Colorado); David Cole (chair, Department of Geography at UNC); David Musick (chair, Department of Sociology at UNC); and other colleagues who made suggestions or helped in editing the manuscript. The final outcome is, of course, my own responsibility.

I would particularly like to thank Monfort workers who trusted me by freely sharing their experiences. This project most likely would never have been undertaken without the encouragement of Viviano Torres. His travails as a meatpacker made my attention to the subject unavoidable, because we were housemates when both of us were recent immigrants to Greeley. Finally, the project may never have been completed without the moral support of Ruby Dickenson, meat inspector at the Monfort lamb plant — my neighbor and valued friend — who retired as this book was nearing completion.

Because of my close association with Monfort workers, I make no claim to neutrality. We learn most about the world when we try to change it. This book is part of that effort. *Meatpackers and Beef Barons* is not intended as an indictment against individuals but rather as an indictment against a social system that degrades us all as exploiters and exploited. Readers may ask why we did not interview Monfort officials in the process of doing research for this book. We had no difficulty obtaining company publications, government documents, and business reports in which the views of Monfort officials were made clear. In addition, Ken Monfort wrote a regular newspaper column during the period when our research was being conducted. In the column, he freely repudiated everyone who dared to criticize the company. Given the magnitude of corporate intrigue exposed in our research, we felt that we needed to maintain anonymity as much as possible. On the one occasion when we did tour the Monfort beef slaughterhouse in Greeley, we were given dubious information about company policy. (We were told, among other things, that workers get a 15-minute break every 2½ hours, which workers say is not true.) On completion of our research, we requested an interview with Ken and Myra Monfort and were refused.

Certainly, the research for this book is not exhaustive. We regard our work as a necessary beginning. We have protected ourselves and the integrity of this book by using information that is documented. We have neither focused on the worst cases nor have we investigated or commented on reports about the personal conduct of members of the Monfort/ConAgra administration. Many such reports came to our attention once our research efforts became known in the Greeley community. Workers' testimony about their own situations, published accounts of company activity, participant observation in the Greeley community, and historical and background information from outside sources have given us a rich and diverse collection of material on which to base this initial analysis of meatpackers and beef barons in the late twentieth century. We hope that readers will take courage from our efforts and support workers in their struggles, speaking and acting in defense of grassroots democracy in community and society.

Carol Andreas

Meatpackers and Beef Barons

Introduction

"Easy money!"

When Lupe crossed the Mexican border into the United States for the third time, she brought her four children with her. She was determined to establish a home together with their father, Feliciano, who had been promised work in a meatpacking plant in Colorado. The couple had previously worked the fields in Texas, either separately or together, usually leaving children behind with relatives. They had tried to bring all the children to the United States once before but had been stopped by the Border Patrol. Patrol officers kept them for days without food or water and never returned their car.

This time Lupe and Feliciano traveled in a more presentable car, hoping to escape suspicion, and they hid the children carefully among the clothes piled in back. As the afternoon sun bore down, the children stuck their heads up out of the clothes like birds in a nest. They remained silent as they peered out the windows, avoiding attention. When conversation waned in the front seat, they dived down under the clothes, hoping to avoid the expected reprimand.

As they approached the Colorado border, the family was high-spirited and looking forward to a new life, free of the insecurity and oppression of the migrant camp. Lupe was in a forgiving spirit toward Feliciano, who had complicated their already difficult lives by fathering a child with a woman in Texas while Lupe was in Mexico. For a time Feliciano had barely communicated with his family and had even been jailed for getting in a bar fight. Now he was not drinking at all and seemed almost grateful to Lupe for giving him another chance to prove that he was a devoted husband and father.

Six months after moving to Colorado, both Lupe and Feliciano were working with several thousand other meatpackers, most of them immigrants like themselves. During the day, Feliciano was trimming fat off slabs of meat that approached his table on a conveyor belt at the rate of nearly four hundred per hour. The table was arranged to accommodate fifty workers standing close together. But many times there were absences or new workers who couldn't keep up with the pace of the line. Meat would pile up, and people would yell angrily at each other. As lunchtime approached and there were fewer heavy carcasses moving along toward the trimming area, the speed of the line would increase. Meat would pile up so much that everyone was dizzy with tension, but they were happy, too, because lunchtime would provide a short respite from the sweat, cold, and noise of the factory line. Then someone would break the tension and grin at the others, yelling above the din, "Easy money!" Feliciano would laugh uneasily as he laid down his knife and headed for the bathroom.

Lupe worked the evening shift. By the time she got home, it was usually 1 a.m. She tried not to wake the children or Feliciano, but it was hard to get to sleep after 8 hours of grueling work, standing in a pool of grease and blood, doing the same thing thousands of times over. While she was working, she was so numbed by the effort to keep going that she hardly noticed that her muscles and nerves were sore. But once in bed, she couldn't find a comfortable position for sleeping. Her shoulder was developing a sharp pain from hooking the meat all day long with her left hand. Her back felt like it could crack at any minute. She couldn't close her hand, but she forced each finger, trying to bend it to see just how much movement she had lost, hoping to regain some flexibility. She also rubbed finger joints where callouses were developing. She used to help Feliciano do this, before she started working herself. She would comfort him when he woke up in a panic because his fingers had lost all feeling. No one had told Feliciano what to expect, and they both had been afraid that he would be disabled for life after working only a month in the plant. She knew that some of her aches and pains might get better if she could figure out how to sharpen the knives properly and exert just the right amount of effort when cutting the meat.

What frustrated Lupe most about work was the attitude of her supervisor. He walked along behind the tables and threatened workers with "pink slips" if they wasted any meat while cutting, or if they didn't move fast enough. If her supervisor was feeling brash, and thought she looked dour, he would lean over and whisper loudly in her ear: "Easy money!"

At the turn of the century Upton Sinclair wrote *The Jungle* — a classic novel about slaughterhouse workers in Chicago. At that time, thousands of Polish and other East European immigrants were crossing the ocean to pursue a dream. The dream vanished before them as they painfully discovered that, even in the vast American frontier, "the poor man was almost as poor as in any other corner of the earth."[1] Disease and despair haunted immigrants' lives. But through their efforts, and the efforts of black and other immigrant workers who replaced them, meatpackers were eventually guaranteed a living family wage, minimal health and safety for themselves and their families, security in old age, and a measure of respect and dignity.

Over the years, beef production came to outrank all other sections of the food industry in the United States in total assets and sales. Today packinghouses are located away from cities like Chicago. In modern plants surrounded by immense feedlots, cattle are fattened for ninety days and then are killed and cut up in fast-paced "disassembly lines." Boxed beef is shipped around the country in refrigerated trucks or across the globe by air or sea. The new immigrant workers are from Mexico, Southeast Asia, and Central and South America. Like their predecessors, they find that the reality of life in the United States falls far short of the dream. Whereas earlier immigrants were disabled by infectious diseases and blood poisoning — as described by Upton Sinclair nearly a century ago — the new meatpackers suffer injuries to their muscles, nerves, and bones caused by a kind of physical and psychological stress never before imaginable.

During the 1980s, the brown and tan faces of new immigrants replaced those of white males in most U.S. packinghouses. Women often outnumbered men as meat trimmers. Output per worker more than doubled, as wages were cut by nearly half. Injuries and illnesses soared along with increases in the speed of production. During much of the 1980s, government statistics revealed that accidents and injuries among meatpackers surpassed those of workers in any other occupation.

Some workers today make as many as ten thousand knife cuts during an 8-hour shift, frantically hooking and cutting up meat on a moving conveyor belt. Often knives are dull and meat is nearly frozen. Trimmers are protected by hard hats and metal mesh aprons, gloves, and arm guards, but it's still easy to cut or stab oneself or to be cut accidentally by someone else. Workers are always in danger of slipping on wet, greasy floors. The noise level from machinery is ear-splitting. Noxious odors fill the air. Line workers sweat from constant movement yet are chilled by cold temperatures maintained in processing areas.

A young Mexican American woman named Rosa Morado worked five years as a meat trimmer at the Monfort beef-packing plant in Greeley, Colorado. She suffered numerous injuries to her arms and hands, which are scarred from several operations. In the summer of 1990, she gave us a description of what her job was like:

> You have to hook your meat and cut one part out. You have to trim it down to specs. . . . The first part has to have so much fat on it, can't have scores in it, can't have blood bruises on it. Then you turn it around and there's another piece where you have to pull a skin off it and you cut that piece off and then it's a longer piece, like this. Can't have scores in it, can only have so much percent fat around on it. Can't have gristle on it. Can't have tissue on the back of it. So if you know how to do it, you can do it okay. Then you have to cut another piece. Your hook is constantly in your other hand and you cut another piece off, a piece they use for hamburger. Then we turn it, and there's a big piece of fat they call a comb fat. You got to roll that off. They want that rolled off because if you cut it off you usually get lean on it and you're overtrimming. Then the last piece you have, you are left with a big chunk of fat and there's another piece of meat you got to cut out and we got to trim that all the way off around on the back to certain specs, turning it around. We have to show lean on it and make sure there's no fat on the belly of it and no gristle.

All of what Morado described was accomplished in 45 seconds with a line speed of at least 365 head of cattle an hour and with nine people assigned to the job. On vacation days, she said, "I practically had to stand on my hand to straighten it out, it was cramped up so bad." Morado was unusually long-suffering. An estimated fifty to sixty people quit, were injured, terminated, or replaced each week at the packing plant where she worked.[2]

When I first came to Greeley, which is located north of Denver on the way to Cheyenne, Wyoming, the odor from the dog food plant where packinghouse by-products are rendered was described to me as "the sweet smell of success." It was not mentioned that people die from falling into the Monfort company's meat blenders or that local medical facilities must accommodate a constant flow of workers suffering from illnesses and injuries contracted on the job. Over time I came to realize that life behind the doors of the slaughterhouse, which is located north of town, is of little interest to most of Greeley's more than sixty thousand residents.

Many people who see slaughterhouse workers' lives only from the outside believe that the workers — most of whom are Mexican or Hispanic — should go back "home" if they don't like working conditions. They find it uncomfortable to acknowledge that Native Americans and Spanish have been in the Southwest longer than their own ancestors. Furthermore, most of those who are now arriving in the United States to work in meatpacking plants cannot return to their homelands. Many have lost or sold land and possessions before emigrating. Often the survival of family members in their homeland depends on the money that they earn in U.S. meatpacking plants.

An unsympathetic community is only part of the problem hindering change. The union at the Monfort slaughterhouse was broken in 1980 when the plant was temporarily closed down. Since the plant reopened in 1982, the threat of a new closure, or the threat of arbitrary dismissal, has kept workers subordinated to management goals of increased production and decreased cost. Besides drastically reduced wages, many work benefits have disappeared. But company profits are at an all-time high.[3]

In 1987, the Monfort company merged with ConAgra, Inc., which originated in partnership with another Greeley-based business. Before the Monfort/ConAgra merger, ConAgra had also purchased beef slaughter facilities that belonged to Armour, Swift, and other companies that survived both the trust-busting era of the

early 1900s and the Great Depression. Eight plants are now part of
Monfort, and ConAgra is the largest meat-processing conglomerate
in the United States. Well over a thousand small meatpackers have
been forced out of business[4] as ConAgra, Iowa Beef Processors
(IBP), and Excel (a subsidiary of Cargill) have come to control 75 to
80 percent of all beef sales.[5] ConAgra has also gained near hegemony in hog, lamb, poultry, and seafood production and is rapidly
expanding and diversifying overseas markets and operations.

In April 1991, Monfort, Inc., released figures that revealed an
injury rate at its home plant in Greeley that was two and one-half
times the industry norm (more than four times the rate for private
industry as a whole).[6] Until it was forced by a lawsuit to reveal its
injury record, the company had been able to convince the public
that Monfort was a pioneer in plant safety. (See Chapter 5 for more
information on this case.)

Despite the fact that the startling information was published
in the local newspaper, there was little reaction from the community. The conveyor belts ran as usual. Nothing changed. Subsequent
callers to the newspaper's editorial office, reporting on specific
events affecting workers' health and safety, were told that the
subject had already been covered. A letter to the editor chastised
the newspaper for paying attention to people who badmouth the
company they work for but who "sure don't miss a trip to the bank
with their paycheck."[7] Because the plant had closed down for
several years in the early 1980s, townspeople feared that attention
to health and safety problems would cause another plant closure,
destroying the base of the local economy.

As small-town residents are held hostage by ever-more-pow-
erful corporations, the concentration of money and power in the
hands of large conglomerates is encouraged by many legislators and
government officials who see deregulation as a way of making the
United States more competitive internationally — or who have a
personal stake in the growth of giant corporations and banks. Farm
business owners and others who believe that they have been
cheated during this process have begun to seek recourse through
legislation and the court system. Consumers have begun to organize against unhealthy products. Environmentalists seek new regulations to protect natural resources — water, air, and land.

Public money that could be used for housing, education, and recreation is used instead for expanding of jails, prisons, and hospitals. Churches and other institutions that are expected to provide facilities and services for industry and social services for the working poor have begun to question the legitimacy of corporate control of community life. Nevertheless, when workers themselves begin defending their right to dignity in the workplace, they are vilified, sometimes even by union officials who are convinced that worker militancy must give way to "realism."

Current conditions are hostile to collective efforts to act against the exploitation and subjugation of workers. Employers argue that individuals who work at Monfort, or anywhere else in the United States, choose to do so freely. Few workers have knowledge about union struggles waged earlier in meatpacking plants. Many feel isolated from political processes in their communities. It sometimes appears that they have consented to their own exploitation and subjugation. Yet, they are in fact the ones most capable of changing the conditions under which they work.

In this book the voices of workers, women and men, will be heard. As they describe their experiences and express their anxieties and hopes, their thoughts will also be placed in the context of an historical process that has brought enormous profit to their employers and enormous disappointment to themselves. Companies that employ immigrants say that such workers are better off than ever and are participating in the Great American Dream, regardless of the sacrifices expected of them. All this is true. Perhaps justice has all too rarely been part of the American Dream. Yet in the light of a so-called New World Order in which corporate expansion is to be given free reign everywhere — regardless of cost — it is more urgent than ever that we redefine the dream.

Although this book is a case study, not a novel, it is inspired by outrage comparable to the rage that impelled Upton Sinclair to write *The Jungle*. This book is based largely on interviews and conversations with Monfort workers in Greeley and on published reports and documents related to company operations and policies.

But it is also a polemic that questions the effectiveness of "politics as usual," including modern-day unions and electoral processes.

Chapter 1 gives a brief history of Greeley and Weld County from the point of view of immigrant workers who were recruited to labor in northeastern Colorado's sugar beet industry in the 1920s and 1930s, and whose ranks swelled with the restructuring of the meatpacking industry in the 1980s.

Chapter 2 tells of the growth of the Monfort family businesses from the Great Depression to the present. Special attention is given to local politics, long dominated by Ken Monfort, who retired as president of Monfort, Inc., shortly after the merger with ConAgra.

Chapter 3 focuses on "efficiency efforts" undertaken by the company in the face of declining red meat consumption, union responses, and increasing concentration of power in the red meat industry. Former workers testify about the strike of 1979–1980, the plant closure, and its aftermath. A former union leader assesses what he learned from a decade of experience as a meatpacker and organizer.

Chapter 4 includes testimony from Monfort workers and from a union representative, especially before and during a 1987–1988 strike at Greeley's Portion Foods plant, where a large majority of employees are female. The chapter discusses the activities of a professional union buster who first came to Greeley in 1983, when union elections were held at the beef slaughterhouse. He was brought back in 1987 to completely destroy the union at the specialty plant and to oversee establishment of a two-tiered employment strategy at a newly constructed lamb facility.

Chapter 5 describes working conditions at Greeley's Monfort/ConAgra beef slaughterhouse in the early 1990s and explains why government efforts to protect workers exposed to one of the most hazardous occupations in the country have not succeeded. Company influence in state, national, and international politics is examined.

Chapter 6 discusses public alarm over the effects of the concentration of power in the red meat industry, the history of meatpackers' organizing efforts nationwide, and the prospects for grassroots coalition building and international worker solidarity in the context of today's global marketplace.

In the early 1800s, fur traders and scouts intermarried with the Cheyenne and Arapahoes who populated the barren plains and hills of what is now northeastern Colorado. During the gold rush of 1859, many native people died of cholera and other diseases introduced by Europeans. Buffalo herds were disappearing as their valuable tongues and skins were shipped down the South Platte River to Saint Louis, Missouri.

At the urging of European settlers, the Territory of Colorado was established in 1861. Cattle ranchers soon replaced prospectors, scouts, and traders. "The first big problem of Colorado cattlemen was to secure the removal of the red men," wrote historian Ora Brookes Peake in 1937.[1] Destruction of the buffalo was crucial in securing the dominance of farmers and ranchers who came from the East. Native Americans resisted the takeover of buffalo ranges by settlers, waging fierce battles between 1864 and 1869; natives who survived were eventually forced to live on reservations. Colorado gained statehood in 1876, thus making "legal" the occupation of the region by fortune-seekers and others who came to dominate economic life.

The coming of the railroad in 1869 opened the way for expanded settlement by Europeans. That same year, Horace Greeley published a proposal in the *New York Tribune* for a western utopia. The proposal was written by the newspaper's agricultural reporter, Nathan Meeker. A bust of Meeker stands outside Meeker House in Greeley today, bearing the following inscription: "I propose to unite with the proper persons in the establishment of a colony in Colorado territory. . . . The Persons with whom I would be willing to associate must be temperance men and ambitious to establish a good society." Meeker subsequently led seven hundred settlers, many from New York, to establish the Union Colony, which later became the town of Greeley. A year after settlement, the first edition of the *Greeley Tribune*, dated November 16, 1870, carried the following statement: "Individuals may rise or fall, may live or die, property may be lost or gained. But the Colony as a whole will prosper, and the spot on which we labor shall, as long as the world stands, be the center of intelligence and activity."

Most of the original inhabitants of Greeley had money and technical skills but little agricultural experience. They learned agricultural skills from earlier residents of the region. They planted trees, fought off grasshoppers, and raised potatoes and a few other fruits and vegetables. Some also raised cattle and chickens, although domestic animals were always in danger of dying during harsh winters. After a heavy blizzard killed many cattle in 1886–1887, farmers began protecting animals in feedlots. German colonists from Russia joined earlier immigrants at the turn of the century and prospered alongside the others. Some of the farmers recruited Japanese workers, who eventually were able to save enough money to establish their own farms and businesses.

By World War I the sugar beet industry overtook other agricultural enterprises. The value of land had increased, while wages had not, so workers could no longer become farm owners. After the war, times were hard everywhere. With the help of the federal government, the Union Pacific Railroad and the Great Western Sugar Company acquired much of the land. They looked for a source of cheap labor and found it in New Mexico.

Before the First World War, communal lands of New Mexican Spanish communities were already being undermined by commercial farming and homesteading by Texas and Oklahoma immigrants. The postwar depression and a terrible drought brought hardship and poverty to once flourishing Spanish-speaking communities.

Secundino (Sal) Salazar is a descendant of sugar beet workers who migrated to Weld County from New Mexico in 1927. As a young man, he and his wife, Maria, worked in the beet fields to support themselves and their children. He later worked as a janitor and meatpacker in the Monfort slaughterhouse. In 1990, Salazar wrote of the 1920s and 1930s in New Mexico, as described to him by his parents and other relatives:

> Once fertile fields where cattle and sheep could graze were now dry and parched. No rain came from the skies, no water flowed in the rivers. Gardens and farming opportunities disappeared. Farm animals were dying. Other employment was unheard of. In these

Spanish speaking communities throughout the state of New Mexico, once prosperous people were now losing their land and all the benefits derived from it.[2]

The Great Western Sugar Company and the Union Pacific Railroad recruited workers by stopping alongside the railroad tracks in New Mexican communities, blaring out to the people with bullhorns that there was plenty of work in the fields of Colorado. New Mexicans were also told that housing was available in Colorado, but in fact the houses had to be built by the workers. Salazar explained:

> They brought, from New Mexico, advance parties who proceeded to build thirteen colonies in Weld County. Mostly, all the "colonias" were built outside existing city limits. . . . What they did was identify those who had skills in building adobe homes. The walls of these adobe homes were 12 inches thick, making them cool in the summer and warm in the winter. They had no cold or hot running water. Wells and cisterns provided the needed water. Heat to cook and warm the homes was done by wood burning stoves and heaters. To have light at night, lanterns filled with kerosene would be lit. The layout of the adobe houses were in rows, with irrigation ditches alongside the roads and alleyways. . . . The deeds and lists for the property in the colonias were owned by the Great Western Sugar Company.

Soon these *colonias* were filled to capacity, yet recruitment of workers continued on both sides of the U.S.–Mexican border. Farmers began to build farm labor housing close to their fields. Those immigrants who located on farms did not have the same opportunity as did those who lived in the *colonias* to establish communities similar to those they had left behind. "Some families found good well-meaning farmers to work for," Salazar recalled, "but many others were exploited by the mostly Anglo farmers of those times. Wages were very low. . . . During the summer and harvest months all of the family would work in the fields together. Sugar beets were the main crops, and all the work was stoop labor."

In the winter, work opportunities were bleak. Families fed and raised chickens, pigs, sheep, and cattle in small pens behind their houses. They built earthen cellars to store food. Children were transported far from home to school. "Knowing only the Spanish language," said Salazar, our people were not readily accepted. They were treated as lesser beings, and were told not to speak Spanish. Their dark brown skin was seen as ugly and dirty. They were taunted and called dirty Mexicans. They were looked upon as those who would fail in school. After all, they were brought here only to work in the fields. . . . In town there were signs in windows that said "No dogs, cats or Mexicans allowed."

Anglo farmers and workers also experienced hard times at the hands of the big companies that were expanding their operations everywhere. Tensions found an outlet in racism, which became intense. Masked night riders would enter the *colonias* and burn crosses, shouting "Mexicans, go back to Mexico!" All Spanish-speaking people were considered aliens. One night, in 1936, a huge banner appeared in Greeley's Spanish Colony: "All Mexicans and all other aliens to leave the State of Colorado at once by order of Colorado State vigilantes."[3]

Townspeople were so fearful of "contamination" from Spanish-speaking people that the Great Western Sugar Company made blood tests for contagious diseases requisite for occupying houses. Blood samples were sent to Washington, D.C., and, according to a newspaper reporter, "all the tests came back negative" and "things settled down a little bit after that."[4]

Most Spanish-speaking immigrants to Colorado were hired as seasonal farm laborers, but some were also working as maintenance workers on the railroads or as coal miners. Working conditions were dangerous and hours were long. The American Federation of Labor (AFL) opposed the importation of Mexican workers and did not attempt to organize them. In Weld County, workers in the Rocky Mountain Fuel Company's Columbine Mine were organized by the "Wobblies," the Industrial Workers of the World (IWW). After a successful strike in 1927–1928, coal miners, many of whom worked part-time in the beet fields, reached out to organize beetworkers as well. Organizations such as the *Liga Obrera de Hable Espanola* (Spanish-speaking Workers' League) had little success in direct negotiations with employers but served as advocacy and pressure groups on behalf of beetworkers. Eventually, the AFL took up the cause of farmworkers alongside the IWW and its affiliates. Striking workers were red-baited or accused of subversion, and violently repressed by police. Miners' wives often replaced their husbands on picket lines and addressed workers' rallies. Unemployed miners were blacklisted from other work. Mexicans who applied for relief were met with discrimination and hostility.

The Border Patrol was established in 1924 by the federal government to restrict immigration from Mexico. In 1935 the governor of Colorado, Edwin C. Johnson, declared martial law along Colorado's southern border to keep Mexicans and U.S. citizens of Spanish descent out of the state. But as Anglo miners who replaced them continued organizing, Mexicans were brought back in. Local beet growers petitioned Congress to retain unrestricted Mexican immigration while at the same time protesting the "invasion" of rural communities by Mexican families.[5]

During the depression years, Mexicans could not buy land and few could find regular employment on Anglo farms. Yet, they survived because they had close family units. Secundino Salazar explained how people gained strength from their families and communities:

> In their communities, there was respect, love and honor to be who you were. You had to go out into that other world and suffer, but you always had your community to come back to. They found ways to cope with a hostile Anglo world. They refused to send their children to school so as to protect them from racism and discrimination. They dealt with their own problems within their communities, but they also shared the joys of life with each other. Our grandfathers and grandmothers would gather in large groups and share history and their own life experiences. They held their celebrations in local households and prayed their religion together in the open, or in the house with the most space. Small stores sold pop for a nickel, and a candy bar for two cents. Health care was provided by women in the barrio.[6]

Although the number of sugar beet farms declined during the depression, production remained steady. Income for the companies actually increased because they used imported labor. The seventeen sugar beet factories operated by the Great Western Sugar Company in northeastern Colorado prospered. In order to improve their living conditions, Mexican women and men established mutual aid societies (*mutualistas*) and a Spanish American Citizens Association. They lobbied for better housing and for wage regulation and filed lawsuits to protect Mexicans as a group from public discrimination.

Minimum wage rates for beetworkers were set by the Jones-Costigan Act in 1934; however, there was no effective enforcement of it. When growers introduced mechanical weeders, they paid less than minimum wage to those who followed behind the weeders on the pretext that the work was easier. Even though some employers showed paternalism toward workers by giving them access to the fields for gleaning after harvest or by supplying them with milk products from dairy herds, workers still were considered outsiders and inferiors. The perpetuation of racism worked to the advantage of farm owners and other employers because it provided a justification for the exploitation of workers and created ethnic antagonism among the workers so that resistance to exploitation was more difficult.

When World War II began, many young Mexican American men volunteered or were drafted into the armed forces. Secundino Salazar said:

> Young Mexican American males now were being recognized and needed to fight a war. The few newspapers and radio which reached the barrios and colonias were beating a heavy patriotic theme. People would gather around car radios listening. Whereas before all Spanish speaking people had been called Mexicans, now they were being called Mexican Americans. . . . In the colonias, isolated by distance and the Union Pacific Railroad tracks, the people rejoiced about being recognized. They were now needed by the outside Anglo world. . . . So many men went to war that many communities were left with only women, young children and seniors. Thousands died or were injured in far away countries, while back home the families lived in poverty. During the summer families would toil in the agricultural fields of Weld County. In the winter, when there was no work available, they would survive on beans, potatoes and tortillas.[7]

Defense industries generally did not welcome Mexican American women, but some found jobs in garment shops or worked in Anglo homes as domestics.[8]

All over Weld County, prisoner of war camps began to appear. Housing for German prisoners had hot and cold running water, which were unaffordable luxuries for people in Mexican American communities. Japanese Americans were relocated from the West

Coast to concentration camps in the Midwest. By the time the war ended, many people found that their homes and land had been stolen or confiscated. Some stayed in northern Colorado and established family farms.

Beginning in 1943, Colorado farmers had the help of the U.S. government in recruiting farm laborers directly from Mexico as part of the *bracero* program.[9] The program was established primarily to alleviate a farm labor shortage caused by the military draft and the growth of the defense industry. Young men came from all over Mexico to recruitment centers. From there the sugar beet company would transport them to the border. Before entering the United States, both the men and their luggage would be sprayed with DDT "as a sanitary measure and to prevent insects from being brought into the United States."[10] Researchers from Colorado State University reported: "Growers found that Nationals were ready and willing workers without a predilection to haggle over wage rates, field conditions, or the manner in which the work should be done. But growers were faced with some additional problems such as meeting housing requirements and supplying such everyday items as bedding, cooking utensils, and toilet articles."[11]

A different way of putting it might be to say that *braceros,* who composed nearly one-third of the farm labor in the United States at this time, could be used to stifle any attempts at labor organizing; nevertheless, migrant families who came "unregistered" were often preferred because the women worked for free as cooks and caretakers for family members who were working in the fields. In any case, different immigrant groups were used to compete with each other for jobs. This gave growers the upper hand and made it possible for them to increase their profits at the expense of the workers.

Although by law *braceros* were required to return to Mexico when sugar beet work ended for the season, some were recruited to stay on and become regular farmhands. Growers almost always took the initiative in such arrangements, because the workers had little power to negotiate. But Spanish-speaking men did begin to get jobs working in animal feedlots or transporting animals to market. Migrant families from Texas and others who came to Colorado annually to work in thinning and weeding operations in the beet fields from May through August provided a source of recruits for a growing cattle-feeding business in the Greeley area.

Joaquina and Pedro Rodriguez and their ten children first came to Colorado in 1958, recruited as summer workers by the Great Western Sugar Company. Pedro was a Mexican national and had been working mostly in canneries in Texas. Joaquina had been born in Texas, as were all their children. In Colorado the family was paid according to the number of acres thinned or weeded. Housing was precarious; they lived in dilapidated buildings without amenities. But the extra income made it worth their while to make the trip every summer for a number of years. Sometimes Pedro drove tractors or trucked manure to spread on the fields when the harvest was over. Then the family would head back to Texas, where they picked cotton or worked in cotton gins before returning to the canneries.

Eventually, the Rodriguez family decided to move from Texas to Colorado and were joined by other family members. In 1969, Pedro and Joaquina's brother, Tomas, started repairing fences at a Monfort family cattle feedlot. Pedro stopped working in 1976 because he was suffering from arthritis and from dizzy spells. He became a U.S. citizen at the age of sixty.

Joaquina's brother worked twenty-two years for Monfort. He fell and injured his back at work in 1989. Even though he was in great pain, the company's rehabilitation supervisor insisted that he continue working. In 1990 he had an operation, but the pain continued. Monfort medical personnel would not support his disability claims, so he was forced to continue working. In October 1991, Tomas became depressed and killed himself. Joaquina says: "I think when someone is really hurting, they ought to be left in peace and not be forced to go on working. . . . My brother was desperate because he thought if he didn't continue working, he wouldn't receive work benefits and insurance. Because of this, my brother killed himself."[12]

One of Pedro and Joaquina's ten children was seriously injured after working ten years for Monfort. He was hit by a cow while loading animals into a train. He has done occasional agricultural work since then and is currently living in an alcohol rehabilitation center in Greeley. A daughter is an office worker at the Monfort plant. A grandaughter worked briefly in the packinghouse but was fired after being absent from work for a day when one of her five children was hospitalized. The grandaughter's husband worked at the Monfort slaughterhouse for fourteen months and was fired a few weeks before he would have received an annual bonus of more than $1,000. He had signed out in advance for a four-day weekend vacation and was told upon returning that he should have reported for overtime work on Saturday. An eighteen-year-old grandson living with Pedro and Joaquina is "threatening" to work at the slaughterhouse because he is unable to find regular employment anywhere else. Joaquina's face clouds as she says: "I'm not going to let him work at Monfort, no matter what."[13]

Only a few of Joaquina's grandchildren speak Spanish. They don't want to, she says. Although Joaquina is a woman who smiles easily and tells me that I worry too much, she doesn't smile when she talks about members of the family who share many of the Anglos' prejudices about Mexico and Mexicans. Joaquina has never been to Mexico, but she is proud of her heritage.

In 1969, Joaquina responded to an article in the local newspaper inviting Chicanos to come together to organize a *Cinco de Mayo* (May 5) celebration in Greeley. Ever since that time, she has been an active member of what came to be known as *Al Frente de Lucha* (at the forefront of the struggle), which has brought cultural programs and opportunities for Chicanos and Mexicans in Greeley: improved healthcare, a recreation center, bilingual education programs, music, dance, theater, and art. In the 1970s, *Al Frente de Lucha* published a newspaper in Spanish and English and met regularly to organize demonstrations to make demands on the city.

Secundino Salazar, who is also a member of *Al Frente de Lucha*, began working at the meatpacking plant in 1966. "Sal," as he is known, first worked night shift as a cleanup man and later worked on what is called the kill floor, where animals are killed, bled, skinned, and debowelled. Several years after transferring to the fabrication section (where meat is trimmed and de-boned), he was elected chief union steward. He later left Monfort to do community service work with *La Raza Unida*, a nationally based Chicano organization, which was supported by Greeley's *Al Frente de Lucha*.

Since then he's had a hard time finding regular work. "Maria, [Sal's wife] was always concerned that I didn't have a good-paying job," he says, with a self-effacing smile, "but she never tried to get me to go back to work at Monfort." Secundino struggles constantly to help his children deal with Anglo prejudice and to maintain pride in themselves.

In 1991, Joaquina, Sal Salazar, and others began again to publish a bilingual bulletin, *Al Frente de Lucha*. They were responding to issues generated by the new influx of Mexican nationals coming to Greeley to work in a "restructured" (that is, a lower-wage, higher-speed) meatpacking industry. In the April/May edition, Joaquina wrote:

> Before 1969 neither *Cinco de Mayo* nor *Dieciseis de Septiembre* [September 16] were celebrated in Greeley. But at that time *Al Frente de Lucha*, which was known as Apostles for Justice, began celebrating these Mexican national holidays by marching to Island Grove Park, where there were speakers, music, and theater. All this was done by the people, without much money from the city. Our unity was what counted. Today the city has taken over and things are done their way. What's important is that at least young people can learn something about Mexican culture and the struggles of our people.

Joaquina was part of a Mexican and Chicano choir that sang Mexican songs at the 1991 *Cinco de Mayo* event. A play prepared by recent Mexican immigrants, depicting humorously the travails of the undocumented, did not appear on the program because a Monfort management employee was on the city's *Cinco de Mayo* committee and said that it was not suitable entertainment. One episode of the play, which was auditioned before the committee, showed how a meatpacking worker was given a job only after paying money "under the table" to an office employee; another showed the insensitivity of those who are in charge of treating workers injured on the job. Objections were raised to the play on the grounds that *Cinco de Mayo* was for "pleasure, not for politics."[14] A car show and a fashion show were the featured events of the day.

During the *Cinco de Mayo* festivities, a Greeley policeman was called on by Monfort supporters who were on the *Cinco de Mayo* committee to stop members of *Al Frente* from distributing free copies of their newsbulletin. (The newsbulletin contained a brief critique of the process involved in selecting events for the city's commercialized *Cinco de Mayo* and an article about an organizing meeting for a local chapter of a new organization, Work Injured Citizens of Colorado.)

The police officer involved was a Chicano, who was reluctant to arrest anyone himself but who, nevertheless, claimed that anything controversial would not be allowed in the park. Serious confrontation was avoided because a hailstorm intervened and everyone went home. Vivano Torres, who had been cautiously handing out bulletins to friends said that there were not many packinghouse workers at the event in any case, because, in his opinion, recent immigrants felt that the downtown park where *Cinco de Mayo* has been celebrated recently was "off limits" to them.

The group that had prepared the rejected play for presentation were immigrants from Mexico City. Some immigrants from the city are college educated, but, because of the economic recession in Mexico, they had been earning less in Mexico weekly as accountants or teachers than they could earn daily working at Monfort for $5 to $7 an hour. Even though they had no experience working in the fields in Mexico, others were topping onions for 14 hours a day and earning less than minimum wage on farms outside Greeley.

One man, whose wife suffered from an incurable disease and required a great deal of medical attention, worked both at Monfort and in the fields. He told us of a friend who had paid $800 to a "coyote"[15] in Mexico City who brought him to Colorado, promising him a job at Monfort and false documents. When they arrived, the contact person in the personnel department had been fired in the midst of a public scandal that had surfaced over the ongoing recruitment scam. The man lost his $800 and had no job.

The fee being charged locally to undocumented workers for a job and protection from discovery more than doubled during a six-month period. We were told that the fee had gone from $150 in November 1990 to $600 in March 1991 — perhaps because of the growing availability of documented workers as the impact of economic recession was felt in Colorado.[16]

At a time when Mexican peasants are being forced off their land by agribusiness expansion in Mexico and unemployment is at an all-time high in that country, Mexican nationals are facing more and more obstacles to northern migration. The migration

continues, nevertheless, enriching employers who are able to ma-
nipulate both the political process and the people who are its
victims.

In the 1980s, Greeley's population increased by seven thousand even though the industrial base of the city was not expanding
to accommodate this influx. Newly arrived Mexican nationals generally lived on the North Side of Greeley in the environs of the
Monfort slaughterhouse. Some lived in *La Colonia,* one of the
remaining colonies established by Great Western Sugar Company
in the 1920s, which continues to be identifiable as a community. A
few adobe houses are still standing but are no longer kept in repair.
An assortment of mobile homes and low-cost rentals are crowded
together where gardens used to be. A homeless shelter, Guadelupe
House, stands in front of the family store where residents can buy
imported food products from Mexico as well as candy and soft
drinks. A Pentecostal church, built in 1930, remains standing, but
no one is there on a daily basis to serve the needs of residents. There
is little left of the cohesive community described by Secundino
Salazar.

Tension exists between those who have lived in *La Colonia* for
many years and those who are transient or recently arrived. Turnover at Monfort is high because most workers cannot keep up with
the speed of production (which has more than doubled since the
1970s, as subsequent chapters of this book explain), so those who
quit or are fired are forced to look for temporary or seasonal work
anywhere they can find it. Temporary work is the fastest growing
sector of Greeley's economy.

Those who sleep and eat at Guadelupe House are not permitted to stay there during the day; they can be found drinking coffee
at fast food restaurants, standing in line to sell blood plasma, or
collecting aluminum cans for spending money. No one can stay at
the center for more than six days. A Monfort worker who has lived
in Guadelupe House himself said: "They're caught out in the cold,
without a home or hope. I know ten people who sleep in an
abandoned mobile home on the North Side or in an unused warehouse only a few blocks from affluent businesses downtown."[17] He
said that the homeless can spend time in the city library if they
don't sleep or beg. Only those who have not lost a sense of hope
take advantage of social assistance programs such as the Women's

Place (a shelter for abused and battered women and their children), Transitional House (a shelter for homeless families), or Guadelupe House, which serves mostly single men. Others turn to delinquency or prostitution.

Police make nightly raids on city parks, arresting drunks, and searching cars for drugs. They allege that youth gangs are flourishing in Greeley for the first time. The county is planning construction of a new jail on the North Side and the expansion of county offices. Officials say that "the driving force behind this move is that law enforcement has been the fastest growing part of government for the last ten years."[18] Alienation of large sectors of the population from the political process is evident at every level of government. Immigrant residents who are not citizens have no voting rights. Electoral districting divides poor neighborhoods. Even politically conservative Hispanics who aspire to municipal government positions are often discouraged. After a mid-term city council vacancy was filled by an Anglo woman, a former city council aspirant remarked: "It would appear that a Hispanic candidate would have to be capable of walking on water in order to get appointed to the City Council here in Greeley."[19]

In the summer of 1991, for the first time since passage of the 1986 Immigration Reform and Control Act, which specifies that companies hiring undocumented workers should be fined, the Immigration and Naturalization Service (INS) began systematically inspecting Monfort employee records. The INS came into the meatpacking plant and worked with Monfort personnel to select lists of workers to call up, one by one, apparently for questioning or deportation. This went on over a period of several weeks. One day, thirty employees were approached by supervisors. Each was led away to the cafeteria in the midst of the other workers' catcalls against the company. Once they were outside the production area, some were treated roughly, handcuffed, and placed in INS vans. Other workers were assured that although their names were on the list, they would be protected from deportation. Many of those who were taken away from their work stations were never able to collect wages owed them.

One man who was deported to Mexico and who returned to Greeley several months later said that he had lost about $4,000 by not getting his annual profit-sharing bonus, by having to pay a coyote to help him get back to Colorado, and by being delinquent on his mobile home payment. He had been caught six times crossing the border during the past ten years but had been too proud to get fraudulent papers.

Although the district INS officer said, "there are more fraudulent documents around now than I've ever seen before,"[20] and although workers themselves testified to reporters that "at least half those who work at Monfort have false papers,"[21] the Monfort company did not receive any fines. No charges were filed against the company. Nor did massive deportation occur.[22]

Although the INS raid was, perhaps, a slight embarrassment to the company, the intimidation of workers and the high turnover of employees assure that wages can be kept low, benefits can be denied, and workers cannot effectively protest the treatment they receive at work.

Monfort workers told me that they thought the INS campaign was designed to force a certain number of Mexicans in the meatpacking plant to go out and work in the fields during the summer. In spite of new *bracero*-type government programs allowing Mexican nationals to come to the United States legally to do agricultural work on a temporary basis, there is still a shortage of farm labor during the summer. Rather than doing farm labor, however, many of those who left the plant forcibly or voluntarily during the weeks of the campaign against the undocumented workers showed up later in Lexington, Nebraska, where a new Iowa Beef Processors (IBP) slaughterhouse was recruiting workers. A Nebraska-based sociologist who is doing a community study in Lexington asked, "What's going on at Monfort? There's a stream of people coming here from Greeley. There's not enough housing in Lexington and they're living out of their cars."[23] A slaughterhouse worker at an Excel plant in Fort Morgan, Colorado (50 miles east of Greeley), said that the same thing was happening there. People coming from Greeley would rent a motel room or apartment, if they could find one, for women and children, while men would sleep in their cars.

Monfort spokespersons said on several occasions that, although a number of workers were being fired or were quitting voluntarily, production had not been affected. "It's difficult to tell which employees have quit because they are illegal aliens and which have quit for other reasons."[24] An INS official declared that the agency would prefer to deport workers "rather than chase them from one illegally obtained job to another."[25] An Associated Press report said: "Employers who hire illegal aliens will get no second chances under a crackdown by the Immigration and Naturalization Service that also targets a booming black market in fraudulent worker documents."[26] The same article quoted Dan Stein, executive director of the Federation for American Immigration Reform, as saying: "We're knee-deep in a recession, the unemployment rate is skyrocketing and community tensions are on the rise. Sanctions enforcement will alleviate those tensions and make sure the deserving people who need those jobs the most will get them."

The wife of an undocumented Monfort worker told me: "We are being treated like criminals. If we were criminals, we would have found ways to steal and cheat in Mexico. We came here because we want to earn an honest living."[27] It is increasingly clear that sporadic publicity about harsh measures taken — or about to be taken — against undocumented workers, their employers, and those who engage in marketing fraudulent documents serves primarily to support and augment the exploitation of foreign workers.

The more raids there are in meatpacking plants, phony or not, the more migration is stimulated from Mexico to replace those who are fired. Greeley is near Denver, Colorado's largest city, and has an established Hispanic community, so Mexicans can come more easily to Greeley than to other small towns where meatpacking jobs are available. When things don't work out for them, many apparently move on to other places. Most Monfort recruits during the summer of 1991 came from Mexico's northern province of Chihuahua. Those who came as part of a family unit seemed more likely to survive than those who came alone. Extended families can more readily overcome obstacles, deal with ruthless landlords, and find opportunities for work.

Jorge Amaya, the director of Rocky Mountain Service Employment and Redevelopment (SER), a federally funded program established in Colorado in 1981 to recruit farmworkers for jobs in year-round industry, said that most migrants were coming to Greeley looking for work in meatpacking or related industries. A family of six doing seasonal work in the fields made only an average of $7,000 per year.[28] If they managed to obtain work at Monfort, the company received federal money to "train" them.[29] But they still did not receive wages high enough to afford adequate housing. In the summer of 1991, SER was looking for public funds to buy a condemned housing complex and make it available to Greeley's immigrant workers, using guidelines established by the government to protect farmworkers from unsanitary and unsafe working and living conditions. Before the purchase could be completed, assurances were needed that the agency would not inherit the fines imposed on the previous owner of the housing complex.

Churches also sought donations to help meet the urgent needs of migrants. A series of articles in the *Greeley Tribune* in July 1991 called on churches to make basements available to house migrant workers, but most local churches balked at this request. Some noted that it was the obligation of employers to make housing available to workers. Others simply said that facilities were in use.

Greeley's only federally funded clinic closed its doors to new patients other than pregnant women and migrant farmworkers (who are eligible under separate programs) in June 1991. The director of the clinic, Ricardo Lucero, said that the demand for services had risen so steeply that it was impossible to offer preventive, diagnostic, and out-patient services usually available on a sliding-scale basis to Greeley's low-income residents. In January 1991 the meatpacking plant had withdrawn the company's support for health benefits available to employees' families. Workers strained to stretch paychecks to cover extra monthly payments for dependents' health insurance or suffered the consequences. Perhaps not coincidentally, reported child abuse, rape, and violence against women soared during this time, as did resentment directed against the disenfranchised poor. Hospital and other social services were curtailed as demand for them outstripped the city's capabilities.

When early Spanish-speaking immigrants first arrived in Greeley, there was one Catholic church in the community. Mexicans were excluded from attendance or were asked to sit in the back row. Immigrants then built a separate church on the North Side. They called it Our Lady of Peace. Our Lady of Peace has gained a place of respect in the community and has several affiliates in small towns nearby. Until recently, most of those attending Our Lady of Peace in Greeley were Chicanos or Mexican Americans — longtime residents who spoke English fluently. By 1990, on any given Sunday, there were rows of young men standing in the back — Mexican nationals, many of whom worked at the meatpacking plant. Young Mexican families, often composed of mothers and children without adult men, also crowded into the back of the church. Four services were conducted every Sunday, two in Spanish and two in English.

Pedro and Joaquina Rodriguez rent a house in Evans, a small town immediately to the south of Greeley, but they drive to North Greeley on Sundays to attend mass at Our Lady of Peace church. Secundino Salazar and his wife, Maria, live in a small rental house on Greeley's North Side, as do most of their children. They attend church regularly at Our Lady of Peace, but Sal sometimes meets with a group on Saturday evenings at the downtown Catholic church, St. Peter's, to discuss plans for economic development that would bring opportunities to Spanish-speaking residents of Greeley.

As attendance by Mexican families increased at St. Peter's in recent years, and as priests took up the cause of immigrants, conflict began within the membership. Since special Spanish-language services were introduced several years ago, many Anglos have left St. Peter's to attend a new Catholic church on the West Side of Greeley. Greeley's West Side is in the "modern" part of town where more affluent residents are likely to live.

Father Peter Urban left a full-time position at St. Peter's in June 1991 to become a "roving Hispanic minister in northeastern Colorado."[30] He said at that time: "My dream is that someday Monfort will have better working conditions, that the powers that be will figure out a better way to do this." Like many others who have been working among the poor in Greeley, he feels that "nothing will change unless Monfort changes."

Monfort today is similar to the Great Western Sugar Company of a previous era. "In Colorado, the beet industry was dominated by one large corporation, Great Western Sugar Company. This company owned all the sugar beet factories in the area, financed the growers, purchased the entire crop of beets, and recruited all the outside hand labor for the fields."[31] As the sugar beet industry declined, the red meat industry grew. At first, a majority of the workers in the Monfort plants were Anglo men. It was considered a privilege for Mexican Americans to find work alongside these Anglos, and the Monfort family provided some of them with stable work, which was unavailable elsewhere. But as small meatpackers like Monfort overtook industry giants that were first established in the big cities a century earlier, competition among them grew, and they turned to the same practices that had brought economic success to their predecessors: super-exploitation of immigrant minorities.

The meatpacking industry in Greeley employed approximately thirty-eight hundred people in 1990. In the same year, Hispanics made up 20 to 30 percent of the town's population. While the white population in Greeley has increased by nearly 14 percent in the past decade, the Hispanic population has increased by nearly 50 percent. The town's total population was fifty-three thousand in 1980 and is over 60,500 today.

Ken Monfort, whose family fortune was built largely with the use of immigrant labor, wrote in 1990: "We are not all rich or poor, white or brown, active or sedentary. A diverse city for a diverse population . . . and I love it."[32] He defended his support of Colorado's "Official English" initiative (which carried in Greeley as well as in the state in 1989) by saying, "Since we are all too dumb, lazy or privileged to learn Spanish, it looks like it's your duty to learn English. The better it is learned, the more promotions and advancements will be earned, I am sure."[33] Most supervisors in the Monfort plants do not speak Spanish; most people who enter the plant as new employees (turnover was approximately forty each week at the time of this writing)[34] speak little or no English. In effect, this assures that newcomers maintain a position as outsiders who cannot expect or demand equal treatment from the administration.[35]

Ken Monfort has often been praised for providing opportunities for minorities. "My image of Hispanics is positive," he said. "New hires . . . are more apt to stay if they're Hispanic than if they're Anglo."[36] When the Eastman Kodak company opened a plant in nearby Windsor, Monfort (according to the *Denver Post,* January 6, 1991) wrote an impassioned letter to the company urging Kodak to hire minorities. Critics, however, maintain that his real motive was to keep wage rates down in the county by making a large pool of cheap labor available, and they accused Monfort of discouraging businesses with established higher wage rates from locating in the area.[37]

In the past decade, Weld County has consistently had lower wages than the rest of the state (and has had among the lowest wage rate in the nation). Food manufacturing employees in the county make nearly 22 percent less than the state average. They have less purchasing power today than they did two decades ago. At the same time, the county has consistently produced more agricultural wealth than any other county in the state, primarily through the sale of livestock and meat products. Weld County's social structure, characterized by wide disparities between rich and poor, can be compared with that of the San Joaquin Valley in California, where agribusiness owners have gained enormous wealth primarily from immigrant labor.[38]

Weld County's Economic Development Action Partnership sends information packets to businesses that might want to locate in the county. The materials advertise the low prevailing wages and the "miniscule percentage"[39] of unionized employment (5 percent in 1990). At the same time, real estate brokers and economists say that the impact of a low-wage structure has a ripple effect that hurts everyone, not only those who are in low-paying or dead-end jobs. The answer, some say, is to "offer businesses government incentives to increase productivity and boost their bottom line."[40]

Weld County's public trustee said in March 1991 that although Greeley had a "seller's market" for new homes, there was an increase in foreclosures on small homes, reflecting the prevailing low wage structure. "While the economy has gotten better, there are still lots of folks out there who have financial troubles. . . . I would think wages would be an issue in this."[41] One apartment building manager boosted the rent on one- and two-bedroom apartments with the explanation that there was a big demand for apartments because lower-income residents could no longer afford to own homes in Greeley.[42] Federal money spent annually in Greeley and Weld County on subsidized housing (for administration and rent subsidies) comes to more than $2.5 million. Waiting lists for subsidized housing have doubled in the past five years. More than two-thirds of the applicants are employed, but their wages do not cover the minimal expenses of maintaining a family. (A superviser of food stamp eligibility in Greeley says that wages are so low at Monfort that anyone with four or more dependents is eligible for food stamps — if they can prove citizenship or have more than five years of legal residency in the United States.[43])

An editorial in the *Greeley Tribune* of June 26, 1991, pushed for government subsidies or tax credits to construction companies as incentives for "construction and maintenance of decent housing" for the county's working poor. This proposal was prefaced with the comment: "Few Americans are willing to perform such work for such wages, yet we are all willing to enjoy the fruits of that labor."

It seems that every solution proposed by Greeley's elite rewards the people who have created the problems in the first place or penalizes the victims. In 1990 a fiscal crisis in local government was dealt with by introducing a special food tax, which is one more way of forcing the poor to subsidize the rich. Employment and unemployment generally rise together in Greeley and Weld County (half of the county's population lives in Greeley). So the rich get richer and the poor get poorer. People sleeping under bridges are perceived as a health hazard to the community at worst and as an embarrassment at best. Those directly affected are the objects of paternalistic concern, of scorn, or of ridicule.

It should be self-evident that employers actively recruit immigrant labor because they can pay immigrant workers less and work them harder than long-term U.S. citizens. Legislation supposedly intended to stem immigration and prevent worker abuse serves, in practice, to terrorize workers, helping to keep them poor and subjugated. Taxpayers — including the immigrants themselves — pay to perpetuate this process, subsidizing employers directly or indirectly. Many citizens affected by increasing polarization between rich and poor become resentful of immigrants instead of questioning the practices of employers. Even those who are advocates for the poor seldom recognize the institutional causes of poverty and racism.

Businesses can appear to be progressive and non-discriminatory by promoting the idea that disadvantaged members of the community can advance themselves personally through initiative and hard work. Those who don't succeed can then be held responsible for their own misery, and business owners can reap enormous benefit from a climate of ethnic tension. Underlying causes for the alienation and marginalization of immigrant populations are deliberately hidden from public view. Political patronage assures that those who are really responsible for creating and perpetuating class divisions are seldom held accountable for the social consequences of their decisions and actions.

The Making of a Modern-Day   2
Company Town

On April 28, 1991, Father Anthony (Tony) Judge of Our Lady of Peace Church stood before a small gathering of union organizers and supporters at Island Grove Park in Greeley. They gathered to commemorate a National Day of Mourning for those who had died at their workplaces. The event coincided with newspaper reports that Monfort, Inc., had been cited for several deaths caused by the company's failure to enforce lockout procedures on defleshing machines and by numerous other "egregious willful" health and safety violations in its Grand Island, Nebraska, facility.[1] No inspection had been done at the Greeley slaughterhouse, but the company's own records (obtained by a local reporter) indicated that the situation there was equally dangerous for workers. Instead of opening their newspapers to learn of one more Citizen of the Year award for Ken Monfort, retiring president of ConAgra Red Meats, Greeley residents learned that the local slaughterhouse was one of the most dangerous workplaces in the nation.[2]

Father Tony had come to Greeley only three months before the memorial event and had already become aware of the terrible damage done to the bodies and minds of workers at the Monfort meatpacking plant. He condemned those responsible as he read from the Bible (Isaiah 59:6–8):

> The evil plots you make are as deadly as the eggs of a poisonous snake. Crush an egg, out comes a snake! But your plots will do you no good — they are as useless as clothing made of cobwebs! You are always planning something evil, and you can hardly wait to do it. You never hesitate to murder innocent people. You leave ruin and destruction wherever you go, and no one is safe when you are around. Everything you do is unjust. You follow a crooked path, and no one who walks that path will ever be safe.

If the city's elites were in attendance that day at Greeley's First Congregational Church, where many of them were members,[3] the morning's news must have loomed over their own service. It would now be necessary to repair the damage done to their carefully cultivated legitimacy.

In October 1988 the *Greeley Tribune* had published a special issue on *Playing the Game: How Power and Influence Work in Greeley.* Headlines referring to the city's Town Fathers, or "top ten," read: "The Cream of Greeley's Crop." A city council member asserted approvingly: "You can't tell who the Democrats and Republicans are on the local level." In fact, a group called The Committee, established in the 1960s at the initiative of agribusinessman W. D. Farr, reportedly made several nominations for seats on the city council and then gave financial backing to all the candidates nominated. "That shows that the group's intent is not to wield power but to get good people to run for office."[4] At that time (1988), Ken Monfort was portrayed as the single most powerful man in Greeley,[5] but both his power and that of The Committee, which was composed of Monfort's close friends, were said to be waning. "People are too suspicious of The Committee for it to have much power, but members influence each other," according to former members.[7]

University of Northern Colorado (UNC) President Bob Dickeson described the city's power structure as a process of consensus-building: "There seems to be — without an actual decision being made — almost a kind of consensus-building approach that takes place. Very informally. And the criteria are pretty clear: Is it good for Greeley?"[8] (Dickeson himself was the beneficiary of a similar kind of "consensus." In 1981 the UNC faculty gave him a near-unanimous vote of no-confidence, yet the Board of Trustees kept him on for another decade.) Ken Monfort was described as a "reluctant leader."[9] Later he commented, in his characteristic pseudo-folksy style: "A friend of mine once told me that you had to be careful and not bitch too much about city government or you could wake up some morning and find yourself as mayor."[10]

The merger between Monfort, Inc., and ConAgra, one of the largest food-processing corporations in the world, took place in 1987, a year before the *Tribune*'s power structure survey was completed. The merger, however, hardly received a mention in the newspaper's report. While Monfort/ConAgra was steadily expanding its operations in the Greeley area, the Monfort family was diversifying financial and real estate holdings, thereby encroaching on the territory of other families and businesses. The Monforts' cameraderie with other prominent business people was cooling even as the family's personal power increased. As they became victims of their own success, they sought to introduce an ideology of pluralism into local politics. When a fiscally conservative opposition group, naming itself The Other Committee, emerged in Greeley, Ken Monfort said: "The Other Committee is interesting, kind of like a little town hall that helps the city look at itself. When I was in the State Legislature, I learned it was easy for a person in elected office to think he's doing everything the right way. The Other Committee keeps them on their toes."[11] This comment overlooks the fact that neither The Committee nor The Other Committee was an elected body, much less a tribunal of the people. In fact, The Committee's membership was known only to themselves and, as the 1980s ended, they represented less and less of a "consensus" even among Greeley's professional and business elites.

By the mid-1980s economic and social disparities brought about by the Monforts' success created lifestyle problems even for the more privileged Anglo population in Greeley:

> Emerging Hispanics, as with any arriving minority, take the low-end paying jobs in our community — the unskilled blue-collar positions. All gainful productive work is good up to a point. The point occurs when we don't have ways for such individuals to better themselves, and when we become a predominantly blue-collar community such as Commerce City [North Denver's industrial zone]. There is nothing wrong with Commerce Cities — we need them. It's just not what Greeley aspires to be.[12]

In addition, Greeley's agriculture-based economy was recuperating from recession at the expense of family farmers and businesses that had lost out in competition to ConAgra and other big corporations. "What we are ending up with," reported UNC economist Ann Garrison, "is bigger and fewer owners of agricultural operations, with an 88% reduction of income going to those who own their own farms."[13]

The situation in Greeley and Weld County is not unique. The expanding U.S. economy during the years following World War II made it possible for prosperity, if not power, to be shared by anyone who was willing to play the game of capitalism. The number of millionaires in the United States increased while the situation of many working class people improved. As production and prices outstripped available markets for goods and services, however, more people slipped out of the middle class into the ranks of the working poor.

Family farmers, business entrepreneurs, and those who worked in the feedlots and disassembly lines were not the only ones whose fortunes took a turn for the worse. When so-called cost-containment initiatives were enhanced in the meatpacking industry in the late 1970s, Ken Monfort wrote in a company publication: "We can do a lot of things a lot more economically in this country if we are turned loose and told to go compete."[14] In the same publication, he defended the use of the chemical hormone diethylstilbesterol (DES) as an additive in beef. Monfort pleaded innocent when the company was charged with systematically violating regulations regarding such additives, claiming that there was a "misunderstanding of instructions" on the part of employees.[15] Monfort complained about policies favoring small companies bidding on government meat business, saying that this would only increase costs to taxpayers, and he lauded the company's success in finding cargo for returning Monfort trucks. At one point, Monfort reported to fellow businessmen that the "backhaul is better than the outbound business anymore,"[16] but he did not explain what kind of back-hauling cargo had been obtained. (Later investigations revealed widespread use of meat trucks to haul toxic wastes from the East Coast to the Midwest.)[17]

Ken Monfort insisted that health and safety regulations and rules limiting competition drive consumer prices up. Yet, as government favored the unfettered growth of big business in the 1980s, consumer prices continued to climb, and the overall economy entered a period of severe contradictions marked by strikes, recession, unemployment, and dislocation of populations.

Economic crisis did not hurt everyone equally. "If Monfort of Colorado is able to buy calves and corn cheap, it means someone else down the line — farmers, for the most part — are hurting," explained a business reporter during the agricultural recession of the mid-1980s.[18] More to the point: "The shakeout among farmers also should help reduce the oversupply of fattened cattle that has depressed prices."[19] In other words, what was good for the Monforts was not necessarily good for the rest of the population.

Monfort/ConAgra's return to stockholders in the late 1980s was as high as that of any company in the United States, and red meat production was the highest share of that profit. In 1990, ConAgra reported its tenth straight year of record earnings. Monfort's president declared that a major goal was to double the profit margin by focusing on efficient production of beef products (increasing the value of meat by processing it more extensively).[20] Because the industry is labor-intensive, profit is derived from sheer volume. Machines are introduced where possible to effect savings for the company; workers, for the most part, must adapt to the pace of the machines. The availability of willing workers near the source of livestock "leaves the Western region in a more competitive advantage than the rest of the U.S."[21]

In order to deflect attention from maneuvers to create advantages for themselves at the expense of others, beef barons sometimes conveniently attribute their success to luck. But the process of building and maintaining an operation that requires the sacrifice of thousands for the benefit of a few requires much more than luck.

When Ken Monfort retired as president of ConAgra Red Meats in 1989, he enjoyed talking about his rise from awkward country-school-boy to "corporate cowboy," as he was called by admirers. He also enjoyed recalling "hard times," perhaps as a way of justifying the family's current wealth. Actually, Warren and Edith Monfort, Ken's parents, had prospered by buying up range cattle during the depression of the 1930s. At that time farmers were beginning to use tractors instead of horses in the fields, so huge supplies of corn once needed to feed draft animals could be used for year-round feeding of cattle. Cattle were also fed sugar beet pulp and alfalfa, crops grown on irrigated farmland by immigrant workers. The feedlot operation expanded into meatpacking in 1960, when the Greeley slaughterhouse was purchased by the Monforts from a Denver-based company, Capitol Pack, Inc.

An undated company brochure from the late 1970s, titled "The Monfort Story," emphasizes "innovations" made possible by fattening cattle and cutting up carcasses in the countryside instead of shipping cattle to big cities for slaughtering and processing. Improvements in refrigeration and transportation also made it possible to cut up carcasses before shipment. Boxed beef could be transported directly to restaurants and hotels, while by-products — bones, fat, and blood — were processed on site to make dog food, fertilizer, and other non-food products.

Of course, relatively unskilled labor was needed to accomplish all these changes in the processing of beef, and unskilled labor could be paid less than butchers, who cut up whole carcasses in grocery stores or shops. The trick was to secure a reliable source of labor that was willing to carry out monotonous tasks at high speed, and the cooperation of public officials. The company was "innovative" in this respect as well.

In the 1960s, Ken Monfort served two terms in the Colorado State Legislature. He was at that time a member of the Democratic party. When a bid for the U.S. Senate failed, he took over full-time management of the Greeley meatpacking operation. He received funds from the state government as an incentive to hire high school dropouts, handicapped workers, minorities, and people under twenty-two years of age or over forty-five. Many of these people were Hispanic men. In Greeley's Portion Foods plant, which had been established in 1965 to process hamburger and special meat cuts, a largely female workforce could be paid less than slaughterhouse workers even though much of the work they did was identical to that performed in the slaughterhouse.[22]

By 1971, Monfort feedlots were purchasing annually some four hundred thousand tons of ensilage (green fodder used to feed cattle after storage in silos or pits) grown on twenty thousand acres of irrigated land. The company's slaughterhouse was disposing of twenty million pounds of sewage per day, twice what the rest of Greeley produced. The city obtained a federal grant from the Environmental Protection Agency to build a sewage plant solely for the meatpacking industry. Monfort assumed payment of interest on the debt incurred, and some operating costs, while continuing to utilize the main city sewage plant as well.[23] A bond issue for another wastewater-treatment plant for Monfort, Inc., in Greeley was approved by the Weld County Commissioners in November 1991. Interest on investments in the $4.1 million plant is tax exempt. In the same month, the city of Greeley issued $6.6 million in water bonds to buy water rights for industrial expansion. The rights were purchased from farmers who agreed to rent the water back from the city until such time as the city's claim on the water would take priority.

In the 1970s, the company had required more capital for expansion than could be secured from local bankers. Company stock was put on the open market after Warren Monfort, founder of Monfort of Colorado, retired as chairman of the Board (in 1972). The Monfort family retained control of over two-thirds of the company's assets. In order to make a major move into the national market, it had been necessary to have a union label on meat products. Warren Monfort had signed contracts with the Amalgamated Meat Cutters and Butcher Workmen of North America. At the same time, Ken Monfort and his business allies lobbied, unsuccessfully, for "right-to-work" legislation so that union power would be weakened (outlawing both "closed shops" and "union shops," which assure that all those working under union contracts belong to the union, pay dues, and abide by union decisions).[24]

When Secundino "Sal" Salazar was elected chief union steward in 1970, he received a letter from Ken Monfort:

> I am very pleased to learn that you have been elected Chief Union Steward. . . . A very great honor has been bestowed on you as your fellow employees have placed their trust in your judgement and fairness. If I can ever be of help to you — my door is open. I am personally hopeful that we, at Monfort of Colorado, will always have the free exchange of ideas and feelings between management and union employees which we have had since the plant opened ten years ago.

During this time, Richard Monfort, Ken's oldest son, who was attending business school at UNC in Greeley, worked in the

Monforts' feedlot in Gilcrest, alongside Pedro Rodriguez. Such cameraderie with workers went by the way, however, as a new era of economic contraction began.

Personal attention, patronage, and a shared work ethic did not assure worker compliance when boxed beef businesses determined to overtake the Big Five meatpacking companies (Morris, Armour, Cudahy, Wilson, and Swift). Once new technologies had been adopted by all those competing for the market, the new beef barons sought to forcefully extract more from their workers. This called for cooperation rather than competition. When one company was faced with a striking workforce, it could count on other companies to purchase its surplus beef.

In an effort to contain operating costs in 1970, Monfort tried to introduce a profit-sharing scheme as a substitute for retirement programs and cost-of-living wage adjustments. Workers refused the deal and went on strike. Under pressure from a new "get-tough" management strategy, workers eventually agreed to a no-strike clause in return for a cost-of-living agreement (also known as a COLA).

When the Nixon administration negotiated massive exportation of U.S. grain commodities to the U.S.S.R. in 1973, the price of grain to feedlot owners "virtually doubled overnight."[25] Beef prices were, however, frozen on government order to control inflation. The use of chemical additives came under government regulation, putting a further strain on producers. Meat consumption remained high, but the number of meatpacking companies declined precipitously.

Ken Monfort proudly recalled later how he had weathered the storm of 1973–1977. He relied on family and personal allies who had reputations as strongmen. Among these were Gene Meakins, a former CIA officer in Guyana,[26] who became director of personnel and public relations, and Roland "Sonny" Mapelli, who brought a Denver-based, family-owned meat distribution business into the Monfort operation and served for a time as chairman of the Board of Monfort of Colorado.

Monfort sought means of influencing legislation that would give meatpacking companies tax breaks, secure deregulation, and increase access to foreign markets. Hank Brown, who was the Monfort company's director of development from 1972 to 1980, also served as state senator from 1972 to 1976. He was a U.S. congressman and member of the Congressional Beef Caucus from 1980 to 1990, when he became a U.S. Senator from Colorado (see Chapter 5).

By the mid-1970s, meat consumption in the United States had reached an all-time high. Neverthless, Monfort began to negotiate aggressively for overseas markets and brought in a Chicago banker, Samuel Addoms, who took over as president of Monfort of Colorado from 1975 to 1980. Meatpacking plants were purchased in Denver, Florida, Texas, and Nebraska.

By the end of the 1970s, the cost of production and transportation in the United States was affected by tight energy supplies and high interest rates. In an effort to contain costs, workers at the Greeley slaughterhouse were forced into a strike, followed by a two-year suspension of production after which former strikers were replaced by a new workforce. The union never recovered (see Chapter 3).

"There's no way you can market your way out of problems. You've got to be a low-cost producer," Ken Monfort said, recalling the crisis of the late 1970s.[27] In 1979, shortly before the standoff at the Greeley plant, Monfort had purchased a former Swift & Company slaughterhouse in Grand Island, Nebraska, which reopened as a Monfort subsidiary. Wages for both management and workers were cut. The federal government gave Monfort a tax break to hire refugees from Southeast Asia at the Grand Island plant. The company tried to make a sweetheart deal with the National Maritime Union and managed to frustrate investigations into a Laotian mafia-type operation within the plant that allegedly threatened workers who signed up with another union.[28]

When it was no longer possible to maintain the liberal image that Monfort and company had been cultivating during the 1960s and 1970s, Ken Monfort and Sonny Mapelli switched from the Democratic to the Republican party and formed part of an Eat Crow Club in Greeley, insisting that the defense of "freedom and democracy"[29] required hard choices and a few "bloodied noses."[30] Of course the bloodied noses were not to be those of Ken Monfort or his loyalists. They hired personal bodyguards to protect themselves from angry workers who were being subjected to an increasingly militarized work regime (see Chapter 3). Monfort spent less and less time on the plant floor.

After the Greeley plant closed down in 1980 — and reopened two years later without a union contract — workers were paid about half the going rate in the industry at that time.[31] They received six paid holidays instead of ten. The factory line reached a speed that UFCW organizer Steve Thomas said was "the fastest kill in the country that I know of."[32] (Business sources estimate that workers were processing between 215 and 340 carcasses per hour in 1982.)[33] Morrell soon followed suit, and his South Dakota plant later came under indictment for under-reporting of injuries. Turnover among employees in the meatpacking industry increased tremendously in high-speed "restructured" plants. Workers, many of whom were Mexican nationals, migrated from plant to plant looking for a place where working conditions were tolerable and wages would cover minimal living expenses. Companies with "floating" work forces prospered.

A former Monfort manager testified at a government hearing in 1984 that high turnover can be advantageous for employers:

> We found very little correlation between turnover and profitability. An employee leaves for whatever reason. Generally, we're able to hire a replacement employee, and I might add that the way fringe benefits have been negotiated or installed, they favor long term employees. For instance, insurance, as you know, is very costly. Insurance is not available to new employees until they've worked there for a period of a year or, in some cases, six months. Vacations don't accrue until the second year. There are some economies, frankly, that result from hiring new employees.[34]

Turnover and the hiring of immigrant workers also inhibited workforce organizing efforts. The Monfort corporation worked hard to maintain a non-union workforce at the slaughterhouse. They did so by selecting employees who could be "cultivated" for promotions while the bulk of production was carried out by short-term workers. Divided workforces could be more readily controlled. By giving bonuses to non-union workers and refusing them to workers who were still unionized, and whose negotiating power was weak, the company could reap extra profits in both union and non-union worksites. In 1982 the *Greeley Tribune* reported: "In an effort to maintain a competitive position company-wide, Monfort says the company increasingly is looking toward profit-sharing and bonus plans as a key element in its compensation plans for non-union employees."[35] Those who aspired to production bonuses kept a check on others, who recognized that worker unity was needed to resist the company's constant push to speed up the disassembly line. Furthermore, once-a-year bonuses were a cheap way to lure workers to plants where turnover was high. Yet, without a union contract, the company was under no obligation to provide bonuses and was under no obligation to retain employees until the time when bonuses were distributed. Company policy could be changed without notice, and employees could be fired without cause.

By the mid-1980s, nearly half the meat-processing workers in Greeley were women, many of them single mothers. At this time, the State of Colorado established a Job Service office near the Greeley slaughterhouse and began processing applications for Monfort. The county commissioner enthusiastically supported the move, referring to Monfort as "our golden friend."[36] The Monforts also brought a state Employment and Redevelopment Office to Greeley by providing an initial $50,000 grant. The U.S. Department of Labor subsequently supplied it with operating expenses of nearly $900,000 annually. The office, known as Rocky Mountain Service, Employment and Redevelopment (SER)–Monfort Learning Center, channeled farmworkers into area manufacturing jobs and offered classes in English and preparation for citizenship exams. This office and the Weld County Information and Referral Service lobbied for government incentives to businesses that hire minorities; money is now received directly by Monfort, Inc., in the form of grants for training each new employee recruited by SER.

By promoting such high-visibility government agencies that serviced Monfort's employees and potential employees, the company could maintain a public profile as an advocate for the poor. When an article appeared in the local newspaper encouraging dropouts to return to school so that they would not be "condemned for life to sweeping the floor of a factory or on the cutting floor at the meat packing plant,"[37] Ken Monfort responded with a letter to the editor: "I happen to sit at a desk most of the day. Sometimes when I go home at night, I really wonder if I accomplished anything. I can guarantee that this feeling is not prevalent at our meat packing plant, where the employees know each day that they have produced something and accomplished something. . . . They deserve our respect — and they have mine."[38]

By 1986, Monfort was described in *Forbes* magazine as "multiplying successes by three or four times compared with the last big change from shipping whole beef carcasses to boxed beef."[39] Monfort was listed as third among beef producers in the nation in profitability, second in growth and earnings per stockholder share, and first in stability of earnings. In other words, administrative changes introduced in the 1980s brought even more overall financial gains to the company than the earlier change from shipping whole carcasses to cutting up beef at the source. This new advance was attributed primarily to "closer management practices and more computer operation," a reference to a computerized disassembly line in which work operations were "de-skilled." Each worker was responsible for a smaller portion of the meat-trimming process but was required to perform at a faster and more controlled speed.

In the 1980s beef consumption fell due to higher consumer prices and increasing consumer concern about the health properties of red meat. Nevertheless, the company's earnings rose by 81 percent from 1985 to 1986. Pre-tax income in the same period was 94 percent higher than the year before. A second shift at the slaughterhouse was introduced later to maintain the lead that had been established over smaller producers.

By the mid-1980s, competition for overseas markets was intense. Monfort was taking the lead in developing a Japanese market, but this was not enough to make the company competitive with transnational food-processing companies such as Cargill and ConAgra (both of which had specialized in grain trading internationally). In 1983, Monfort initiated an anti-trust suit against Cargill, whose Excel Corporation also had meatpacking operations in Colorado. The suit, which was heard in 1986, lost in the U.S. Supreme Court, and in 1987 Monfort of Colorado merged with ConAgra, whose farm chemical component had originated in Greeley decades earlier.

The 1987 merger with ConAgra was beneficial to both companies because it facilitated diversification in holdings, which meant that greater overall control of food production could be achieved. Monfort already had established an advantage in "hierarchical integration" of beef production by owning feedlots as well as slaughterhouses and processing plants. After purchasing Monfort,

ConAgra became the second largest food-processing firm in the United States and the fourth largest in the world.[40] The company went on to buy out Beatrice Foods, which was already involved in meatpacking, and consolidated its control of other acquisitions such as Swift & Company and Armour. By 1990, ConAgra's revenues approached $20 billion annually; its return on equity averaged over 22 percent in its eleventh straight year of record earnings.

ConAgra's largest workforce was still in Colorado's Weld County, which ranked number one in the nation in the value of livestock, poultry, and their products. At the same time, ConAgra was able to do what businesses call "global sourcing" for cheap labor, minimal environmental and safety regulations, and natural resources.

By 1991, ConAgra had joint ventures in Australia, Canada, Chile, France, Japan, the U.S.S.R., and Thailand. It had taken over hog production in the United States in the same way as it had moved into poultry and beef in the 1980s, forcing other companies into bankruptcy or making strategic acquisitions.[41] ConAgra had, in fact, surpassed Iowa Beef Processors (IBP) as the nation's largest meat packer (if one includes poultry and seafood products in addition to red meat).[42] By marketing new, labor-intensive meat products with non-meat additives and labeling them "Healthy Choice," ConAgra intended to increase its margin of profit in meat processing, "moving quickly" to "stay out in front of the pack."[43] The company also needed to move quickly in the face of pressure on legislators to restrict use of the word "healthy" in labeling.

After the Monfort/ConAgra merger, most beef and lamb operations that had been owned or purchased by ConAgra became Monfort plants, but the Monforts now had big investments in other food products as well. In 1987, after the merger, the Monfort family's share in ConAgra was about 10 percent, making them the largest stockholders in the company.

Ken Monfort's son, Richard, who had been running the Grand Island plant, began heading the Greeley operation after the merger with ConAgra. The Greeley slaughterhouse was still the most profitable of all the red meat plants owned by Monfort/ConAgra, although poultry and hog operations in Portugal were reportedly the parent company's most profitable operations.[44] Charlie Monfort, Ken's second son, assumed responsibility for ConAgra Red

Meats International Sales Corporation. He sought state funding for a trade office to facilitate sales to Japan and sought government support for expanding the market for U.S. beef in the Soviet republics. But he also began making personal investments in non-food areas, such as a major league baseball team in Denver (the Colorado Rockies). The family increased investments in real estate and became more involved in banking and other local businesses such as restaurants and bars.

None of the Monforts were indifferent to local politics, but they no longer had the "legitimacy" that had once been accorded Monfort rule. As the lives of more and more people came under their direct control, it appeared that they were more feared than respected. In 1991, two special elections were called to determine the fate of new development projects in Greeley. Initiatives promoted by the Monforts prevailed, but there was enough acrimony to break apart old alliances.[45]

While Richard and Charlie Monfort were increasing the family's assets in Colorado, their sisters, Kaye and Kyle, took over responsibility for the Monfort Charitable Foundation. Kyle also served as president of the local United Way. Involvement in community projects such as the Dream Team, which rewarded students for staying in school, gave the Monforts increased leverage over community organizations that might otherwise have become sympathetic to Monfort workers' increasingly precarious lives.

In 1987, when Greeley's Portion Foods workers went on strike (see Chapter 4), they couldn't get United Way personnel to sign a petition calling for the company to negotiate. Strikers went from house to house with petitions, looking for support from the public wherever they could get it. One striker told us:

> I had done some temporary work at the Girl Scout agency. I took petitions in there and they all signed them. Then I took petitions into United Way and they told me "no" they could not sign them, and I said, "Why not? Just because Ken Monfort is one of your largest contributors?" and they said, "Yes, the money we get from the packing plant each year is a lot of money and we can not afford to lose that," and I said, "Ken Monfort doesn't give that money. His employees do, because he has a drive there every year. He loves it if you contribute to the United Way, and I'm sure he gives a great deal of money, too. . . . " But they would not sign it.[46]

Monfort was able to abate controversy over an expensive proposal for a a new civic center in Greeley with a gift of $1 million. Others contributed a total of $7 million, and taxpayers paid an additional $8 million (plus upkeep in perpetuity). Predictably, the center's auditorium is named Monfort Concert Hall. In 1990, after the North Colorado Medical Center, Greeley's only hospital, had written off $27 million in unpaid accounts from the previous year, the Monforts gave the center $1 million.[47]

Ken Monfort continued to be the major spokesperson for the Monfort company when he became president of ConAgra Red Meats after the merger with ConAgra. In 1988 he was also elected president of the American Meat Institute, an organization with headquarters in Washington, D.C., that lobbied on behalf of the meatpacking industry and oversaw nationwide television advertising campaigns for red meat (another "innovation" of the 1980s).

Monfort was happy to take credit for the company's survival in the 1980s, saying with pride that he'd always been a "terrible loser"[48] and enjoyed taking business away from the competition. But when he retired as president of ConAgra Red Meats in 1989, he said: "I've never been very impressed with bigness. I don't think it solves things or makes anything better. I was always very suspicious of bigness. Big business. Big government. Big anything."[49]

By sounding the theme of the humble, small-town advocate, and by increasing philanthropic activities, Ken Monfort was able to maintain a certain charismatic hold on local politics even as the number of his adversaries increased. When the sale to ConAgra was completed in 1987, he said that his father "would have approved," but that "Mom, on the other hand, would have thought it is too big. She always thought we worked too hard as it was."[50]

Certainly a great deal of hard work was involved in building the Monfort/ConAgra empire. But the hardest work was not being done by corporate executives. And those on the production line were receiving little benefit from the company's success. ConAgra recorded an annual average return to investors of 35 percent during the ten years after it began investing in red meat production. Each year the margin of profit increased as productivity was enhanced through what businessmen call "closer management." Workers were being driven harder and were receiving lower wages, farmers were getting lower prices for products they sold to meatpacking companies, and consumers were paying higher prices for meat. Fewer and fewer companies gained more and more control over resources and markets.

Ken Monfort had been upset about Cargill's expansion in the early 1980s, saying that red meat prices would eventually be driven up by industry concentration. He later insisted that "the way the meat business functions is the way business is supposed to function . . . it's competitive."[51] Critics said that some competition did still exist, but that "the sector [was] certainly not open to new organizations."[52] After a decade of frantic takeovers in the industry (see Chapter 3), and the threat of government intervention to prevent further concentration in the meat industry, the American Meat Institute took the predictable position that concentration should be curtailed but that established companies should not be broken up.

As a result of the concentration of wealth and power in Weld County, corporate farmers were locked into growing feedcrops on contract to ConAgra, a process called "forward contracting." In an effort to retain both flexibility and control, Monfort became an advocate of government subsidies for feedgrain producers. "I didn't think I'd ever hear myself saying this," said Ken Monfort in 1986, when he encouraged "our growers" to use government wheat and feedgrain programs to tide them over until he could "pick up the slack."[53] An enemy of government bailouts such as that of Chrysler Corporation, he was happy to take advantage of government largess when it could help further his own company's expansion.

Under the Reagan administration, government agencies looked the other way when patterns in cattle pricing indicated the use of inside information by big meatpackers to drive small- and medium-sized ranchers out of business and to bring about further concentration in the industry. At one time, the company proudly stated in an illustrated brochure: "Monfort . . . is the only major beef producing company encompassing cattle feeding, beef and lamb processing and local distribution on a nationwide basis."[54] This practice of concentration became more generalized in the 1980s. One Colorado rancher remarked: "Whenever the market strengthens to a certain point, they quit buying our cattle and they kill cattle out of their own yards. Then they break the market."[55]

These processes are not abating in the 1990s. Five hundred farmers and ranchers were driven out of business in Colorado between 1990 and 1991, according to the National Agricultural Statistics Service. In Weld County, the amount of income going to those who owned their own farms suffered a dramatic decline as concentration in land ownership increased. Corporate dynasties were, however, strengthened.

Often big businesses have survived at the expense of competitors by deliberately stimulating overproduction. Lower prices would then cause competitors to go out of business, and prices would go back up. Even as the demand for red meat decreased, aggressive meatpacking companies would open up second shifts and take temporary losses until a competitor dropped out of the picture. This happened in Greeley during the transfer to ConAgra. It also happened in a number of other places where Monfort/ConAgra took over established plants. For example, Monfort took over ValAgri in Garden City, Kansas, where IBP was also operating a beef slaughterhouse. Farmland Industries (a cooperatively owned enterprise), which had previously shown good returns, was then forced to close down its Golden City plant.

Monfort had the edge initially in Colorado because the company "owned the animals from start to finish."[56] ConAgra, as a transnational "family of companies operating from farm to table,"[57] was in an even better position to drive out competitors. In Greeley, besides the beef and lamb plants formerly owned by Monfort, ConAgra operated a chemical plant, feed and fertilizer companies, and retail stores. Investigations were underway in North Dakota, South Dakota, Montana, Minnesota, and Iowa, challenging the legality of such integrated corporate structures.[58] In Colorado and Nebraska, however, where Monfort and ConAgra were headquartered, "synergy" (as the advantages gained from mergers and takeovers came to be called by business reporters) escaped serious scrutiny. It continued to be flaunted by Monfort with pride.

When corporate economic power becomes the dominant reality in daily life, democratic governing processes, freedom of the press, and freedom of speech all come to be treated as mere frivolities. Any challenge to corporate interests will be met with the marshalling of whatever social institutions are affected to defend those interests. In Greeley, the relationship between ConAgra and UNC reflects this process, showing how patronage operates to link business and academic institutions.

In 1989, one year after I came to teach in the sociology department at UNC, a one-page article appeared in a student publication, *Hispanic Horizons,* about a new unionization drive at Monfort. The article was written by a recent graduate of the School of Journalism. It included a brief history of company-worker disputes over the years and a commentary on working conditions at the company's plants, as described by several workers. Gene Meakins, vice president of personnel and public relations at Monfort, was quoted in the article as saying: "They're just trying to stir up trouble; it's all hogwash."[59]

The university administration withdrew the publication from circulation after only a few hundred copies had gone out, and removed the offending article. The director of the Hispanic Cultural Center went along with the recall, commenting wryly: "Our purpose is not to shape the social conscience of the university."[60]

At the time these events were unfolding, it was rumored that the Monforts were about to make a big contribution to the university. The administration dodged questions about any impending gift from the Monforts, but Claude Johns, the vice president for university relations, said that the article in *Hispanic Horizons* was inappropriate because Monfort is a "corporation that has done so much for the university and the community."[61] A few months later the president of the university, Robert Dickeson, announced a $10 million fund-raising campaign and revealed that a pledge had already been received from the Monfort family for $1 million. The gift was for the establishment of an endowed "executive professorship" in the College of Business Administration. The president said: "Our program will become enriched because this support from the Monforts will allow us to bring people from the business world into the classroom to share their knowledge and experience with our students."[62] The president also published an October 11, 1989, speech that he gave to faculty, "Legacy of Promise," in which he said, "I am unaware of a university anywhere that has a better relationship with its Chamber of Commerce. . . . The Greeley–UNC relationship is reciprocal and symbiotic. One cannot truly understand this institution without appreciating the quality of that connection."[63]

Journalism graduate students writing for the student newspaper, *The Mirror,* did the best they could to take a critical view of the cozy relationship between the university and the sacred cow north of Greeley; they also published letters praising the corporation and supporting the university president's "vision of the whole picture, a concept young reporters often miss."[64]

By December 1990, the School of Journalism had lost its graduate program and *The Mirror* had been effectively reined in. In March 1991, *Hispanic Horizons,* the same publication that had been so unceremoniously censored two years earlier, carried a full-page article praising the Executive Professor Program, which was by then underway. The first invited lecturer was Bill Coors, chief executive officer and president of the Adolph Coors Company of Golden, Colorado, who spoke on the free-enterprise system. The Coors company has been notoriously successful in breaking unions and gives support to ultra-right-wing movements and governments throughout the world.[65] It has at times been the object of boycott campaigns demanding an end to race discrimination in the workplace and an end to discrimination against women and homosexuals.

Myra Monfort, Ken Monfort's second wife, who served as legal counsel for the company in the 1980s, was interviewed regarding the gift that the family had made. She said: "What we wanted to do was bring someone with real life experiences into the classroom. The only ones aware of the complexity of a situation are those who have lived through it."[66] Obviously, she wasn't promoting the idea that students should be exposed to the testimony of union leaders, minority activists, or injured workers in meatpacking plants or beer factories.

Ken Monfort himself served as a distinguished professor in UNC's School of Business in 1978. He also served for a number of years on the Colorado Board of Agriculture — which governs Colorado State University (CSU) in Fort Collins, the University of Southern Colorado in Pueblo, and Fort Lewis College in Durango — and received an honorary doctorate from CSU in 1987. The next year the family gave $1 million to establish an endowed chair in agriculture at CSU. Monfort personally recruited Gary Smith, an animal science researcher who had worked with the company for many years, to the chair.

After joining the CSU faculty, the Monfort recruit took the case to the media that red meat does not cause cancer and that U.S. beef is healthy and safe for U.S. consumers. (U.S. beef was banned in European Common Market countries, which cited the use of chemical additives and unsanitary production methods.)[67] A bill (HB 1176) was introduced in the Colorado State Legislature allowing punitive damages to be exacted from anyone who makes claims about environmental or health hazards of perishable food products without "reliable scientific facts and scientific data." Although the bill was publicly identified with apple-growing interests, it was backed by the Colorado Cattle Feeders Association, the Colorado Farm Bureau, and the Colorado Cattlemen's Association. It received little opposition in the state but became a source of embarrassment nationally and was vetoed by Colorado's governor, Roy Romer. Had the bill passed, small-scale research efforts could have been effectively squelched through intimidation. When competing studies about controversial subjects existed, only those armed with corporate-financed research facilities would have been deemed credible, and others would have had to relinquish what meager resources they had to pay the corporations who brought suit against them.[68]

Ken Monfort waged a campaign in 1988, when he was president of the American Meat Institute, to "streamline" beef inspection.[69] Inspection is intended to detect diseases and contamination in meat. The streamlined system gave more responsibility to packers, rather than to U.S. Department of Agriculture USDA government inspectors, for examining meat. It also introduced spot checking as a replacement for the inspection of all carcasses. Monfort plants were part of a pilot program to test the new method.

A meat inspector at Monfort's Grand Island plant, David Carney, testified in 1990 before the USDA's Food Safety and Inspection Service that the Streamlined Inspection System (SIS) was designed to increase line speed in the processing of beef, not to assure quality control. He said that "beef has never been filthier."[70] Another inspector at the Grand Island plant testified that he was fired after he refused to accept for inspection meat that had been improperly processed under the new guidelines. Nine USDA inspectors signed an eleven-page letter to the secretary of agriculture outlining their assessment of the SIS as it was being implemented in the Monfort plant. They concluded: "In an industry caught cheating so many times, we do not believe that higher profits and lower government inspection costs are good enough reason to move meat inspection toward a corporate honor system."[71] David Carney's sixteen-page affidavit explained that the inspectors were not acting simply out of self-interest in condemning the SIS; their jobs are protected by civil service regulations. He explained:

> It's a lot less work to just watch cattle whiz by than to cut and trim raw meat. With SIS they can get paid a full salary for going through the motions, but they're not happy about it. They want people to know what this program means, because they don't want their family and friends, or consumers all across the country, to eat the kind of diseased and filthy beef they can't condemn anymore.[72]

ConAgra received a "dishonorable mention" award from the Council on Economic Priorities (CEP) in 1991, in part because of Monfort's advocacy of streamlined meat inspection. A CEP press release of April 4, 1991, says: "Whistleblowing USDA inspectors claim the company has falsified records, harasses employees who seek safer regulations, and have found meat inspected under the new system with microbial contamination rates up to ten times higher than normal." Nevertheless, the SIS remained firmly in place.

On April 30, 1992, ABC's *PrimeTime Live* aired a segment targeting "Dirty Meat," including film footage from Monfort and other plants participating in the SIS. This was followed several days later by a Denver-based TV production defending the company's health standards. A *Greeley Tribune* columnist declared: "Film of meat being dropped on the floor of a meatpacking plant was provided by a federal meat inspector. Was he concerned about a health issue or losing his job?"[73] Actually, USDA inspector Dale Gorman was removed from the worksite in Greeley's Monfort plant because of his cooperation in getting the ABC–TV film crew into the plant. He was threatened with a month's suspension by USDA officials in Colorado, then was transferred to another state instead.

Gorman says that he had been stonewalled in earlier attempts to call attention to unsafe and unsanitary conditions in the Greeley plant.[74]

The *Greeley Tribune*'s Sunday Business/Agriculture section often reads as if it had been provided directly by Monfort's public relations department. For example, school children recently competed for prizes in an essay contest based on information given to them by the Weld County Cowbelles about "water use by the beef industry and benefits society receives from that use."[75] Although the newspaper provided no general review of Jeremy Rifkin's *Beyond Beef: The Rise and Fall of the Cattle Culture,* published in the spring of 1992, it ran a series of diatribes against people such as Rifkin, who "would like us to eat what they feel is good for us — who have an ultimate goal to convince us they are superior to all the rest of us."[76] Warning the public not to succumb to the "scare tactics" of environmentalists and health advocates, a Denver member of the National Cattlemen's Association said that only big ranchers and feedlot owners would survive a major reduction in beef consumption.[77] A spokesperson from Greeley's slaughterhouse said that a reduction in meat consumption would affect mostly smaller companies, asserting that Greeley's plant was "fairly safe . . . assuming no stringent, new local regulations are put in place."[78]

Although the *Tribune* occasionally prints news or opinions that are less than complimentary to the Monfort company, it granted editorial space on a biweekly basis for a number of years to Ken Monfort, who therefore had the opportunity to comment regularly on public issues involving corporate interests. Although Monfort was still on the Board of Directors of ConAgra and was involved with new investments in Australia when he began writing the newspaper column, he often identified himself as "a retired businessman" and referred to Monfort, Inc., as "my old company." The columns were mostly devoted to damage control. Monfort also commented on local, state, national, and international politics, extolling foreign investments as a patriotic cause, and humanizing corporate affairs, corporate leaders, and the elected officials of their choice. The image Monfort projected of himself was that of a loveable defender of homegrown values, appealing to the prejudices of his readers in a self-conscious way, or — in a reversal of the Archie Bunker tradition — weaning them gently from liberal illusions: "A person in our society has an awful hard time making certain points," he wrote, "without being called a racist or a bigot."[79]

Monfort's criticism of a college professor who occasionally took the company to task was blunted by an affectionate reference to him as "my good friend so-and-so" (to the chagrin of the professor discussed, who had met Monfort once at a social event).[80] Professors who spoke out against corporate greed were invariably identified as "Communists" and "Socialists." Monfort's attacks against environmentalists identified them as "Hollywood types" who didn't have to worry about economic matters.[81]

When sidestepping issues was not feasible, Ken Monfort assumed innocence. As president of the American Meat Institute, he was interviewed by a *Chicago Tribune* reporter who questioned him about soaring workplace injuries in the industry. Monfort answered: "I would guess there was a little thinking that packinghouse work was tough and hard and dangerous, and that's just the way it's gonna be. . . . Until the government started keeping statistics, I don't think most of us knew how bad we were."[82] Yet, the company did everything in its power to avoid government oversight.

Another of Monfort's public roles was that of defender of business morality and, by implication, of businessmen's right to govern. He regularly commented on corruption by public figures, distancing himself and his friends from such behavior and — incidentally — attempting to exonerate the system that puts such people in power. When his own close friends or associates were charged with corruption, he maintained a discreet silence or offered advice: "The public is awfully forgiving to those who admit a mistake."[83]

A union organizer, commenting on the way that Ken Monfort was able to use charisma to overcome distrust of corporate power, said: "He's been good at it. Give the devil his due."[84] Ken Monfort's charisma is, of course, not always enough to win public confidence when crucial issues are at stake. Water pollution from feedlots has become a critical concern of Weld County residents, who are also faced with the depletion and contamination of underground water supplies and with threats to fish and wildlife from the diversion of stream water for urban use. When a Texas-based corporation, National Hog Farms, began to set up facilities for hog-slaughtering operations near Greeley, some residents challenged the efficiency of its manure-disposal system. In March 1990, Weld County citizens rejected an initiative that would have required National Hog Farms to construct a waste-treatment facility near its operations southeast of Greeley. Environmentalists generally favored the initiative, but it also had the support of beer magnate Joseph Coors and railroad tycoon Phillip Anschutz, who own hunting ranges near the site where National Hog Farms was locating. The last day that new material related to the controversy could be submitted to appear in the newspaper before the vote, a full-page ad was run with more than fifteen hundred names opposing the initiative. Most of the names were Hispanic, and alongside them ran a bold-face legend, "PAID BY US (NOT ANSCHUTZ)."[85]

What the ad did not say was that Monfort supervisory personnel had circulated among employees to solicit signatures and donations. Supervisors told workers that if the hog farm were required to construct a manure-treatment facility, Monfort would eventually have to do the same, and the money would come out of their pockets in the form of reduced bonuses or no bonuses at all. A former manager said:

> The supervisors didn't know anything about it. They felt there was such pressure coming on top they might be fired if they said no to some things. A lot of the supervisors on night shift don't even live in town. They didn't even know the signatures were going to appear in the newspaper. . . . They were just going around and asking people to sign a piece of paper that said they support the hog farm. . . . Most people who signed it had no idea what they were signing. A lot of these people don't even speak English.[86]

When Monfort has been embroiled repeatedly in controversies about water use, water pollution, or air pollution, they often attempt to skirt the law or, if necessary, rewrite it.[87]

There are regulatory standards for odor pollution in the State of Colorado. However, citizens who complain to officials about odors emanating from the Monfort plant are told that to try to enact more stringent regulations would be dangerous because legislators could (and presumably would) use this as an occasion to make the already loose standards even less stringent. In May 1990, in spite of the fact that the Weld County Health Department's "odor sniffers" included Monfort employees as "trained volunteers," the company was cited five times for odor violations. According to state law, each violation requires a fine of $25,000 to be levied against the offending party. Monfort's legal office asked for a hearing, which was to be held the following October. Meanwhile, the office negotiated for a postponement of fines while the company sought to replace odor-control equipment with state-of-the-art technology. The date for compliance with the agreement was moved ahead a number of times, and the company paid a total fine of $5,000 before new equipment was in operation by July 1991.

Odor problems are usually brushed off by the town's elite (who tend to live on lakefronts outside the affected areas), as nothing more than the "smell of money" or, at worst, as an image problem that plagues Greeley. The director for environmental protection of the Weld County Health Department, Wes Potter, told us that his office received an average of twelve calls a day complaining of slaughterhouse-related odors.[88] These were regarded as a "nuisance," because, he said, the department was doing all it could to contain the problem. A recording device had been installed to take off-hours calls, which could then be screened for "repeat offenders" (that is, people who called too often complaining about odors).

Residents who live downwind from the rendering plant (where meat by-products are processed into dog food) had to shut their windows on hot summer evenings to avoid vomiting from the smell.[89] Yet their problem was regarded by municipal and county officials as "psychological" and not a "real health hazard."[90] The *Greeley Tribune* normally took a benign view of the situation and gave warm praise to the company when new odor-control equipment was finally installed. One day, however, a short article appeared in the paper without a byline:

> Monfort Odor Blamed on Open Plant Door — The Weld County Health Department did not find any odor violations at Monfort Inc. on Wednesday despite numerous complaints by northeast Greeley residents. . . . A Monfort official said today the problem occurred when a blood dryer stopped working for about 10 minutes. While

workers were repairing the part, a door was accidentally left open and the odor escaped from the plant in north Greeley, said company attorney Ron Lambden. "The problems was solved as soon as possible," Lambden said. But there was no way that once the genie, so to speak, got out of the bottle, to get it back into the plant.[91]

Potter sent a certified inspector to the plant after residents of the downtown area and east Greeley began complaining about the smell. He reported that although the odor was strong, tests showed that the levels were not high enough to be violations. "A steady breeze and some gusty winds hindered the tests," Potter claimed.[92] A year later, the odor from the plant had not abated, and Potter had accepted a position as vice president of ConAgra Red Meat Cos. in charge of environmental operations.

Ken Monfort could cite environmental awards that he or the company received from the Greeley chapter of Trout Unlimited or other organizations to which he belonged. He even received an award from *The Environmental Monthly* for "voluntarily moving the world's largest feedlot" from North Greeley to sites in small towns within a 15-mile radius of the slaughterhouse — at a cost, reportedly, of more than $5 million.[93] Actually, the decision to move was made after a year-long campaign waged by a group called Citizens for Clean Air (who, one might imagine, received no more than a "nuisance award" from the Weld County Health Department). Small towns where feedlots were established discovered, too late, that pollution controls promised by the company were insufficient to protect the health of residents.

Controversy over odor pollution occurred recently at a privately owned wastewater-treatment plant southwest of Greeley near Milliken, where Northern Colorado Brine illegally accepted brine water from Monfort on a daily basis for over a year, until it was cited by the Weld County Health Department.[94] Even though the Monfort company has consistently underestimated the potential environmental cost of expansion projects undertaken, and even though it has been blamed regularly for polluting rivers,[95] violating Food and Drug Administration standards, and engaging in subterfuge to avoid prosecution for offenses to the community,[96] company spokespersons insist that the public "benefits greatly from a cooperative rather than adversarial relationship" with corporations.[97]

As the Monfort company has grown from a small family operation to the most lucrative subsidiary of one of the biggest transnational corporations in the world, the illusion of corporate beneficence has been challenged on many fronts. Each time the company faces a real threat to unencumbered expansion, however, those who are asked to make the biggest sacrifice are the company's own employees, whose "loyalty" can no longer be taken for granted.

When the Greeley slaughterhouse closed down in 1980, Ken Monfort declared: "If we don't sell and we reopen it, as far as I know we have a legal responsibility to negotiate with the union."[1] The legality of the situation remained unclear, however. When the plant reopened in 1982, Monfort said: "We're in one of those businesses where the fittest survive, and we hope to be one of the fittest."[2] Being one of the "fittest" meant refusing to recognize the union (United Food and Commercial Workers International Union — UFCW) and refusing to hire former workers who had participated actively in the strike that preceded the plant closure.

The company hired a new work force and bombarded workers with dire warnings about the consequences of unionism. All new employees were shown video footage of the plant closure that followed the 1979 strike and were told that if the union got back into the plant, they would lose their jobs to former workers. They were made to understand that speaking to union organizers could cost them their jobs.[3]

Threatening the newly recruited workers was not enough to assure that the union could be kept out of the slaughterhouse. At least an appearance of community support for the company management was needed to oppose the union's reorganizing drive. On June 6, 1983, the following "Open letter to Monfort Employees from Citizens of Greeley" appeared in the *Greeley Tribune*:

> The company cited economic reasons for the closure, but everyone in the community knew who was really at fault — the union. . . . Business in Greeley suffered greatly. Former Monfort employees certainly were not buying houses or cars; few could even afford basic necessities. For two years, the Greeley community suffered as the plant doors remained shut. . . . The City of Greeley out-of-the pocket cost because of the City of Greeley Police Department activities directly related to the strike during the 75 day period from October 31, 1979 to January 14, 1980 consumed 4500 man hours plus the costs of call up [of riot control forces] to handle potential disturbances

during the employees' coming back to work day represents an approximate minimum cost of some $44,635.00 with actual cost probably exceeding $50,000.00. These figures do not take into account the additional above budget costs incurred by the Weld County Sheriff's Department. In addition for the calendar year 1980, the sales tax suffered a shortfall of more than $500,000.00 which can be attributed directly to the unemployment which was created by Monfort's problems. It is easy to see the Greeley merchants during that period of time suffered some $25,000,000.00 or more in loss of sales that can be attributed to the plant closing.

Now, only one year after the plant's reopening the same union is trying to get back into the Monfort plant. We in the community believe that unionizing again could result in the same disaster we all saw before.

Ken Monfort personally maintained a low-key posture with regard to "restructuring" of the work force. He told reporters that labor costs "started becoming a problem" after Iowa Beef Processors (IBP) broke a strike in Dakota City, Nebraska, in 1969. Reduced wages and benefits were necessary to keep the company competitive, he said, and "the less-than-rollicking economic times makes people hang in there a little longer" — referring to workers who are in such desperate circumstances that they will tolerate worse conditions of employment.[4] (Former union members say that Monfort at one time told them that he would have resisted following IBP's tactics if the union had "held the line" in competing plants; union representatives pointed out that Monfort was always willing to buy IBP beef when the union was striking IBP. In any case, Monfort took the position in 1982 that "we're a lot smarter now than we were in 1980.")[5]

Although they did not dispute the disastrous effect of the strike and plant closing on the community, union members had a somewhat different story to tell about the background to these events. Jim Spohr, who worked at the slaughterhouse from 1970 to 1980, recalled the frustration that workers felt when Monfort was trying to force cutbacks on them before the strike. The union offered to consider accepting cutbacks if Monfort would let them look at company accounts.

We told him, we said, "we understand that people can hurt. That happens. Sometimes it's not their own fault. And we're reasonable people so just give us the books. Let us have a look at the books. Maybe we can cooperate and see if we can collectively figure out what the problem really is, you know. Are we really getting paid too much? Are we asking too much? Or are you maybe spending too much here where you should be maybe spending over here, whatever." And, of course, he [Monfort] said, "well, looking at the books is out of the question, take my word for it." And we said, "well . . . if you could show us some proof of where the problems really lie, we'll talk. But other than that, no, we are not going backwards," which is what he was asking us to do. We asked for no pay increase for that last contract. All we wanted at that time was to maintain, hold on to what we already had, not give it up.[6]

Although Monfort claimed that the company had suffered financial losses, union members pointed out that he had recently bought a jet airplane for $1.5 million, a whole fleet of trucks, and two new meatpacking plants. (A third plant was purchased during the course of the strike.) Altogether, the company added 30 percent to its assets in 1979 and doubled its production capacity. Steve Thomas, the union's business representative, said: "I know money doesn't grow on trees, so they must be getting it from somewhere."[7]

The company agreed to disclose overall financial records, but would not provide a division-by-division breakdown on income and expenses. Workers were convinced that the books had been tampered with in any case. Monfort's president, Samuel Addoms, who had been hired specifically to oversee the company's expansion during "hard times," later declared: "There were more than sixty major packing firms in the meat industry in the early 1960s. There will be only ten large packers in the 1980s . . . and Monfort intends to be one of them."[8]

Before the contract negotiating time expired on Halloween 1979, Jim Spohr said that there was an "incredible speed-up." "Boy, did it ever speed up! You wouldn't believe it. There was meat fallin' all over the floors out there. The tables were runnin' all over. There was no possible way to keep up. They were firin' people at a rate of ten a day just for anything, any little thing. . . . I guess he was making a point there [referring to Monfort]."

A gradual speed-up had been going on throughout the 1970s. Joe Benavidez, who began working at the slaughterhouse in 1966, said:

> We were doing our best, but it was just too fast for us. So the meat would just pile up. We'd just have to stack 'em up. I remember this one time, this supervisor . . . he got a piece of meat, and he threw it at me. And I had the knife in my hand, and it hit my knife and the knife went up in the air, and just about cut my face with it. I got so mad that I grabbed the knife; I went after him. I told him, "If I get my hands on you, I'll cut your ears off!" So he took off. I thought he'd turn me in to the office, but he didn't. . . . I didn't see him for about three or four hours. . . . That's one of the only times that I ever got into it with any of my supervisors. I used to get along pretty good with mostly all of 'em. This one thought he was doing his job by trying to make us work faster. But that wasn't his job to do.[9]

Steve Thomas, who started working at the plant in 1969 and who was first elected as a union steward in 1974, said that speed-up was not an issue at the formal bargaining table. Instead, he said,

> One of the ways we did bargain with them, we slowed that chain down. That was our way of getting our way. . . . I think the company felt a little out of control because the union was so strong. . . . I mean when it got too hot on the kill floor we just quit working, went downstairs and cooled off. We didn't talk about it. And I still believe, I mean, that's how you get a strong union. Everybody sticks together; it's not the officers. I mean everybody likes to blame the officers.[10]

After 1975, Thomas served as full-time business representative for the union. He says that when he first started working at Monfort in 1975 they were killing 120 head of beef an hour and by the time of the 1979 strike they were killing 192. "Already in 1975," he said, "with a kill of 150 per hour, we were totally maxed out. . . . I was always tired every night when I went home."

It was after the union won some increases in pay and benefits following a fifty-six-day strike in 1970, and again in 1973 negotiations, Thomas said, that the company "really started changing their attitude. . . . They had these quality control people . . . it was so much bullshit. . . . They also hired a security force; the first group they hired even carried guns. We all joked about that you know, but they, just, I don't know, kept watch in effect I guess, and they really tried to streamline their operation."

When so-called efficiency experts were brought into the plant to do time studies, workers were angry. Jim Spohr recalled:

> Those people were, they were animals. I don't think there was a sensitive nerve in their whole body. I just can't think of a nasty enough term to use for people like that. Their job was to get people so scared that they would do anything they were told. And that's when people really started quitting. There were probably even more people fired.

The "efficiency drive" was accompanied by a turnover in supervisors. Some were transferred out of the Greeley plants to other Monfort operations. They had come up through the ranks as workers who had once been union members themselves, either at Monfort or in other packinghouses. In the 1970s new, specially trained supervisors were brought to Greeley, and others were sent away for training. The new approach, according to Spohr, was:

> You will do it or you will not work here. . . . Most of these people had no experience butchering whatsoever. Their method of supervision was "anybody messes up you simply fire them." That's what they were there for and that's what they did. . . . Employees weren't the only ones under pressure. The supervisors were also under pressure from the upper echelon of management. The mid-managers, they were under a lot of pressure, too. So, I could kind of see why we were pushed like we were. It didn't necessarily come from our supervisors. It came through our supervisors.

Spohr recalled that when he was working on cleanup, he would clean fat off the floors while people were on break and get things straightened up so the shop would be ready when they returned. One of the new supervisors saw him sitting in the locker room after break time smoking a cigarette all by himself after everybody else was back at work. "The supervisor said, 'What are you doing here?' I said, 'Well, I'm the cleanup man. I take my break afterwards.' And he says, 'You're telling me when you're taking a break?' " The supervisor took him to the office and said:

"I want this man suspended for a day." Well, the personnel manager wasn't there, so his assistant or whoever had me suspended for the day, which was fine. I just went home. And then when the real manager got back (Norm Peterson, that was his name) . . . when Norman got back, I explained what happened, and he said, "Well, just try not to get in his way; you'll get your day's pay of course." . . . Two or three times things like that happened. I think they wanted to look like they were doing a good job.[11]

Speed-up affected the pride that workers had in the job they were doing. Spohr explained:

When I first started working at Monfort, it was a quality product. You made the right cuts the right way; if you didn't, you sent the meat back to make it right. Then all of a sudden they became much more interested in production as opposed to quality. It got to where you couldn't recognize some of the cuts coming down the table because people had to go so fast that they didn't have time to do it right. . . . When a piece of meat falls on the floor, there's a certain procedure that is used to clean it because we use salt on the floor. The floors are wet most all the time and the salt is to keep people from slipping. . . . Well, when the meat falls on the floor consequently it picks up the salt and everything else on the floor. Traditionally, we would take it over to the sink, wash it off good, dry it, the inspector would look at it. He O.K.'d it, and we could use it. It got to where that wasn't even happening anymore. Meat would fall on the floor, they would pick up the meat, wipe it across the front of their frock, throw it on the table, bag it and ship it. . . . The supervisor could be standing right next to you, and he never saw it.

Workers who had been at the plant for a number of years resisted the changes in part because they felt that they had given their best to the company in good faith and had been betrayed. Joe Benevidez said:

In the earlier years, the packing house was a great place to work. It was. Kenny Monfort was a great guy. . . . He'd go out to the "kill floor" with us, wherever we were at, come and talk to all the employees. . . . If you had any complaints, if you had to go over somebody's head, you could go all the way to Kenny Monfort if you had to. He would listen to you. Of course this was in the early years. The work got harder, 'cause he made you work faster; he made you put out more work; he put you to the limit, at the end.

When Benevidez was asked what kind of power the workers had to control the speed-up process, he said:

Well they would speed up, we would complain, and they would slow it back down, you know things like that. And then they brought in these "efficiency experts." They'd come out and stand right behind you with their time clocks. They'd time this guy, and they'd time somebody else. And the fastest guy, that's who they would go by. . . . There's always some guy there that wants to show off, you know. Sure, anybody can bone out a strip in ten or twelve seconds, a few times, but you couldn't do it all day long. They couldn't expect you to do it eight hours. . . . Some of these guys thought it was pretty funny; they didn't take it that serious. They didn't know how serious it was gonna be.

Everyone who testified about working at the slaughterhouse had ongoing health problems that originated on the job. Besides the direct effects of speed-up, there were many other work-related injuries and illnesses. Steve Thomas fractured his skull when an air pressure hose broke while he was snipping off hind legs of beef. The coupling of the hose came loose and started whipping back and forth from the air pressure. "I ducked and stood back up and it came back and hit me right here, knocked me out. If it hadn't been for a guy named Jim Hager standing up over it, who caught me when I fell off the bench . . . well." Thomas recalled other problems, which he says were "not serious":

That was the only serious injury I had, I mean I stabbed myself in the groin once, and I stabbed myself in the knee, and my thumbs and fingers were cut. . . . My hands bother me still, you know, from pulling that hide and I still have arthritis in my hands from that, and from the cold..Other than that my back is really bad. I have a ruptured disk. My left leg is numb all the time [because of the ruptured disc in his back]. But I never missed work from any of these things. It's just a matter of hurting. There isn't anything you can do.

Thomas added that his hearing is "fucked up" (from the noise of the machinery, the air knives, and the chain that carries the meat along the disassembly line). "But I'm not in any way disabled. I have plenty of friends that are."

Joe Benavidez takes medication every day to control pains he has in both shoulders. "After twelve years in the packinghouse," he says, "I got rheumatoid arthritis. I was about two years away from the packinghouse when the arthritis started bothering me really bad. The pain is in all my joints." He has scars on his hands from operations he had while working at the packinghouse. "My wrists used to swell up so bad. I couldn't hardly move my hands." He also had a heart attack while working at the plant. Since then he's had another.

> I had to have open-heart surgery; I had to have a triple-bypass. I'm not saying it was all from the packinghouse, but a lot of it might have been a result of the hard work and the stress. . . . Just when you got used to doing one job then they'd put you on another job. That was later on. Before, you would bid on a job; and once you got the job, that was your job. Nobody could take it away from you. If you wanted to bid on another job, you had the right to do it. You had a three-day trial period. If you didn't like that job, you went back to your old job. There, toward the end, you worked where they put you; that was it.

Jim Spohr avoided knife work as much as possible.

> I tried to get the easier jobs. . . . I don't care for knives, they're too sharp. I had a hard time keeping a knife sharp, especially when things got speeded up, which means you work even harder trying to saw through the meat rather than cut through it. When the line ran slower, you had time between cuts to keep your knife sharp. You even had time for a little chit-chat if you wanted. Anyway, later on, I spent a lot of time on cleanup, quite frankly.

That didn't keep him from getting hurt, however.

> Once I was working on the night shift on cleanup. After they get done they have a crew come in and wash the blood all down, wash the tables all off with this high pressure water hose and I remember I was back in the blood pit washing it down and they had these grates across the floor. You had to take these grates out so you could get down in underneath to wash. You wash from the top but you could direct your hose down there to clean it. Well, it was really cool in there that evening. I'm sure it was in the fall. And the steam from

this hose was just clouding up everything. You couldn't see more than a foot or more in front of you. It was just that cold in there and the water was hot enough to create a considerable amount of steam. Remember, I was washing it down and I turned around to wash something else and stepped back into that hole I just created. And it was about two or three feet deep. I just stepped right into it. I fell back. Cut the back of my head real good. I think I got nine or ten stitches in it. They sent me up to the hospital. This was at night. The doctor came in and sewed it up and sent me back out to the plant.

He didn't come in the following day and was given a hard time about that. "My head still hurt real bad, and I could tell he [the supervisor] didn't believe me. But there was no way you could prove it. They're not a sympathetic lot out there."

During the strike that began in November 1979, Monfort workers suffered various forms of harassment that increased antagonism between the union and the company. Monfort cut off the company's contributions to medical insurance for workers. Strikers were cited by the city for burning refuse in open containers to keep warm on the picket line. Twenty-four strikers were arrested on various charges ranging from "criminal extortion" (verbally threatening a security guard) to misdemeanors such as trespassing and "attempted vandalism." A Monfort truck driver tried to run over picketers. A bullet was fired into the front window of Steve Thomas's apartment.[12]

Roland Mapelli, who became chairman of the Monfort Board of Directors in 1972, was thought to be responsible for hiring thugs to intimidate workers and was blamed for much of the heavy-handedness in the administration at Monfort.[13] A haystack at the Mapelli ranch was apparently set on fire during the strike, and Mapelli later said that he received threats on his life.

Monfort's final offer was presented to the union in early January 1980. In return for eliminating the cost-of-living allowance, workers were offered a 20 cent per hour wage increase each year for three years. This was unacceptable to workers because inflation at the time was 13 percent annually. The offer also proposed eliminating the afternoon rest break and cutting back in the number of work hours guaranteed to employees annually. Vacation time was to be cut, a birthday holiday was to be eliminated, health insurance and other benefits were to be reduced, and the company proposed to contract out sanitation jobs to non-union employees and to eliminate job security clauses in the contract. New hires were to be given a lower base wage, threatening the security of those already employed. "If I was working out there beside a guy who was doing the same job, but making $2.50 an hour less than me, I wouldn't feel too secure in my job," said Steve Thomas.

Because workers knew that the company had purchased another beef plant in Grand Island, Nebraska, in preparation for the strike in Greeley, their options were extremely limited. By the time Greeley workers were confronted with this final offer, Monfort had expanded the Grand Island plant and had invited a union (the National Maritime Union) with no history in meatpacking to represent the workers. A contract was signed at the Grand Island plant behind the workers' backs, at rates far below those prevailing in the industry. Steve Thomas told Monfort's Greeley employees that in the Grand Island plant, "to promote good relations with its employees, [the company] gave this sweetheart union a desk inside the plant . . . and arranged periodic beer busts and other happy little occasions."[14] At other plants that had been purchased in April and December of that same year (in Florida and in Denver), "company unions" were also in place.

Monfort had already begun hiring replacement workers in Greeley when the January offer was made. Most of those who had gone out on strike were convinced by then that the company wanted their union out of the plant at any cost. They decided to frustrate the company's plans by going back to work without a contract, prepared to protect their jobs and their working conditions through their own efforts, with or without union assistance.

Thomas said that by that time workers were unhappy with the union. The Washington office had reportedly negotiated with Monfort before the final offer was made. The national president of the union, William Wynn, had not supported the local union's plan to send truckloads of strikers to the Grand Island plant to shut it down, nor had he supported their drive to initiate a boycott of Monfort products (although he did call for a boycott two months later when the plant was about to close down indefinitely).

When Greeley strikers reported back to work on January 14, 1980, they did so determined to protect their long-term interests. They planned to battle for a new contract from inside the plant.

Failing that, they would go down fighting. The company was surprised by their move and locked them out for several days. Although replacement workers had been told to report to work that day, Monfort said that production couldn't begin because not enough government meat inspectors were available. The city sent a riot control force to the scene, complete with face masks and bags containing gas masks. They expected a confrontation between strikers and scabs.

After production resumed on January 15, 1980, workers reported constant harassment, especially of union stewards who were attempting to defend workers' rights. When a major speed-up was initiated by the company, workers retaliated by slowing down. Steve Thomas said:

> I remember one time Gene Meakins [director of personnel and public relations] calls me at my apartment in Greeley and says, "They're all standing up on the tables. They won't go to work. It's anarchy! It's anarchy!" and all this stuff, you know. It really bothered them that they didn't have control. . . . He fired 160 guys that day, and it wasn't even a matter of money. It was the fact when they said 'jump,' the guys didn't."

When the workers' demands for slowing down production were rebuffed, they engaged in sabotage. Steve Thomas explained: "This one guy figured out how to make a drop of water fall on this 440 box and shut the whole thing down about every hour. It took them about a week to figure what was going on. It was an electrical thing. It was pretty slick." When the workers won a round, they shouted, " 'Let's hear it for the union!' 'Yeah!' — 'Let's hear it for the company!' 'Boo!' — Five hundred people shouting. It was a great thing, it really was."

Jim Spohr recalled:

> He [Monfort] wanted us out of there under whatever conditions it took and that's the way it was going to be. I'm sure he was dead set on breaking the union. . . . I think at that time if we'd said, "gee, we'll take a 50 percent wage cut," I don't think he would have allowed us to continue working with the union as our representation. I'm sure that was exactly what he had in mind.

Years later, Monfort skirted charges that he was a classic union buster by saying that high interest rates were responsible for the plant shutdown. "The nice easy way is to blame it all on the unions," he said, "but that, frankly, wasn't true."[15] Addressing himself to investors, he defended the company's maneuvers by promising them stable returns: "We're trying to turn the cattle business into something for widows and orphans."[16] He assured his supporters: "We're not broke, we did not file Chapter 11 bankruptcy, and I do not beat my wife."[17] The question of whether the company closed down because of the strike or because of economic pressures to cut costs was crucial in deciding whether workers were eligible to receive unemployment benefits (and back pay, once the plant reopened). Both the union and the company disputed these issues in the courts for years, distracting attention from the more fundamental question of whether the company had conspired to break the union at the time of the strike.

When the Greeley plant closed down "indefinitely" in March 1980, long-term workers were able to withdraw savings accumulated in a profit-sharing fund where their money had been held in trust by the union (another benefit that Monfort was trying to rescind). Those who left town had a hard time selling their homes, because the real estate market fell apart due to the plant closing. Local businesses would not hire former Monfort employees, at first for fear of retaliation from Monfort and later because they were regarded as having caused the plant closing through their militancy during the strike. One former union member said at the time: "I've had people take the applications right out of my hands when they find out I worked at Monfort."[18]

Unionists predicted Monfort's long-term plan. Steve Thomas told former strikers and their supporters: "At the very worst, the company has a huge tax write-off from which it can benefit. Or it can keep the plant shut down . . . and then later on . . . using some pretext, try to reopen it without a union."[19] His words were prophetic.

Jim Spohr went back to apply for a job at Monfort when the plant reopened two years later, but, like many other union members, he was told that he didn't "qualify." He's now working at a nursing home and rehabilitation center, counseling alcoholics. "I compare working at Monfort to being on a rock out in the middle of a river. You're not going to go anywhere and you're really afraid to jump off that rock out into the river 'cause the water's swift and cold and there's not many places to jump to. So most people just hang to that rock for dear life. And they say, 'It's the worst job in the world but it's the only job I got!' "

Joe Benavidez had decided after two months on strike that he would not return to work without a contract; he took the money due him from the union's profit-sharing fund and opened up a bar near the Monfort plant. He named the bar Union Hall Lounge. It had one pool table and a seating capacity of about twenty-five. When the plant closed down in March, he was confident that it would reopen "in a couple of weeks." "Maybe it's my imagination, but it seems like when it's good weather, everything works out better."[20]

Although the Union Hall Lounge prospered, it was not because the plant reopened "in a couple of weeks." Public Relations Director Gene Meakins announced on April 1: "It becomes a matter of allocating your resources where they will make the best return on investment."[21] While the company pleaded poverty during its attempt to break the union, reports to the stockholders painted a different picture. Before the company-union dispute began, Monfort President Samuel Addoms had written in a company publication:

> In 1978 we were able to improve productivity as a result of cost containment initiatives started in 1977. . . . Although results were impacted by explosive inflation in the underlying costs of raw materials and by the effects of hedging activities, we were able to absorb these impacts and still report a modest profit. . . . At the same time, increases in the company's underlying inventory values have allowed us to initiate longer term plans for future growth.[22]

This summed up what the workers knew, that the company was prospering even as the country in general, and the meat industry in particular, were experiencing economic contraction, and that this was happening at the cost of their bodies and minds. In an address to the Colorado Meat Dealers Association in August 1979, Ken Monfort had said: "It is imperative that any of us who wish to survive in this business will need not only to buy well, sell well and produce efficiently . . . we will also need a tough and competitive labor strategy." The wife of a striker said several months later: "They [the workers] have to live their lives in their bodies. They want something left when they retire."[23]

The company had installed cameras and listening devices in the plant as the showdown between workers and management was approaching. Families were suffering from "strain, heartbreak, and unbearable tension every day in the plant and every day in the workers' homes."[24] The company that the workers had helped build was determined to prove them expendable. And it became more and more apparent that the union was also letting them down.

The Amalgamated Meat Cutters and Butcher Workmen of North America, which had represented Greeley slaughterhouse workers for almost two decades, had merged with the Retail Clerks International Union less than a year before the Greeley slaughterhouse closed down. The new union established as a result of the merger was called the United Food and Commercial Workers union (UFCW). The two unions had been competing for membership over the years. Union leaders said that the merger would end their competitive status, while giving workers more strength through numbers. Both parties to the merger belonged to the AFL–CIO labor federation, which has incorporated most organized workers in the United States and Canada since 1956. The UFCW became the largest AFL–CIO union on the continent.

Membership in the Meat Cutters union had been declining in the late 1970s. One out of every three meatpacking companies had gone out of business. This was partly due to decreasing demand for red meat and partly due to the location of new meat companies in "right-to-work" states, where laws designed to discourage union organization allow employees to refrain from joining unions even where union contracts exist. Ironically, the decreasing demand for red meat was brought about partly by high prices to consumers. Increased "efficiency" in production did not lower retail prices. As the newer companies more than doubled their share of the market, the price of red meat increased.[25]

While membership in the Meat Cutters union had been decreasing, membership in the Retail Clerks union had increased, because service jobs were beginning to replace manufacturing jobs in the 1970s. The AFL–CIO encouraged organizing efforts among service employees, many of whom had been working for minimum wages before unionization.

After the union merger, the headquarters of the new UFCW union was in Washington, D.C., where the Retail Clerks headquarters had been. The Chicago offices of the Meat Cutters union were closed down. The president of the new union came from the Retail Clerks union. Twenty-five international vice presidents of the Retail Clerks and twenty-three international vice presidents of the Meat Cutters retained their positions. Meatpackers had to wage a power struggle within the union to avoid subordination. They needed to retain an emphasis on bargaining with established companies for "master contracts" in order to improve newer companies' wage and benefit structures. (Master contracts or pattern contracts are those negotiated simultaneously for a number of plants within the same industry.)

In October 1979, immediately before the union contract in Greeley was about to expire, the UFCW negotiated master contracts in Midwestern slaughterhouses that established similar provisions for wages and benefits in a number of plants. John Morrell & Co. agreed to an accord covering eight thousand workers that called for a series of wage increases over three years; an improved pension plan; more paid vacation time; and increased dental, health, and welfare benefits. The contract also required employment of a union steward or officer of a local union as a safety specialist. The company was prohibited from closing a plant and then purchasing the same or similar products made in the same plant by a different (or "bogus") company. These provisions laid the basis for similar accords with Wilson Foods Corporation's 7,000 employees, George Hormel & Company's 7,000 employees, and other meatpacking plants, including Hy Grade Foods Corporation (2,500 employees), Swift & Company, Armour and Company, and Cudahy Company (20,000 employees altogether).

If Monfort had not been able to keep the newly purchased Grand Island plant going and to begin production in Florida and Denver at the same time, it's unlikely that the company could have broken the union in Greeley when it did. The new president of the UFCW (perhaps responding to Monfort's personal appeal when he went to Washington, D.C., in December 1979) undercut the successful efforts of meatpackers during the first months of the UFCW's existence. Instead of encouraging workers to remain firm in the face of corporate scheming against hard-won workers' rights, the UFCW encouraged conciliation and concessions. The attitude that subsequently came to characterize the union is revealed in a remark by UFCW President William Wynn: "Where companies are in trouble, we're prepared to be responsible and understanding."[26] The problem was, the union was in more trouble than the companies that got concessions.

The constitution of the UFCW allowed for the appointment by top union leaders of local representatives who negotiated on behalf of workers. The local leadership of the Meat Cutters Union had been elected directly by plant workers. The merger thus replaced a democratically controlled workers' organization with an enormous bureaucracy. At first, representatives who had been elected previously by workers were reappointed by the new union leaders, but as political maneuvering took place within the union's upper echelons, appointments were made arbitrarily without worker input. There was also encouragement for union locals to become submerged in larger organizing units. Over a ten-year period, the number of locals went from 900 to 550. Greeley's Local 641 was phased out and became part of the UFCW's Local 7, which by the end of the 1980s encompassed twenty-one thousand workers, most of whom were retail clerks.

When Monfort's Greeley slaughterhouse reopened in 1982, business magazines reported that total labor costs would be 25 percent less than in 1980, "while new operating methods unrestricted by the union's contract should, by themselves, increase productivity 25%."[27] The closure of the Greeley plant, one of the largest in the nation, was followed by a frenzy of plant closures and a juggling of assets throughout the Midwest. In August 1982, *Business Week* reported:

> Swift Independent Packing Corporation (SIPCO) reopened two slaughterhouses that Esmark had closed and renegotiataed their union contracts, cutting labor costs by about 50%. . . . At Wilson, the company's new management has closed uneconomical plants in Denver, Des Moines, and Oklahoma City and has concentrated its production at more efficient facilities, such as in Marshall, Mo. There, Wilson has doubled output while increasing the payroll by only 50%.

Many companies bought plants that were temporarily closed down and reopened them, declaring them new facilities. *Business Week* reported: "Unencumbered by old wage contracts, they can hire a new labor force. This can produce spectacular cost savings. Esmark closed both its Guymon, Oklahoma and Moultrie, Georgia slaughterhouses in April, 1981. When SIPCO reopened them a month later, it was able to slash labor costs to an average $7.50 per hour, 50% less than Esmark had been paying."[28]

The undercutting of labor unions and the cutting of wages and benefits was accompanied by a rapidly accelerating concentration of ownership in the meatpacking industry. In many cases, companies that closed down did not have outdated facilities, as news reports indicated. The plants reopened and resumed production immediately with a "restructured" labor force. A. V. Krebs wrote:

> No better example of the practices that have become almost epidemic in the meatpacking industry was seen than in December 1983 when the Greyhound Corporation shut down its 13 Armour Food Company meatpacking plants, eliminating 1500 union members whose earnings averaged approximately $10 an hour. Two days later, the corporate agribusiness giant ConAgra, with over 30,000 employees, purchased Armour and reopened 12 [of the same] plants with a nonunion workforce of some 900 employees whose starting pay began at $6 an hour.[29]

Other companies filed for bankruptcy in order to restructure their workforces and reopen with reduced wages, two-tiered wage structures (lower base wages for new hires), and without cost-of-living agreements. Following the example of Monfort in Grand Island, Nebraska (see Chapter 2), companies actively recruited minorities and immigrants who were willing to work under such conditions.

In 1980, IBP which already owned nine beef plants and had overtaken Swift & Company as the nation's largest beef producer, opened the "world's largest beefpacking plant" in Garden City, Kansas. IBP hired Vietnamese immigrants, Mexicans, and Central American refugees. An idle packing plant in Garden City was then reopened as Val-Agri, which was later purchased by SIPCO, and later purchased by Monfort. Initially, migrant workers in these plants were young single men (just as they had been in Grand Island in 1979 and in the Greeley plant when it reopened in 1982); increasingly, young mothers joined their ranks.[30]

Turnover was so high at non-union plants that organizing was almost impossible. Because of continuing speed-up, some plants experienced a turnover of 100 percent every few months.[31] While the UFCW continued to represent a large majority of organized meatpackers, the number of meatpackers who were organized continued to decline. In an effort to turn this situation around, the UFCW accepted low-wage contracts in return for union recognition. Critics call these arrangements "backdoor deals," which weaken the bargaining position of other UFCW locals and sometimes force plant closures in higher- wage packinghouses.[32]

In the 1970s, IBP began its rise to predominance among meatpacking companies by fighting the union in its plant at Dakota City, Nebraska, by keeping new plants unorganized, and by bringing in the Teamsters union to undercut wages in a Kansas slaughterhouse. ConAgra emerged in the 1980s as the most aggressive in buying out established companies and undercutting union agreements. ConAgra entered the red meat business after having established itself as a multinational conglomerate in other food commodity sectors. It then waged "the most aggressive acquisition campaign in agribusiness history."[33]

Before merging with ConAgra in 1987, Monfort of Colorado had not been in decline. But Monfort was fearful of being outmaneuvered by bigger companies. While ConAgra was purchasing twenty-one Armour facilities and reopening them with non-union work forces, Monfort was engaged in an antitrust lawsuit against Excel. Excel, the red meat division of Cargill, was vying with IBP for top place among meatpackers in North America. After the Cargill suit was lost, a new frenzy of buyouts and buybacks took place, including the Monfort/ConAgra merger. Commenting on the "concern" he had with regard to business concentration as he was fighting Cargill, Ken Monfort said:

> I thought at the time that it was going to lead to too much concentration — to two-firm concentration. Of course, we fought that all the way through the Supreme Court, and the Supreme Court said we were wrong. So that changed my mind a little. But, in addition to that, it seemed to me that if the industry was going to be concentrated there should be at least three large players instead of just two.[34]

In 1987, Monfort/ConAgra purchased sixteen SIPCO facilities as well as E. J. Miller Enterprises in Utah. That same year IBP gained (temporary) predominance in hog-slaughtering operations. While this new shakeout among meatpackers was occurring, the UFCW, spurred on by rising militancy among the rank and file, regained some initiative in bargaining. But almost half the time the union was still losing in contract negotiations. The general economy in the United States was improving and the big meatpacking companies were making record profits every year.

A 1985–1986 strike at the Hormel hog plant in Austin, Minnesota, was a watershed for the union in that it provided an opportunity to turn things around for workers. Hormel was operating at a profit after having received a loan from employees (in the form of a temporary wage cut) to expand operations. Nevertheless, the company insisted on extending the cut in wages and reducing benefits. Because Hormel workers' wages were above the industry norm, the UFCW did not give full support to the workers who were on strike. The Austin local felt that only an industry-wide effort could save their jobs — and revive the union movement. They successfully mobilized workers in other plants to support them in their drive to shut down production at Hormel and to prevent the company from signing a contract with scabs. Because some of those who showed solidarity with the Austin local had no-strike clauses in their contracts, the UFCW national leadership decided that it was necessary to collaborate with the company in repressing its own members.

Lewie Anderson represented the UFCW in the Hormel dispute. He presided over the Austin local's expulsion from the UFCW for going over the heads of national leadership in building a strike solidarity movement. But when repercussions from these events were felt throughout the country, Anderson determined to "stop the concessions."[35] He began publicly criticizing the union's top leadership. After being demoted by the union's president, he wrote a position paper, *Back to the Jungle.* He also established an organization, Research, Education, Advocacy, People (REAP), with a newsletter that has been published monthly since May 1990. The organization denounces the high salaries of union officials,[36] the infrequency of meetings among officials and delegates, and the oligarchic nature of the union's leadership structure. It also serves as a watchdog on union giveaways to corporations.

Neither REAP leadership nor the national UFCW leadership reflect the changing composition of the work force in meatpacking plants such as Monfort/ConAgra of Greeley, where young foreign-born workers — many of them women — are the large majority.

When the Greeley plant reopened in 1982, the company's manipulation of new hires, high turnover, and general suppression of organizing activity made union reorganization difficult. The transition the union itself was experiencing further complicated the reorganization drive.

Steve Thomas had left the union after the plant closure of 1980. He thought that the UFCW had made a big mistake when it chose to protect the Monfort company from "going broke" (which he thinks might have happened if Greeley strikers had been encouraged to promote a shutdown at the Grand Island plant). "Either they would have gone broke or we would have got a contract," he said. In any case, he didn't want to participate in the power struggles that were beginning to take place in the union at the time. He moved to Cheyenne, Wyoming, and opened a small business. Two years later, he returned to Greeley and helped organize for union elections in the plant, temporarily leaving the business in the hands of his family.

Thomas and other UFCW organizers spent an entire year waging an uphill battle to contact new hires and convince them that the union could offer them more protection than the company, which had turned its back on its own workers two years earlier. The morning that the union election was to take place, in June 1983, Thomas felt elated because he was sure of a victory. UFCW Local 7 organizers had obtained signed cards from 80 percent of the Greeley slaughterhouse workers authorizing a union election. "This is a miracle," he thought. "We just organized a bunch of scabs!" The union had tracked down the names of workers by copying down car license numbers and going to people's homes. He was certain that a majority would vote for the union. But on the morning of the election, Monfort called a meeting of the entire work force and told them that if they voted for the union he was going to fire them all and hire back the former workers. "We had no time, of course, to respond," said Thomas. "The atmosphere during the election was just one of intimidation. They had these great big supervisors pushing guys around and shoving the tables around and the whole thing was really intimidating. That . . . lawyer Sykes planned the whole thing, and he had these big thugs with him."

Charlie Sykes was a well-known union-buster who had opened an office in Denver after working for years with IBP and other packers in Iowa, Nebraska, and elsewhere.[37] When the vote in Greeley was lost by 396 to 301, the union challenged 94 of the votes and charged the company with "patterns of racketeering." Specific charges were brought against Charlie Sykes, but those who had agreed to testify against him never did. Charlie Sykes continued to be associated with the Monforts into the 1990s (see Chapter 4).

The National Labor Relations Board (NLRB) eventually ruled that Monfort, Inc., had committed "numerous, pervasive and outrageous" violations of labor law.[38] The company was found guilty of "discriminating against applicants from its preclosure unionized work force by disparately and more strictly adhering to its hiring criteria when considering those applicants." The company also "engaged in a continuing pattern of violations including unlawful termination of union supporters, interrogations, threats of plant closings, promises of additional benefits and improved working conditions, unilateral changes in working conditions, threats of discharge, solicitation of employee complaints, and grants of unlawful aid and assistance to one of two competing unions" (referring to the company union that existed for a short time at the Grand Island plant).

One worker, who testified at NLRB hearings that she had been refused a job when the plant reopened in 1983, was later reinstated. But when she continued organizing efforts on behalf of the union, her locker was broken into and literature was removed. Her work equipment was stolen. She was cited several times for "parking too far from the curb" in the plant parking lot. She was forced to work double shifts for days at a time. She was finally fired for tardiness, even though she had called in and had brought a medical excuse.

When her children went to work for the company, they were also harassed out of their jobs.[39]

Findings against the company were still on appeal ten years after initial charges were filed. In April 1990, Monfort contested an order to hold new union elections in Greeley and to rehire or compensate up to 350 former employees. In April 1992, Monfort lost this appeal but vowed to delay payment through further litigation.[40] Regardless of the outcome, the company's union-busting scheme — however illegal — had already paid off handsomely. Many workers felt that criminal charges should have been made against Monfort officials.

Labor disputes in the 1980s were characterized by increasing acrimony everywhere in the United States, but worker militancy was generally discouraged by the unions. The prevailing odds were weighted in favor of the companies, who did not hesitate to demand that state and national troops be used against strikers. Already in the Monfort strike of 1979–1980, the governor of Colorado had authorized the Colorado State Patrol to aid Greeley police in "controlling traffic" the day that replacement workers were to have reported to work, when confrontation with strikers was expected. An observer said during an IBP strike in Iowa several years later: "It's not justice when an army may be called on to insist that the workers obey the law, and it takes years to resolve whether a company will obey the law."[41] By the end of the decade, unions continued to rely on legal struggles, and workers found themselves unable to wage effective battles without union leadership.

After spending seven years commuting between Cheyenne and Denver to testify in union disputes, Steve Thomas has little patience for lawsuits. He thinks that workers have to reclaim their own power in the unions.

> You know, nobody likes violence by any means but that's when gains were won, when people were tough, and they would do what they had to do. . . . I was always taught you give a good day's work, you work hard for your pay, but you don't have to eat bullshit from anybody. . . . Really the downfall of the unions is not the leadership,

because the leadership would be changed if there was strong grass roots.

Thomas left the union because it began to feel more like a job than a cause. He said:

> The union president's even got his private jet, and they buy them either a Corvette or a Cadillac, whatever they want, the vice presidents and the president. . . . They don't talk about the ideal or brotherhood or anything like that. They talk about money. That's really the problem with that structure — it's created these mercenaries, and mercenaries aren't loyal. And, you know, we've done that, because in the unions we talked about money all the time, we talked about "we're going to get you more money." We forgot to talk about, you know, "let's put our arms around each other and we're going to fight this son of a bitch together." People can't be loyal to dental insurance or optical insurance. I mean it's not in human nature. They can be loyal to a cause, but they can't be loyal to money.

Thomas said that he decided early on that if union work ever became more of a job than a cause, then he would get out.

> That's what those high salaries do to you, you know. It's hard to give that up. . . . It's hard to shift gears and say, "Wait a minute — this organization is all fucked up!" when you've been fighting for it with every breath you take for years, you know. It's hard to make that change.
>
> These guys always tell themselves they got the best interest of the worker in their heart, but you can justify damn near anything, you know. "You take a two dollar an hour cut, but we're saving your job." I mean you can justify just about anything in your mind but sometimes it works well to step back and take a look at what you are actually doing, and what your actual motivations are; that's what they don't do. . . . The goal, I believe, was to keep the dues dollars coming in so they could protect their jobs, and that's why they became afraid to take on a fight and why they became afraid to lose membership and they would sign these sweetheart deals.

In retrospect, Thomas added:

> One thing about the organization, it's still the only game in town. So you almost got to go with it and hope that you can make it good

enough that you can live with it because the alternative is having no union or having a company-dominated union or maybe having a union that is so weak that it's ineffective. . . . Maybe the union needs a checks and balances system of government like the constitution has in this country. Or maybe the structure of the organization is so bad that it needs to be torn completely down and start over again.

The union defeat at the beef slaughterhouse in Greeley reinforced meatpacking barons' resolve to move ahead full-speed with industry concentration and workplace restructuring. But Greeley meatpackers were still to wage another hard struggle in the 1980s, when the Portion Foods work force went on strike and confronted Monfort/ConAgra in 1987.

Standing Together, Body and Soul   **4**

At a public meeting held in the basement of Greeley's Our Lady of Peace Catholic Church, October 19, 1987, a worker from Monfort's Portion Foods plant testified before co-workers and church leaders about workplace conditions. Her name was Christine Gallegos. She asserted that it was impossible to go on cutting loins with dull knives, working at a table that was constantly understaffed. Like many others, she was having problems with inflamed nerves in her arms and hands, brought on by exertion from cutting meat all day long at a pace that required too much of her body. Her back and legs were also under strain; psychological stress and danger from the never-ending push to work faster and faster were taking a toll on her body and mind.

Gallegos described her experience of the prior week, when there were only four or five people working where there should have been eight. She had asked the cleanup man for a box (a "combo") where extra meat could be kept for cutting up at the end of the day. "You fill up your board where you're working and you don't have no more place to work so they put you a box so you can stack your meat in there," she explained. When the supervisor came by, he objected.

> He told me, "Don't you dare attempt to put any meat in that combo!" I said, "I'm not going to stab myself or stab anyone else. . . . I'm going to throw a piece of meat in there if I have to." And he said, "Don't you dare do it!" So I let it go at that and I kept stacking my meat to where I only had this much room to work on the table. So finally I told my partner that was working with me, I said, "Come on . . . what are you waiting for? Let's do something!" I said, "If he sees that we're trying to work on this little space he's not going to get us any more help and he's not going to let us put any meat in that combo." So my friend and I started throwing meat inside the combo and he came back and he said, "Didn't I tell you not to throw anymore meat in

there?" I said, "I'm not forcing myself. I can't sleep at night anymore because I'm hurting so bad." So I kept throwing all that meat in the combo and he just looked at me and said, "Well, if you have to do it by yourself [after work], you're going to do it," he goes, "because the rest of those people aren't going to help you." I said, "Fine, I'll do it," but then we had a breakdown [the conveyor belt stopped functioning] and he brought our red hats to help us do all the meat that we had put in the combo. [Red hats are "lead men" who help the supervisors.]

Gallegos explained that although the people at her table gained some satisfaction from standing up to the supervisor that day, the table was still understaffed, and there was never enough time to sharpen knives so that the work could be done properly. Other workers testified that the company had taken away their rough steel and ceramic knife sharpeners, claiming that it was costing too much to replace worn-down knives. At the same time, meat was often half frozen from being kept in the cooler too long, so it was more difficult to cut. Management was unresponsive to complaints and workers found the so-called open door policy to be a sham.

Gallegos had gathered 150 signatures on a petition to present to the plant manager. She explained:

> You can't keep your knives sharp, you can't cut your meat, and you use strength to make your cuts and then your hand, your wrist is taking it, your joints are taking it. You do that for eight hours. . . . I mean, you can't keep your knives sharp when you're working with frozen meat is my point. So what is the result to yourself when you're trying, you're hurried, you can't do the job? At night your hand goes to sleep. At three o'clock in the morning you're numb.

The petition was overruled by the management. "That's what happened, and that, I assume, would be something like an 'open door policy!'" she said. "The petition I took with all these signatures didn't do any good." On further questioning, Gallegos explained that the smooth steel sharpeners that they were permitted to use worked fine if the meat was soft and if the chain was running slow. "But if the meat is frozen and the chain speed is going too fast for the amount of work they want people to put out . . . well, you can't do a piece of meat good if you're waiting for the other one and you're stacking up [pieces of meat]. You're just a mess out there, and then they want quality! They can't get it."

One by one workers testified that they were blamed for everything that went wrong in the workplace. Even when they were giving everything they had, they could feel no satisfaction for having done a good job. Over and over workers testified that the chain speed was "the whole problem down there." They also said the plant's "safety committee" was ineffective.

> They say the safety committee is made up of workers. Would they be people you could go to and say, "These are unsafe conditions because the chain is moving too fast, the knives aren't sharp enough?" No. They have one person walking around who is the "safety commissioner" and he's never been in a packing house in his life, and he says, "You ain't got earplugs, you're not safe." Like, if you wear earplugs, you're safe! If she doesn't have her hair up [entirely covered with a net], write her up! [for an infraction of safety rules]. . . . You can't go and talk to them about your problems. They have no consideration that people are being cut, or that their hands are gettin' torn up, that there's too much work.[1]

When workers got sick or were injured, the company did everything possible, workers said, to avoid having claims made for workers' compensation. Their problems were minimized by company doctors, and if they were too ill to work, they would be told to seek medical attention on their own, so that they wouldn't be eligible for workers' compensation.

A woman who had been employed by Monfort for five years testified at the church hearing:

> On Friday I went to work. I hadn't been feeling good for about, oh maybe three weeks. I have this pain in my chest. I needed to go to the nurse's station and ask for a pain pill, but I thought I could make it to break. Then I got this real hard pain in my chest. I couldn't even breathe, and I felt myself . . . like I was going to faint. And I thought, "Well, I'll try to last 'til break," and I didn't. I fainted and they took me out. They told me to go to my own doctor, not to the company doctor. I know it's work related, and they know it's work related, but they didn't want me to go to the company doctor. So I went to my doctor and I had an EKG and some other tests run and all that. My problem is that I have arthritis in my chest wall. So, well, I'm going to call in sick tomorrow 'cause I think I need another day, so I don't know what's going to happen, whether I'll get fired or, I don't know.

When the moderator of the hearing asked whether she wasn't
allowed sick leave, he was told:

> On the job I'm doing, they're working us very hard. I'm like, I'm like
> pulling double count [doing the work of two]. My foreman knows
> that, and he helps every once in awhile, but Thursday . . . the meat
> was falling all over. It was getting dirty. It was stacked up, it was
> falling on the floor, it was all over. . . . I guess what I'm trying to say
> is that I'm more overworked than an ape. . . . What they do is pick
> on their best workers. The one that can work the best is the one that
> they'll work the hardest, and if they have a favorite then they'll let
> them do whatever they want, you know, like they can go and wash
> a piece of meat every two or three seconds while you're standing
> there working 'cause you know you're not a favorite, or you don't
> know someone, you know.

Workers testified that Monfort doctors were consistently loyal
to the company, not to them. In effect, "the Monfort doctor will tell
you, 'Well, we know you're hurting, we know you got tendonitis
[the first stage of carpal tunnel syndrome, a crippling nerve dis-
ease], but you know, I don't care. I just want you to go back and do
your job, you know — suffer, suffer — If you want to make money,
suffer. I don't care whether you hurt or not.' "[2] When they went to
other doctors on the company list, they found out that their treatment was the same. One worker who had lost his fingernails twice
and who had lost his ability to tie his shoes or open cans of soda
pop or clip his own nails, talked about his experience of trying to
get help:

> He [the doctor] just writes a prescription and that's it. I went in there
> the first time and he felt my hand a little bit, and he told me I had
> tendonitis. I could have told him that! So he wrote me a prescription.
> It was anti-inflammatory pills, or something like that. So I took them
> and it helped for a little while but then the prescription ran out and
> then I went back to my job and it was still gettin' worse to where I
> couldn't grip. I still can't grip. I went back the second time to a
> different Monfort doctor and he just looked at my hand and wrote
> out a prescription. It didn't take no longer than two minutes. So I
> took them [the pills] and they were gone and the same thing
> happened again. It kept gettin' worse, and I went a third time to a
> different one, and he just wrote me a prescription and he said, "Well,
> that should take care of it," so I took them, and after that my body

was back to the same thing again, and at that time they gave me light duty, for two weeks. Then they put me back on the same job in which I got the tendonitis, and it's been getting worse ever since. . . . My supervisor, he says "Whatever the doctor says — and the doctor says you can go back to work." . . . I was gonna wait and see if they sent me to a different doctor that knows anything other than writing prescriptions. If I go to a different doctor, I have to take time off, and I don't know whether it causes conflict or not. That's why I've waited so long.

This testimony was interrupted by another worker, Delia Ann Martinez, who said that she had called in sick and

before I even explained, you know, what the matter with me was, he [the supervisor] tells me, "Well, you don't sound sick to me." I was really mad and I said, "I didn't know you were a physician." And he goes, "What's the matter with you?" and I tell him, "Well, I'm going to my doctor and when I find out I'll let you know, too." I was really hurting and when I did go I couldn't walk at all, and they found out I had a bone spur, which was from pressure of all the time just standing in that one spot. I figured if he were to fire me [for going to the doctor], well, you're a person, you're not just a thing that they can use. I went to my own doctor. I thought, "To heck with them," you know. When you go to the nurse's station, well, when I was in the service we never had that many people in the sick line!

A common complaint of those who testified was that they couldn't go to the bathroom when they needed to. "They told us that in order for us to go to the bathroom that we would have to be relieved by a supervisor. Well, where do you find a supervisor, you know?"[3]

It wasn't uncommon for people to be expected to work 8 or 10 hours extra when there was more work to do. Ruth de Vargas explained: "Thursdays and Fridays we used to put in 18 hours a day, two shifts in one." Overtime was compulsory: "I told the foreman a couple of times, 'Hey, I have kids at home. I have a husband. I want to go home! 'Go ahead and punch out!' he would say. Meaning I could get fired."

Workers were never sure what their work schedules would be. One man complained that for awhile they were pushed to finish work early, doing a full day's work in 7¾ hours, so that they wouldn't get the full 8 hours' pay. The same worker testified that meetings held with supervisors every month or so are

> just a bunch of baloney. They're a waste of time. It's really not the supervisors' fault that the line is going that fast, and the main reason [for all the problems] is because the line is going so fast. . . . They always tell us in our meetings, "Try to help us out, you guys, and when we can, we'll try to help you out," and the first few months, you know, I said, "Well, I'm going to go ahead and try to do my best and help them out," but I noticed I help them out and we don't get any help when we really need it. . . . We're working really hard, and then they don't want to give us 8 hours so I tell the rest of the people, "Well, let's just stack up so we at least get the 8 hours in because we're doing, you know, more than we're supposed to." . . . I'm at the wing table. They're supposed to have fourteen people and they have eight people right now. Somebody's always sick. . . . Within a three-week period, three different people on the job I was at got cut. . . . And the bad thing about it is if the cut ain't that bad and they get three or four stitches they still make them work full-time. . . . It's very simple. They wouldn't have 50 percent of the problems they have out there, health problems or anything, just slow the chain down. Give us a chance. Give us a break. You're just working, working, working. If they cut down on production they would get better quality, because half the stuff that is going down looks like garbage anyway.[4]

A woman who testified that she had been injured three times at Monfort believed that she had been sent back to work too soon every time. Once, when she had had back surgery, she returned to work when her back was still bleeding.

> Another woman who's married to one of the bosses and had the same surgery, she was off work for three months. I got five weeks. I had vacation time coming and I told the doctor I didn't feel like I was ready to go back to work yet, I'd just take the vacation time. But I got sent back to work. The favoritism there was obvious. . . . And then they denied it was a workers' compensation case.

The application form for employment at Monfort included the following question: "Do you have any reason to believe that you will be unable to work for sustained periods in areas of extreme cold, heat or dampness?" Evidently the company thought that this absolved it of any responsibility for the effects of heat, cold, and humidity. Obviously, prospective workers were expected to answer "no" in order to be hired. At the hearings in 1987, a worker testified:

> It's pretty cold in there, but it doesn't matter that it's cold because after an hour you're sweating anyway. You can't feel the cold. You go to break and come back and then you start gettin' the chills because you already cooled down. And after two weeks of working there I got a cold and I had it for a month and a half. I still have that cough really bad . . . people are consistently sick.

Injured employees generally had to wait for the nurse, workers testified, and sometimes there was no qualified nurse on duty at all. Besides, one worker said, "the nurses are company, just like all the rest of them." A woman at the Portion Foods plant testified that when she was starting a new job, she stabbed herself in the stomach:

> I was cleaning a knife and it slipped out of my hand, and it flew and stuck in my stomach. It went in about an inch. Well, I pulled it out and put it on the table and I turned around and told the girl next to me what happened, but there was no blood. I went like this and no sooner did I do this and it got all full of blood, and she took me down to the nurse and the nurse got all mad at me because I pulled the knife out of my stomach. She wanted me to go down with the knife in my stomach! And they were coming up from break, you know. They could have hit me and pushed it in further! Well, she took me in and I think I had five stitches put in, and they took me home and I was all full of blood. They brought me back to work. They just sent me home to change my clothes and come back and cut. Then the next day they put me back to bone guard. . . . I told them about my stitches but they still left me there. We were picking up about forty or fifty pounds [of lamb] every five, six seconds. It's quick, and my stitches ripped on me. They didn't put me on light duty or nothing. I told my foreman that my stitches were bleeding. He just says, "What can I do, babe?"[5]

As long as workers' testimony did not go beyond the closed doors of the church basement where complaints were heard, their concerns were unlikely to be addressed. Most of the workers who made the complaints were willing to have their testimony, and their names, made public. Workers at the Portion Foods plant had some protection from being harassed for testifying because they were members of the UFCW and could ask union stewards to file grievances on their behalf. Although the union had been defeated seven years earlier at the slaughterhouse when it was closed down, Greeley's Portion Foods plant was never closed, and Local 7 continued to represent the workers there. A short report on the hearing appeared in the UFCW newspaper, but word of the event never reached the general public.

Four months after the hearing, the union at Portion Foods was broken. Father Gary Lauenstein, who was pastor at Our Lady of Peace Catholic Church at the time, explained how he was involved in organizing the hearings, how he became interested in the union, and how he felt about events that took place during that winter of 1987–1988.

> About 98 percent of the people in my church are Hispanic. Most of them are poor, and maybe half have worked at Monfort at one time or another. I was always hearing stories about people not being able to get workers' compensation for injuries they had. They were coming to the church for assistance, and many of them were permanently disabled. One day the union leader, Ron Bush, came to leave off some materials and we got to talking about the situation. We decided we needed documentation. My job was to get some other clergy involved, and a doctor if possible.[6]

They decided to hold a meeting in the church basement. Father Gary was unable to get a doctor to attend the meeting, but he did get a number of other ministers. Ron Bush passed out leaflets at the plant to advertise the meeting. "I probably wouldn't have called it a 'hearing,' like he did," said Father Gary.

> Anyway, that's a minor point. . . . The next day I got a call from the president of one of their subsidiary companies who was a parishioner of ours in Ault. It was Sonny Mapelli [who was also president of the Board of ConAgra Red Meats]. . . . He was challenging my right to do such a thing, you know. "A church shouldn't get involved in those kinds of things," he said. "You don't know anything about it," and I said, "Well, these are my parishioners. How can I ignore this?" He talked to me for a long time. He was pretty ticked off and dropped out of the church, and he's still ticked off to this day, I understand.

Mapelli attended Our Lady of Peace mission church in a small town north of Greeley. But Father Gary was soon contacted by Joel Meilinger, a vice president at Monfort who was an active member of his own church and who had been called on the carpet at a meeting of the Monfort Board. Another parishioner warned Father Gary that if he didn't leave town within a year, he'd be dead. "So I found myself in a tug of war all of a sudden for which I wasn't well prepared."

The shock of the pressure from the company triggered a physical reaction in Father Gary.

> I had had ulcers in '81 or so and apparently it retriggered them instantly. . . . I became very ill over that weekend and had to get another priest to come in and say mass. I ended up going to the hospital and they finally calmed me down, gave me some kind of medication, but I couldn't do anything for about two days and that frightened me. So I did not pursue the issues as vigorously as I might have. I decided to content myself to hearing both sides of the story and then just giving the union paper some things, you know.

The testimony of the workers was never mentioned in the local press. "You get to a point you don't know who you can trust," said Father Gary. "They had someone at the meeting. I know because we had a meeting with Ken Monfort later and I said, 'We had this hearing and we had about 60 people present there and Monfort says, 'Well, the number we have is more like forty.' That showed me they had somebody there." Father Gary continued:

> When Mapelli talked to me, I realized I was in over my head, 'cause he would throw out things in our phone conversation that I had never heard before and I didn't know anything about labor law, and then he would say things like, "I spend my whole life building up my business and you're destroying it." You get these high-powered people calling you and telling you that you're ruining lives and that you don't know what you're doing, and I thought, "Good heavens, what did I get myself into?" and I kept thinking, "Well, my only concern is the welfare of the workers." . . . I kept going back to that, you know.

Father Gary's meeting with Ken Monfort (held at the corporate headquarters soon after the hearing) was also attended by

Fathers Leonard Urban and Peter Urban of St. Peter's Church, Reverends Steve and Sue Brown of Family of Christ Presbyterian Church, Myra Monfort (the company's lawyer), and Eddie Aragon, a parishioner who was manager of the company's dog food plant. At first the meeting was "friendly." Ken Monfort said that he wasn't aware that there was a problem with the knives and that he would look into that. He said tendonitis was a problem in many work-places and that his company was way ahead of most doing research on it. Father Gary reported that Monfort said that he always tells new hires, "it's tough work, and if they can't do it they shouldn't be in this line of work."

At one point, one of the ministers said, "You think you can justify all of these things for your profit?" "Mr. Monfort got a little hot under the collar then," said Father Gary, but when Father Gary told Monfort that he himself would be supporting efforts to unionize the slaughterhouse, Ken Monfort became very defensive and even-tually walked out declaring, "This meeting's over!" Myra Monfort was still present, and Father Gary recalled that he told her: "He has a problem that he has to work on with regards to unions because you can't be in this business without having to deal with unions, you know." Father Gary explained, "That didn't go over real well with her, either."

> Anyway, he came back in and asked us to leave and I said to myself, "How could there be what they call the open door policy? How could some little guy on the line who wants to complain go in and talk to him when he won't talk to us, you know?" So together we concluded there's no way the interest of these people can be represented without a union.

Testimony at the church hearing had revealed that in a two-year period after the Greeley slaughterhouse reopened, total turn-over was higher than in the twelve years before the plant closure, when the work force had been unionized. Because the Portion Foods plant remained unionized in the 1980s, its work force was relatively stable. More older people worked at Portion Foods than in the slaughterhouse. About 85 percent of the workers were women. Some had worked there for twenty or more years, had relatives working in the plant, and felt a certain loyalty to the company. Nevertheless, as contract time neared in the fall of 1987, Monfort was taking a hard line toward the workers.

Wages at the Portion Foods plant had been frozen for six years. The annual bonus had been taken away. A two-tier wage system had been introduced, which meant that new hires would never make as much as older workers, who were feeling pressure to quit their jobs. The probationary period for new hires had been extended from thirty days to ninety days so that medical and other benefits were available to fewer workers. An afternoon break had been cut out. The number of workdays guaranteed for each week had been cut back.

As revealed in testimony at the church hearing, the attitude of management personnel had hardened; injuries were more and more common, and more serious. One worker on the cleanup crew had fallen into a hamburger grinder after safety controls had been removed to reduce cleaning time. Half of his body was gone by the time the machine was stopped.[7]

Workers at Portion Foods were aware that Monfort was itching for a strike so that the union could be broken. But they were at a point where they believed that they just couldn't continue to make concessions. "People just wanted *something,*" said Steve Clasen, who had worked nine years at the Portion Foods plant and who was a union steward at the time. "The company was giving them all this punishment and they felt betrayed."[8]

Sharon Hill was on the negotiating team for the union. She said that the company stalled for time so that workers were pressured to agree to demands for concessions. Charlie Sykes, the same man who had assisted Monfort in defeating the union's reorganizing drive at the slaughterhouse in 1983, was brought in as negotiator for the company. Even management personnel who had participated in negotiations with the union previously complained that they were not being consulted this time around. The workers knew that they were in big trouble.

Monfort and Vice President Gene Meakins (the ex–CIA official, whose relationship with Monfort dated back to college days — see footnote 26, Chapter 2) called workers aside individually and in small groups to talk with them about why a union was not beneficial to them, feeling out their loyalties. By the time Charlie

Sykes took over, he had a psychological profile of the work force and was able to deal with workers accordingly.

"They never claimed poverty," said Hill.

> But they never agreed to anything. . . . If they'd just said, "We know you guys are making our company, and we want you here, but at least let's take a wage-freeze." . . . They were just taking everything away and didn't want to give anything. Charlie Sykes is a cool character. He doesn't give you the impression that he's a union buster. He was cool and collected until something would start to trigger him.

Because Sykes had no familiarity with the jobs that workers were doing or the part that they had played in past negotiations, members of the negotiating team felt as if they had no leverage and got no respect for what they had contributed to the company.[9]

On November 16, 1987, workers went out on strike. The company hired "permanent replacements" without even informing strikers. "And then," Hill said,

> on January 20th they finally agreed to meet with us again. That was the first mention of us being permanently replaced. And it was like . . . . He said it in a manner like, "Well, this happened since the 17th of November, when you didn't appear at work, that you were permanently replaced," . . . He said it, just like that. It really floored us, the words they spoke and the manner in which they spoke them, because it was just, like, "Well, yeah, you've been permanently replaced. Didn't you know that?"

Workers asked for mediation and were offered a deal where the strikers would be accepted back at work as vacancies occurred. "It would have been like a rabbit in a wolf's pen," said Hill. "So we voted, and everybody chose not to accept that contract and that was when negotiations quit completely."

Meanwhile, a vote had been taken inside the plant, based on a petition started by a small group of workers who had crossed the picket line and gone back to work.

> When they voted and chose not to have union representation, those on the picket line weren't allowed to vote. We didn't know the petition was there . . . they didn't give us that option to vote. So the

ruling percentage of people inside . . . they didn't want the union in there, of course, because all 130 people outside on the picket line were going to come in and take their job . . . so they voted the union out then.

The union fined those who had crossed the picket line after having signed an agreement to go on strike. With company backing, the "scab" union members challenged the fines and the union went on trial three years later. The main testimony brought out at the trial was about the "rudeness" of strikers who had yelled at fellow workers when they were crossing the picket line. A sixty-five-year-old woman was chosen by the company to be the first one to bring her case to court. The judge ruled that the word "Monfort" was not to be permitted in testimony, nor were any workplace issues to be addressed. The victimization of Monfort employees in the workplace was declared a "non-issue," as was the right of workers to unionize and go on strike. Their use of obscenities on the picket line became the focus of attention; union lawyers and former strikers who testified were unable to change this focus.[10]

Sharon Hill recalled that Betty Hubbard, the chief union steward, a mother of seven who had been a widow for fifteen years, was questioned about things that went on at the picket line.

> Betty was not a gutter mouth. And I am. I spew out a large amount of gutter words. But she just never talked like that. She's an older woman. She's had seven kids and even with all those sons, she just never achieved a gutter mouth. . . . So, they were asking her, "What kind of language was used?" And she said, "obscenities." They asked her, "What kind of obscenities?" and she said "Cuss words." And they said, "Could you say those cuss words?" And she said, "No, I don't use those words." She never would say the words she heard. Finally, she said she had heard someone say "s.o.b." They'd ask her, "Well, did they say 'you s.o.b.,' or would they say the words?" And she said, "They said the whole words," but they could never get her to say the cuss words. And that didn't even come out and impress the jury, that not all of the picketers used the language.

The union lost on the first round and then settled out of court so as to prevent the strikers' defeat from having wider consequences by affecting case law or going on to a higher court. Hill's comments about the outcome of the trial and about the outcome of the strike reveal the frustration that workers felt in a situation where all the cards were stacked against them. During the strike, picketers had been subjected to physical attacks and psychological abuse, for which no one was ever prosecuted. Hill explained:

> One of the new hires had pulled a gun on some of our people. One of the women who was most active on the picket line got her face mauled when she was beat up by a scab. But we were the ones who got arrested for disorderly conduct. . . . Sure, some of our people wanted to use physical violence. They wanted to bar the gates so no one could even enter the plant. But federal law prohibited us from doing that. It was discouragement from day one. It really was. We wanted to defend our plant.

Sharon Hill had walked the picket line during the 1976 Portion Foods plant strike. She said that in 1976 there were no scabs. The plant was kept open with people from the personnel department working. The picket line was maintained twenty-four hours a day. The company didn't even let anyone come in to work. During that strike the workers got a raise, more holidays, and a contract bonus. Hill said that she thinks Ken Monfort's attitude changed after that more than the union changed. In 1987

> he was determined to eliminate the union. He did not like unions. He succeeded when he busted the union at the packinghouse. So he figured, "Well, if I can bust seventeen hundred men, I can surely break two hundred women." After the packinghouse went down, I think everybody's attitude in Greeley — they were poor now — they couldn't go out and buy cars, they couldn't go out and spend money at the mall. I think everybody's attitude changed in Greeley, about unions. 'Cause I can remember everybody was pro-union in the seventies, even pro-Monfort, because he paid the best wages around. I mean, how much can you really enjoy your work, sticking cows? But I didn't hear people really complain about their job.

During the Portion Foods strike of 1987, a letter to the *Greeley Tribune* editor complained, "It is absurd to hear people say, 'Oh, my if I don't make $15 or $20 or $25 an hour, I'll lose my poor little $100,000 house and fancy car. . . . So, Monfort, crush this union garbage!"[11] The letter was terribly offensive to strikers, who had a hard time getting their side of the story to the public. Christine

Johnson was a worker who had become loyal to the union only gradually as she realized that "doing 150 percent didn't get you anywhere." She went house-to-house in Greeley during the strike, gathering signatures on the petition that workers had prepared, urging Monfort to return to the negotiating table. She said: "People were totally unaware, and people we talked to and told them how much a woman who had been there nineteen years made, $7.95 an hour . . . a lot of people were floored when they found out. They thought we were making fifteen, eighteen dollars an hour." She added, "It's true they have one of the higher wages in town, but only for the fact that it's the only industry, the rest of them are minimum wage."

People also didn't understand that there was never a sense of security working for Monfort. Johnson explained: "It's like you could work for a year straight and be working 50 hours a week and then all of a sudden you're laid off it could be for a week, it could be for six months. It's just sporadic. There was a couple times I was afraid to get my car fixed because, it's like, well, what if I get laid off next week and then I have a house payment coming up, I can't spend the money so I better save it.

At the negotiating table, money was the main issue. But the morale of workers had been broken by the increasing danger of the work and by their inability to challenge management prerogatives that put them at risk. Machinery was not kept in repair. "Meat tenderizers were notorious for grabbing gloves and pulling some- body's hand down into them and no one knew how to tear them [the machines] down except the maintenance people. . . . We wanted people trained so we could get the hands out," Christine Johnson explained. She and others said that everyone was upset that people were put on lower-paying jobs when they were injured at work and that workers got yelled at when they were injured instead of being treated with sympathy.

Union members were unable to build effective outside support for their cause. During the strike, they couldn't even get checks cashed at local banks.

When Ken Monfort and ConAgra President Charles M. Harper spoke to 450 Greeley businessmen and others invited to an event sponsored by the University of Northern Colorado Foundation, strikers picketed the event. When they were told to disperse, they refused to do so and seven of them were arrested.

Although some members of the university faculty and other community leaders supported the strike, workers were dismayed to see that the state gave residents of a Community Corrections Center leave to work as scabs. Governer Roy Romer, a fraternity brother and personal friend of Ken Monfort, wrote a letter disavowing his support for the use of work-release prisoners as scabs. He said that it was beyond his authority, however, to stop the practice in any given locality.

Female workers faced other problems that never became public issues during the strike, problems toward which even the union had often been insensitive. For example, employees were not allowed to miss work when children were sick, and sexual harassment at the plant was extreme. "Production people reduced women to tears over nothing really," said Christine Johnson. She remembered a supervisor who always called the women "cunts." He would threaten men: "We're going to put you over in packaging with all the cunts." One woman, who had problems with tendonitis after working on her feet for five years, asked to be put on a sit-down job. "She worked for awhile with the cast on and walked with the cast, and he [the supervisor] told her there was no such thing as a sit-down job, that women should not be in the plant, and the only job he had where she could be off her feet was on her knees under his desk." The woman filed sexual harassment charges but "she ended up dropping them because he harassed her continually, and she felt by dropping them maybe he would lay off, and he didn't. He pushed until eventually she called in and quit. If she hadn't quit she would have been fired. He just kept on her. He would follow her around." Sharon Hill told about a supervisor who commented, when she leaned forward to reach over the table, "Oh, you don't have such small titties." Then when she tightened her apron, he said, "Why did you tighten your apron?" She complained and reminded him that her boyfriend was working in the plant. He said: "I only want a piece of it!" She finally got angry and then he started criticizing her work and "writing her up" [putting complaints about her in her file]. Hill eventually asked for a transfer to another area. She says that when harassment charges were filed, there was no sympathy or understanding. Women, including Hill, were humiliated on a daily basis, but they felt that there was no way out of the situation.

Workers said that there were no female supervisors at the Portion Foods plant at the time of the strike. Both racism and sexism were used in an attempt to undermine worker solidarity. In the 1980s, some Mexican nationals began coming in and, according to Steve Clasen, "the company would use migrants, of course, to justify keeping the wage structure low." Betty Hubbard, the chief union steward at Portion Foods, was a Chicana who carried out her responsibilities without regard for the nationality or gender of union members. She inspired co-workers with her fairness as a union steward and with her determination and courage during the strike. But she was unable to inspire union officials to the same degree.

Many workers believed that the union hierarachy did not give Portion Foods strikers the kind of support that they needed to hold the line against union busting. Steve Clasen, who was active in pushing workers to strike, recalled: "They [union officials] were throwing a screaming fit about giving us strike benefits and giving us any kind of long-term support." He is aware of the manipulations engaged in by the whole meat industry, "playing workers off against each other to break unions, switching names [of companies], playing a lot of games on the corporate level," but he's also critical of the UFCW.

> How these people get elected and all this kind of stuff varies a great deal within the unions, and within the United Food and Commercial Workers there are some real power struggles that go on. There are big locals where there's a lot of money that goes in and out of them, and people that get those higher positions, they get sometimes . . . they are hardly any better than the corporate executives that you have to deal with.

Ron Bush, who was a UFCW representative for Portion Foods workers from 1979 to 1988 (when the union collapsed at the Portion plant) said that they were "some of the strongest union members I've ever met. . . . It came out of a sense of need to be together, really getting together and protecting each other."[12] He felt that it was impossible to win any gains during contract negotiations in the 1980s:

The company's main motivation was to put these people out as an example that it did not pay to belong to the union. They couldn't afford the union making any real gains at Monfort Portion Foods for fear it would impact their negotiating, their attempts to keep the other plants non-union. . . . Things that the company would try to do to break the union workers' spirits in that plant, if it did anything, it solidified them. Here was this island of workers who steadfastly just thumbed their nose at Monfort, no matter what he threw at them.

Bush believed that the UFCW hierarchy failed to recognize the importance of the Portion Foods strike: "They did not handle this as a big enough problem. I think there were some other pressures that could have been brought on, but the International failed to do so." As far as the workers were concerned, he said:

It didn't matter what it cost them, they were going to take their last shot at Monfort. I never saw people stick together as tough as I did on that Monfort picket line. . . . I had the responsibility of standing in front of them and said, "Look (and I was very truthful), I can't promise you a damn thing. It is very likely you'll lose your jobs." And the hierarchy of this union was pressuring me into getting them back into that plant at all costs. . . . I was not going to pressure them into "saving the union" (as it was put to me by a union official). These people were the ones that had to work there; they're the ones who have to endure that every day, endure that betrayal by Monfort. . . . I think we save the union by letting those people do what they wanted to do. They may not be working union jobs right now [referring to former strikers after the defeat of the union]; they may not be getting the best pay. But the union is here. It's in their heart.

During the Portion Foods strike it became obvious that, for most workers, their ultimate loyalty was neither to their jobs nor to the union as such, but to themselves and each other as human beings who have a right to live with dignity and respect.

Ron Bush left the union himself for a period of time after the Portion Foods strike, but he went back to work as a butcher in a Denver supermarket in order to get back in the trade and run for the presidency of Local 7. "It's kind of a battle," he says. "Fighting the company, fighting the union, and trying to keep the workers in a frame of mind that they have some real feeling about the union and what the labor movement ought to really mean."

A number of Portion Foods strikers did eventually return to work at the plant, after the union had been broken. They faced taunting from new hires. Martha Valencia went back to work for one day and was so badly harassed that she never went back again.

> About thirty of them were in front of me, hollering at me, giving me the finger. . . . At first, when I got there, the lady from the front office told me, "If anybody tells you anything, you tell the foreman." I called him about three times to tell him, and nothing was ever done about it. . . . They just kept it up and kept it up and they were never, never stopped. . . . When I got to my locker, they had put cupcakes all over in the cracks, chewing gum on the handle. Cigarettes and ashes were all over inside. That did it.[13]

She went up to the personnel office. "The foreman was sitting there and he told me, 'Well, Martha, you should have known what was going to happen to you. You did a lot of stuff like that when you were out there.' "

Valencia's brother and others who were working in the plant encouraged her to reapply for work later, which she did. She was never called. When a friend inquired, a supervisor reportedly said: "I don't think Martha needs her job." Since then, she has been doing seasonal agricultural work, bagging carrots and onions. Sometimes she does housecleaning or makes burritos on contract. She's not young and she really went out on strike more "to support the young people" than for herself, she says, but she gained a lot of pride from being part of the struggle.

Paul Apodaca, who began working at Portion Foods in 1974, and who went back to work several years after the 1987 strike, is still a strong "union man." He said that some of the workers who crossed the picket line after the strike began had been recruited as strikebreakers by Charlie Sykes.[14] Others who were organized in what Apodaca called "the committee to bust the union" now have supervisory jobs. He thinks that terrorizing is a bigger weapon than bribery, however, in getting workers to oppose the union. He was once suspended for three days without pay for having turned in a form on which some information was missing." I hadn't filled in every blank," he said. He assumes that the problem was actually that he had been talking to people about the union.

Apodaca said that there are still not as many Mexicans at the Portion plant as there are at the slaughterhouse, and Mexicans are definitely the objects of discrimination. A Mexican, for example, was refused permission to go to the bathroom and was then fired when he urinated on the job.

> He asked him [the supervisor] two or three times if he could go, because he was working in the cold, ice cold in there. And so finally, he didn't let him go, and he urinated in his trousers. And out the door he went. . . . One of the lead persons said that he was urinatin' in the drain, so I don't know exactly which way. But when he told me, he said he even went to the health department in Greeley, and to the National Labor Relations Board in Denver, and they just laughed at him. That's what he said.

Apodaca said that he himself had been taken off a "plush job" in receiving (in the warehouse) just because the supervisor preferred having a white person in it. "He was always putting a white person in there. I said, 'Why can't you put Larry there? Larry has more seniority.' The supervisor said, 'I put whoever the hell I want to!' " Paul went to the Civil Rights Commission in Greeley about it and was told that he'd have to have more evidence than that. "I felt a discrimination right there," he says, "and I never did push it any further."

Workers testified again and again that those who are recent immigrants from Mexico or other countries are expected to work harder than anyone else. One worker said: "They rode him and they rode him because he was from Mexico. He was called a 'wetback.'[15] This gentleman was a good hard worker. He worked harder than most of the young guys they hire. He got so frustrated that he quit because of the way they treated him, just because he was from Mexico."[16]

Apodaca thinks that the problem is bigger than racism. He said that the United States is progressively becoming a country of just "rich people and poor people, a situation here as it is in Mexico. I can't see just sittin' back and just lettin' this happen." He thinks that racism distracts people from seeing that their real interests lie in sticking together and fighting for their rights as workers. During the

1987 strike, when Jesse Jackson was running as a minority candidate for the presidency of the United States, he came to Greeley to support the Portion Foods workers. Betty Hubbard emceed the rally. Several strikers told me that they had never felt so good in their whole lives as they did when Jesse Jackson spoke to them.

Apodaca said that he and other workers were affected in a big way by the support they got at the rally, but he got the impression that a lot of people who weren't there "took it more as a laugh or a joke." He said that even the Hispanic people "have been set back to the point where they don't have knowledge about these situations. They think, 'Well, let them handle it — let somebody else handle it,' . . . and they don't get involved politically or even support people when they're on strike."

Ron Bush remembers how Ken Monfort played on people's willingness to think that there were no real problems between workers and management or between rich and poor:

> He played this nice folksy little guy in town that happens to run a little packing plant. And I can remember going into the Holiday Inn and Kenny walking into the restaurant, bestowing his blessings on the little folks in town, and doing it in such a folksy way that they'd walk around afterwards and say, "He's just like one of us!" And all the while, the man was a performer, working the crowd. Come in with his white socks, and his pants too short, and his shirt a little rumpled, and "How you all doin?" It was just incredible to me; and this guy is probably the shrewdest corporate executive in the country, considering how he's escalated his interests, linking up with ConAgra and all.

Many of the new hires at Portion Foods later went to work at the Greeley lamb plant, which opened after the Portion Foods union was broken. At the lamb plant the company used another tactic to keep the work force divided, to keep wages down and, ultimately, to keep the union out. A two-tiered system was inaugurated in which half of the workers are working for Monfort and half are working for another company.

The "captive company," MSP Resources, hires new workers at the Monfort lamb plant. Union organizers say that MSP (an acronym whose meaning is unknown to the public) is controlled by Myra Monfort, Charlie Sykes, and Gene Meakins, who attempted in 1989 to oust UFCW workers at a Marshalltown, Iowa, Monfort plant by using MSP. Marshalltown had invested $2 million in sewage-treatment facilities and job-training subsidies for plant expansion before Monfort leased the plant to MSP and negotiated a contract with the Teamsters union, firing eight hundred employees who belonged to the UFCW. Residents protested, and workers were rehired.[17]

MSP employees are on a lower-wage scale than regular Monfort employees. At the Greeley lamb plant, workers whom the company wants to retain are eventually offered jobs on the Monfort payroll. Other MSP employees are treated as temporary workers. The MSP employees wear gray hard hats and the Monfort employees wear white hard hats, even though they may be working side by side. Thus, the two-tier system has been formalized at the lamb plant in such a way as to give maximum flexibility to the company and minimum security to workers.

Management personnel at the lamb plant are mostly Anglo, and line workers are almost 100 percent Hispanic. About half the lamb plant workers are women, although on the kill floor (where sheep are killed, disembowelled, and skinned) most are men.

At the beef slaughterhouse, where there were no women at all on the disassembly line in the early 1970s, and practically none when the plant closed in 1980, women now constitute 30 to 40 percent of the line workers. A packinghouse organizer said that the company thinks women are "more prone to tendonitis," so men are now given preference where possible.[18] Women are more likely to quit because of problems with childcare, but they put up with problems at work — and at home — because their options are extremely limited. Recent immigrants are not eligible for welfare, even if they have legal papers for work.

A social agency in Greeley that has been involved in trying to make childcare services available to working women learned that the company was reluctant to provide childcare facilities at the worksite because of "insurance problems." A "survey" that was conducted by putting a notice on a bulletin board, in English, resulted (predictably) in "little interest." One worker said that she felt so hostile to the company that she didn't want her children anywhere near the plant. "My main goal is to get out of there with no nerve damage and all my fingers intact."[19] Another worker said, "[the packinghouse job is] the only real job I ever had. I feel like I don't have a choice. I'll probably stay at Monfort until I can't move anymore."[20] She had injured herself more than once from hooking meat (meat trimmers cut with one hand and pull the meat over with a hook held in their other hand). She felt that she was vulnerable because "I think they're hardest on some of us who've been there the longest." Her dream is that none of her children will ever have to work at Monfort: "I try to really encourage them. Anything but Monfort. I hope I never see them work down there."

At a workers' compensation hearing held in Greeley in the fall of 1990, I spent some time between sessions talking with a nurse who was administrator of the company's "rehabilitation program." She told me that most of the women who work at the plant are young single mothers and "they're just looking for a man." The young men, she said, are "only interested in getting enough money together to buy a car. . . . Mexicans working at the plant now a days aren't seriously interested in their jobs." As I took notes during our conversation, which was also being witnessed by a translator who accompanied one of the lawyers, she said that "people used to put up with aches and pains. There didn't used to be all these complaints about 'tendonitis' and backaches," which she regarded as evidence that workers were being coddled for imagined ills.

It seemed ironic that a woman who was so insensitive and uninformed had been given responsibility for the company's "rehabilitation" program. Her loyalty to the company clearly outweighed any other considerations as a qualification for her position. During the hearings she sat beside the Monfort lawyer, taking notes as the lawyer systematically interrogated young men and women who had been injured, in an attempt to discredit their claims. Although with few exceptions responsibility for injuries is not at issue in workers' compensation claims, it appeared that the lawyer was trying to punish the claimants, making them feel guilty for having become injured.

Everyone we talked with who works on the floor at the beef packinghouse realized that strained relations among workers due to the pressure on individuals to keep up with the machines' speed and to avoid supervisory censure increased tension between ethnic groups and between women and men. Some put the blame on workers for allowing this to happen. A white man testified that he was expected by other workers to "learn faster" because he's physically big.[21] Until he walked out on the job in frustration, and was brought back by the supervisor, the women on his table were asking him to do what he thought was "more than his share." A South American man told us something similar, that women gave him a hard time, especially at first. He thought that this was because he was perceived as an outsider but also because he is a man and "should have been able to do it better."[22]

We asked some women to respond to what we had heard from these men. Rosa Morado said:

> Well, I think that's the way everybody is down there, especially if somebody is new or something. They give you so much time to be able to do the job, to be able to keep up, but after you've been there for so long they start saying, well, you've been here awhile, and they're working harder because of you or something like that, and that's when people start getting hard on new people, the people that can't . . . it can get pretty nasty. They're saying, "If I can do it, why can't you?" And especially if it's, you know, "Say, look at this man, and I'm a woman and I can do it, why can't he?" That is an attitude they have. I see some women cut some men down pretty . . . real low.

The same worker, when telling about her own experience as a new employee at Monfort, said: "When I started there on my job, years ago, there were more men than there are women. Every day I wanted to quit, but I couldn't so I just fought back the tears. Now there are more women than men. . . ." I think it's because there's a lot more women out there with kids that don't have anybody else taking care of them."

Because of the precarious work conditions for Mexicans in the United States, family life is unstable. Women resent the fact that they are left with the extra responsibilities that result. One young woman, whose husband had also worked at Monfort, was left alone with three small children when her husband was arrested and taken away by police. She never heard from him again. She paid a neighbor to take care of her children. She had fallen on a greasy floor at work and sustained a back injury, but she continued to work instead of going on welfare. "I have a ride to work every day with a friend," she said, "but nobody has time to take me to the welfare office."[23]

Because the situation of women is even more precarious than that of men, some women feel as if they have to prove themselves more than men in order to feel secure on the job. They are therefore more reluctant to complain and are slow in developing solidarity with other workers. This attitude can be used by the company to help "shame the men into following orders. The company will promote women who are fast workers to lead positions as "red hats." After an employee has become a red hat, cameraderie with other workers is entirely out of the question. One such employee told a young man that he was a *llorona* (sissy crybaby) when he asked for permission to go to the infirmary to get pills to relieve a pain in his shoulder.

Kenneth Warembourg, a former supervisor, said that women can advance to be red hats but that they're ignored when they apply for management level positions. He said that, for one thing, they are thought to be "too conscientious": "I was sometimes asked to take meat that's two months old, that's been sitting in the cooler, put it in a combo, and repackage it as if it's fresh meat."[24] He thinks that the company would be reluctant to ask a woman to do something like that. When he complained about putting false labels on meat, he was told, "aged meat's better for you."

Warembourg also said that people in management positions who make sexist remarks about women, or those who go along with such remarks, have told him that they just do it to keep their jobs. "When they talk like that in the office," he says, "and even if they expect you to know better than to do it on the floor, those attitudes are going to come out. . . . If a woman, or anyone else, is getting a little too sharp, she'll just be harassed out of her job. . . . I've been given instructions to watch someone like a dog, and fire them for whatever I could get them on."

A black worker said that one of his supervisors used to "watch him a lot": "I used to see other people throw out dirty bones and really cut the strip up where they can't use it. And he wouldn't take them upstairs [where workers are reprimanded when supervisors write them up or "pink-slip" them]. But, when I did something, he'd take me upstairs."[25]

One Mexican American worker, who was born in Texas, said that he quit his job at the plant because "they treated me like a goddam wetback."[26] He had actually engaged in a fist fight at work with someone he called a "wetback." When asked what the foreman did about it, he said that the foreman didn't care, "he just walked away." Viviano Torres observed, "I guess it makes them feel better when everybody's fighting and hollering at each other. That way no one has time or energy to develop friendships and defend themselves at work."

Union organizers understand that divisiveness among workers will have to be overcome in order to build solidarity against company intransigence. However, most union policy-makers are older white males, far removed from the plant floor. Few union officials speak Spanish. If today's meatpackers are to be organized from within their own workplaces," they may have to do so — at least initially — with little assistance or encouragement from the union.

The 1990s: "You're paid to work, not to think"

In January 1987, Pamela Nelson, who had worked more than four years at Monfort's Grand Island plant, requested access to the company's injury logs. She had developed severe back and neck problems from trimming livers and hanging them on a moving chain above her head. Even though the work was "easy," by her own definition, her body was suffering from stress due to the speed of the chain and the tension of being pushed to produce like a machine hour after hour, day after day. She was a victim of what, in business lingo, is called "de-skilling." Workers call it speed-up. Nelson wanted to know how many others experienced debilitating diseases from stresses that were not sudden and dramatic, but were caused by constant and repeated movements.[1]

Nelson had been "written up" a number of times for absences when she was receiving treatment for her injuries. She had documentation from doctors for all the absences. In defending her job, she discovered that the company had no record of her original complaints about her back and neck. At the same time, she learned about fines being exacted against Monfort's competitor, IBP, for under-reporting of injuries and illnesses. She decided to check Monfort's records to see if similar patterns could be found.

Her request to see the company's injury records was never acknowledged. At IBP, workers who requested access to injury logs had been required to sign statements indicating that they would not hold the company liable in any way as a result of information obtained by looking at the records. Although such a statement could not hold up in court, workers who were not aware of their rights could be intimidated by it. Monfort, however, dealt with Nelson's request by simply ignoring her, so she was forced to call on the Occupational Safety and Health and Administration (OSHA) for assistance. Eventually, Monfort was fined $10,000 for denying Pamela Nelson access to injury logs, but by 1988 the fine had been reduced, on appeal, to $100. Nelson was by that time working full-time in the organizing office of the United Food and Commercial Workers (UFCW) union in Grand Island.[2] Largely through her efforts, the UFCW began tracking injuries at the plant, which remained unorganized while National Labor Relations Board decisions citing company violations of labor law were on appeal. Meanwhile, employees at the union's organizing office urged workers to insist that machines be fitted with closing controls, emergency switches, and guards to prevent deaths like the one that had occurred in Greeley's Portion Foods plant in 1987 (see Chapter 4). The union also lobbied in Washington, D.C., to revive concern for the enactment of government regulations that would force companies to install lockout devices on dangerous machinery. The widow of a Grand Island man whose head had been crushed in a defleshing machine testified that only one of five lockout systems designed to prevent accidental operation of the machine was attached to it when her husband's death occurred. She said that the company had exerted constant pressure on her husband to keep the production line going at maximum speed and had disregarded his complaints about inadequate protection.[3]

Because of the company's disregard for using safety controls in hide-defleshing and other machines at Monfort's Grand Island slaughterhouse, several more workers were killed and others lost limbs.[4] OSHA finally conducted an inspection on the use of safety devices at the Grand Island plant. This resulted in a major decision against Monfort, which was announced March 27, 1991. The company was charged with 197 specific safety violations, most of which were regarded as flagrant violations involving a lack of training workers in safety procedures and a lack of interest in protecting workers. Fines against the company totalled $1.1 million. Monfort would have been liable for $7 million if the OSHA decision had been handed down a few weeks later, when new schedules went into effect. Even so, OSHA's findings were contested by the company in an effort to reduce penalties; they are still on appeal at the time of this writing.

Among the cases cited against Monfort in Grand Island, besides grisly deaths, were those of employees who were totally disabled from back injuries, mangled limbs, and chemical burns. More typical, however, is the case of Patty Stander, who suffered a partial loss of use in both her hands from trimming beef livers. When she developed a paralysis in her arms, she was given heat treatments and "light duty" at several other jobs, but was eventually told that she was "not cut out for packinghouse work."[5] The company would not assume liability for her condition, which has worsened over time; ongoing medical bills are being paid through wage garnishments at the nursing home where she secured work after leaving Monfort.

Repetitive motion injuries nearly doubled between 1989 and 1990, nationwide. The incidence was highest in meatpacking.[6] In Greeley, back and shoulder injuries caused by repetitive motion seem to be almost as common as injuries to arms and hands. One injured worker told us that his supervisor was under so much pressure to keep him working without a break that she had informed him that his therapy sessions were over, that he was not supposed to continue going to therapy. Later, the therapist asked him why he had not come in. The supervisor, he said, had simply lied to him to prevent him from going to therapy.[7]

A worker who slipped and fell on a blood-soaked, greasy floor, hurting his back, said that the supervisor cleaned up the floor and threw some salt on it to make it less slippery but didn't ask him how he was or if he needed help.[8] Marvin Smith said:

> If you're bleeding quite a bit, they reluctantly go ahead and take you off the table. But if they think you can put a Band-Aid on and wait until break time, they'll tell you to put a Band-Aid on and get it checked after work. It's like a shameful thing if you get cut. You try not to let anybody know. . . . A lot of times when people are hurting and get put on light duty, the supervisor will treat them differently. . . . A lot of guys, when they get hurt, they'd just rather take the pain than go through the mental part they put on you for getting hurt.

Sometimes government meat inspectors intervene to insist that workers be sent home when they have infections on their fingers, hands, or elbows and have not been allowed to take time off from work to heal.

One of our informants was an older man who had become partially disabled working at Monfort in the 1970s.[9] He is now self-employed as an interpreter for Monfort workers who are undergoing treatment at the Northern Colorado Medical Center in

Greeley. He put us in touch with people who had suffered knife wounds inflicted by themselves or by other workers standing next to them, shoulder to shoulder, without adequate protection. Others had lost fingers while cleaning or operating machines. One woman had repeatedly complained of loose railings that allowed carcasses to fall off. Her complaints went unheeded, and one day a carcass fell on her and injured her back. Typically, Monfort dealt with such situations by paying off employees who were no longer able to work, in exchange for their agreement not to hold the company liable in any way. One woman explained: "They offer you so much money on a piece of paper. You sign this paper saying you are quitting and whatever happens to you later, it's not their fault."[10]

Unless workers insist, no liability at all is assumed by the company. It was only after OSHA intervened that Monfort was fined $740 for failing to enforce an existing lockout procedure in the death of Roberto Rodriquez, whose body literally had to be scraped from the meat blender into which he had fallen.[11] Workers said that the man's wife, who was in Texas, was unable to persuade the company to pay for shipping his remains to Texas "because her husband was illegal," so fellow workers at Portion Foods took up a collection.[12]

A man who had a heart attack while working got no help because "they thought he was on drugs." Our informant said: "Either way, heart attack or drugs, he was still on the floor and they didn't do anything!"[13] Another worker remarked, "Really, it's not a slaughterhouse of cows. It's a slaughterhouse of people.[14]

A pregnant woman who began bleeding and was not allowed to leave work had a miscarriage at the plant.[15] Women in such circumstances hesitate to initiate lawsuits against the company for fear of losing their jobs or jeopardizing family members who also work at Monfort.

A young woman named Robin, who "felt her back give" while working, was told to keep going. She felt worse that night and asked to be put on light duty the next day. The supervisor refused her request and said, "You're tough! You can handle it!" She got pain pills from the nurse, but was walking stiff-legged. Finally, she quit the job. She agreed to sign papers saying that she was leaving voluntarily, so she was unable to get workers' compensation. Since then, she hasn't been able to lift anything and has gone to live with her mother.[16]

Guadelupe Valdez, a mother of three small children, was pressured to quit work after she injured her leg and back in a fall while working at the trim table. After the fall, she was sent home instead of to the clinic or hospital. When her leg turned blue, she got an ambulance to come to her house and take her to the hospital. She returned to work after two weeks so that she wouldn't lose her job, but she was in constant pain. At home Guadelupe couldn't lift her young children or sit down comfortably. The company claimed that her injury occurred after she was sent home, so she was denied workers' compensation. She continued working with a brace on her back so that she could pay doctor bills.[17]

An older woman who quit working after a similar experience couldn't get her job back when she reapplied. Her experience is like that of many others who lost their jobs after having been injured at work and who were subsequently unable to find work elsewhere. One woman, who had worked two years as a meat trimmer, had to have an operation on her hand.

> When I went back to work, they said I had missed too much and they fired me. Now I can't lift this hand without using the other to lift it. . . . I can't work anywhere and it hurts more when the climate changes. I can't use it at all. . . . They treat the workers like they were people of iron and you had to do as they say, at such a rapid pace. . . . You're working as fast as you can and they tell you, "If you can't keep up with the beef, get off the fuckin' table." They pink-slipped me [for an infraction of discipline] for telling the foreman "How would you like it if I talked to you like that?" They wrote me up. . . . It looks like to me that while I was able to work I was all right but as soon as I got hurt they shoved me in a corner and put a box over me. That's how I feel.[18]

Because injured workers are typically poor, and often undocumented, public concern about them is even less than it might be otherwise. Workers transferred from Greeley's Sunrise Clinic to the Northern Colorado Medical Center say that they are referred to as "clinic cases" instead of by name. Workers report being turned away at the Greeley Medical Clinic if they come without an interpreter. Many prefer, when possible, to seek treatment out of town. Neither the workers nor the company are eager for publicity. When the plant is evacuated temporarily because of an ammonia or carbon dioxide leak, there may be a short notice on an inside page of the local newspaper, but there is no long-term follow-up on the condition of unconscious workers who require treatment or hospitalization.[19]

If cases where dramatic and life-threatening events occur do not stir public consciousness, it is even more difficult to create public awareness about the so-called mundane effects of speed-up in meat processing, which was the issue of most immediate concern to Pamela Nelson when she first requested access to company illness and injury logs.

Repetitive motion illnesses — disorders of the musculoskeletal and nervous systems caused by doing the same thing hundreds or thousands of times a day — have risen dramatically since the 1970s. The increase in reported repetitive-motion disorders in the United States from 1981 to 1989 was sevenfold, and government officials estimated that only a small fraction of such illnesses were reported. Pressure on companies to take preventive measures have succeeded in bringing about small changes in the design of workplaces but have failed to bring about a general reduction in the pace of production.[20]

In 1987 government statistics revealed that injuries and illnesses in meatpacking were more numerous than in any other occupation in the United States, due largely to the high incidence of repetitive motion disorders. Even back injuries were sustained most often, studies indicated, because of cumulative trauma disorders, or "CTD." An Associated Press writer said that, increasingly, workers were being treated like robots: "They treat arms and hands like they're part of a machine. But you can't oil a person's arm or hand."[21]

Ken Monfort, as president of the American Meat Institute, said: "It's obvious that we probably accelerated the problem in the last 10 or 15 years as we broke down the jobs into pieces and said you do this one thing all day." He urged government agencies to give the industry time to deal with the problem, saying, "We're already more cognizant of how the chain speed affects people and quality of work. . . . Probably the plant manager and his supervisors have a very difficult job. We expect them to get 300 an hour whatever he's doing. . . . And we expect perfect quality and [for him] to treat his people well, not to hurt them, not allow them to hurt themselves."[22]

Evidence had accumulated by 1987 showing that 40 percent of meatpacking workers suffered some form of CTD. Yet, several years later, the risk management director at Monfort's Greeley plant, which was by then processing up to four hundred cattle an hour, declared unashamedly: "There have never been any studies done linking chain speeds and repetitive-motion disorders."[23] In the same vein, a doctor testifying before a congressional committee in 1989 hesitated to indict companies directly even though he was obviously aware of the relationship between factory speed-up and increased incidence of CTD:

> Congressman — "My question is, as you increase the speed, which presumably increases productivity, do you also contribute to the medical problems that we are dealing with?"
> Doctor — "You increase the risk within — I think the difference is when I talk about repetitiveness, that means, for example, a number of motions you do in a day, so if I say repetitive . . ."
> Congressman — "So you mean increased speeds?"
> Doctor — "We mean the same thing. If we go up to 20,000 motions of the hand . . . that's probably a higher risk than 15,000 motions of the hand during the day."
> Congressman — "Right."
> Doctor — "Though the precise relationship between repetitiveness and risk is not completely worked out."[24]

Monfort rivals Iowa Beef Processors (IBP) and John Morrell were cited by OSHA in 1987 and 1988 for bad record keeping and for various health and safety violations. Congressional hearings revealed that government policies initiated in the early 1980s, exempting businesses from OSHA inspections if they had "above average" safety records, had encouraged under-reporting of injuries and illnesses. In an effort to reduce "waste" in government spending, the number of OSHA inspectors in the field was drastically reduced during the Reagan administration. OSHA administrators adopted a "non-adversarial" stance in relation to corporations, issuing "guidelines" instead of regulations. OSHA's director of safety standards, speaking to corporate executives, said: "Your comments and suggestions on how we might be more effective in assisting employers and employees are welcome. . . . I know very well that you know more about safety and health in the meat industry than I do."[25]

Confronted with mounting evidence that its policies were not working, OSHA nevertheless negotiated to reduce fines levied in 1987 and 1988. Eventually, IBP paid $975,000 instead of the total of $5.69 million originally suggested. In return, IBP agreed to initiate an "ergonomics" program to "better adapt the workplace to the capablities of workers" and negotiated with the UFCW to allow "ergonomics monitors" into its plants.[26]

Even before these deals were completed, Monfort got the message and hired a full-time director of ergonomics in Greeley. The main feature of Monfort's much-publicized program was the introduction of an exercise program for new workers, who were told to do finger and hand exercises for several weeks before beginning work and who were instructed to continue these exercises on company time for a month after employment. They were then given certificates as "industrial athletes." OSHA does not provide any oversight of the ergonomics program.[27]

The company claims that the morale of new workers has improved since the industrial athlete program was instituted.[28] But workers say that once the initial break-in period is over, so is the concern for their morale. "What really hurts is that once you know how to do the job and get a little bit fast at it, that's when it's bad. 'Cause that's when they start pushin' you," one worker said. "I think they're just taking more of an interest so people won't think so much anymore and say, 'Yeah, they're trying to do something.' . . . I think that's all it is."[29]

The company's ergonomics program does not include any effort to make sure that there are extra people available to take up the slack when workers are absent or to adjust line speed to workers' capabilities. Government guidelines for meatpackers, issued in 1990, mention both of these as issues that need to be addressed, but no standards are suggested and no means of enforcement are provided. In the question and answer section of the OSHA guidelines, company managers are told, in answer to the question "Does this require slowing down the line?" that "This is *one* of a wide variety of control measures that can be implemented to address specific, identified problems. Modifying line speed is one means of work method design that may be appropriate after a systematic worksite analysis has been conducted to determine the nature of existing problems." No time schedule for this "worksite analysis" is given.[30]

Monfort's "worksite analysis" has been going on for more than three years while workers continue cutting up meat at breakneck speed. The UFCW had hoped that a company-wide unionization agreement could be reached with Monfort/ConAgra after the company was cited for massive health and safety violations at Grand Island and for pervasive violations of labor law at several of its plants. But Monfort was intransigent and legal processes were slow. OSHA has answered several specific complaints since 1987 at the Greeley plant and has cited the company, but no penalties have been exacted. No general inspection has ever been carried out.[31] OSHA has been provided with evidence that falsification of injury records occurs regularly and that workers are often treated on the floor instead of being sent to the infirmary. Yet, no formal action has been initiated against the company regarding these practices.[32]

In a letter to Monfort, Inc., dated October 16, 1989, the regional OSHA office wrote: "On review of your company's 1988 OSHA–200 reports, it is evident that you may have an excess of cumulative trauma disorders recorded. We have decided that because a national settlement is imminent with ConAgra, we will not address this apparent indication of a hazard at this time."

Four years later, the "imminent settlement" has still not been reached, nor has any general inspection been conducted. Gene Meakins, in an effort to downplay the seriousness of charges brought against the company for safety violations in Grand Island, and hoping to deflect future criticism of its operations in Greeley, said: "The UFCW told us as late as yesterday that they would stop what I call the 'slander campaign' if we would agree to recognize them without a vote by the workers."[33]

Knowing that revelations about the plant's injury rate could be made public by the union at any time, Monfort/ConAgra administrative personnel confirmed to a reporter in April 1991 that the most recent accident and illness records from the Greeley plant exceeded the industry norm by more than two and one half times.[34] Company spokespersons insisted, however, that Greeley was its "star" plant in matters of safety and health. The statistics, they said, were a result of over-reporting as part of recent health and safety initiatives at the plant, where cumulative trauma disorders were being "tracked." Accidents, they said, had actually been "reduced by 56% in the past three years."[35]

OSHA apparently accepted the company's explanation that "preventive treatment" after an initial complaint could be reported as an "asymptomatic" situation. Gene Meakins said, "We feel we are ahead of the industry and OSHA in this area, just as we were with hearing testing several years ago."[36] An audiologist contracted by Monfort said that the testing program is set up to identify workers who may have acquired hearing problems previously, from exposure to gunshots while serving in the military or while hunting, so that this information can be used to protect the company later if such workers complain about hearing loss suffered in the workplace.[37]

Shortly before Monfort's dismal safety record was exposed by the press, Dr. Fred B. Groves was named corporate medical director for ConAgra Red Meat Cos., in charge of Monfort's five beef plants. As a former head and founder of the Corporate Health and Medical Programs, Inc. (CHAMPS) at the Greeley Medical Clinic, Dr. Groves had been Monfort's preferred "company doctor" for seventeen years. He is the one person whose name surfaced over and over in our interviews with Monfort workers who were suffering from cumulative trauma disorders (including carpal tunnel syndrome). He is the one doctor who was most despised by workers. They said that he took the company's side in every dispute over injuries and illnesses, downgrading the extent of workers' suffering. He was slow to authorize necessary treatment and reluctant to recognize outside opinions.[38] Groves was a member of the State Grievance Committee, which processes complaints brought against physicians. Groves is president of the Weld County Medical Society and a member of the Colorado Medical Society Workmen's Compensation Advisory Committee.

Many workers consulted doctors outside Greeley, at their own expense, when they were ill or injured; they felt that most Greeley doctors were under pressure, directly or indirectly, from Monfort.[39]

Although medical journals are full of studies about causes and consequences of repetitive motion stress on bodies, companies and company doctors have been extremely slow to recognize the specific nature of cumulative trauma disorders. They make workers feel that whatever problems they are having on the line are their own fault.

In the fall of 1990 workers were given a leaflet informing them of a new "safety incentive plan." They were offered a week of paid vacation if they could go a whole year without making any workers' compensation claims, without arriving late or leaving early from work, and without "being observed in violation of any safety rules." Workers recognized that this was an effort on the part of the company to absolve itself from responsibility for work stress. "Everybody knows you can't go a year without missing work or getting hurt in a place like this," one worker said.[40] The leaflet was taken as one more indication that they would be scoffed at rather than given sympathy when they were in pain.

Regular breaks from work are mandated both by law and custom, but meatpackers are seemingly exempt from such "privileges." When interviewed by reporters in 1988,[41] Ken Monfort said that slaughterhouse workers get a 15-minute break every 2½ hours. When we toured the Greeley packinghouse in 1991, we were told the same thing.[42] Actually, ever since the union was broken, workers at the Greeley plants get one 15-minute rest break and a 30-minute lunch break during an 8-hour workday. There is no break during the last 4 hours of work. Pay is figured from the time the chain starts to the time the last carcass leaves the kill area. The extra time that workers spend completing work on the line; trading in and sharpening knives; putting on boots, frocks, mesh gloves, aprons, earplugs, hairnets, and hats; setting up stands and arranging table boards to specifications — or engaging in whatever other preparations are required for work — is not counted on company time. Nor is the removal and disposal of clothing and equipment. All this has to take place during breaks as well as at the beginning and end of the workday. One worker explained:

> On the 15-minute break, when the horn sounds, you have to take all of your equipment off, because you can't take your equipment to the lunchroom or the locker room. . . . Then you have to walk all the way. . . . So, really you don't have that much time. By the time you

do all these other things, you really get 5 minutes to yourself. And you have to be back on your table and ready when the horn sounds again.[43]

The break is hardly a time for respite in any case, as Marvin Smith explained: "The locker rooms are so hot you sweat before you even go out to the floor, where it's cold. And the roaches are so bad. You open your lockers up and they fall. And then, they're on your clothes. You have to shake your clothes off to put them on. And sometimes, if you don't shake your clothes good, you can put your frock on and feel a roach crawling on you." Although the locker rooms are uncomfortable, workers sometimes break the rules and eat lunch there rather than in the cafeteria, where the smell is worse:

> The kill floor's on the other side, and the doors to the cafeteria are open, and the smell from the kill floor is terrible. . . . I go upstairs to my locker room. It's bad up there, too, because it's hot and you've got roaches to try and avoid. They have signs up in the locker room saying "No eating, No drinking" or anything, but everybody does it anyway.

Workers say that only if the chain breaks down for some reason do they get a rest. Even then, they can expect that the chain speed will be increased later, as Viviano Torres explained: "Later on they'll speed that chain up really fast to catch up." If the chain speed is set for 360 an hour officially (and this is limited only by the number of government inspectors available), workers can still be working at the rate of four hundred an hour or more for part of the day. The company will cut days short, sometimes for weeks at a time, to get more work out of them for less pay.

After getting their 1990 annual bonus, workers said that they had worked more hours than the year before but had been paid less. They discovered that the bonus was set according to the price of meat, not according to the amount of work they had done. So all the pressure that they were putting on each other, at supervisors' urging, was not necessarily going to result in a bigger bonus. At "line meetings" the supervisors made workers feel guilty collectively for injuries and absences. Workers were told that they would be rewarded if they worked hard. Rosa Morado, who had worked five years at the slaughterhouse, commented on the line meetings with a laugh: "They'll tell you about all the improvements they're planning on making and how good everything is going to be." Another said that they were told that there had been thirteen injuries at their table in one week and that all of these had been caused by carelessness. One of the workers had fainted and fallen down and hurt herself. This was considered to be her own fault, because it was assumed that she had been on alcohol or drugs. This same worker had been feverish several times and had gone to the infirmary, where she was given pills and was sent back on the line.

Workers who dare to complain about working conditions or who try to make suggestions are told: "You're paid to work, not to think." Those who are supposed to do the "thinking" are not interested in hearing workers' opinions about the organization of production. One man, named Robert, who was working the day shift at the "gut table" in May 1991 said that they had been doing four hundred per hour regularly when a group of managers from another Monfort plant where the speed was 320 per hour were brought in to observe how speed could be gradually increased. Robert's supervisor drew "happy faces" and "sad faces" on a paper towel, indicating whether the work was going well or not. The criteria for achieving the "happy face" kept increasing. A fast worker would be singled out for being "number one" and would get a piece of candy. Some workers risked displeasing the supervisor by refusing the candy. The game had been all for show anyway, Robert said, because speed-up had been effected at the Greeley slaughterhouse by yelling and by firing anybody who couldn't keep up.[44]

A young man named Marvin Smith had suffered from back and shoulder injuries and had accepted "light duty" periodically even though he was paid less for it. Smith said: "They're always on us. You hardly ever hear 'You're doing a good job, keep up the good work!' You hardly ever hear that." He was also bitter about getting less money just because he'd been injured at work: "I can't understand that. You get hurt on the job and they cut your pay. Doesn't make sense." He said that he was the only one left at his table after a year. Sometimes people throw down their knives and walk away crying, he said, then come back at the urging of friends or relatives working in the plant. But sooner or later, nearly everyone quits or is fired. The work force is mostly young people. Even if they want to stay, their bodies get used up and they can't go on.

"It's scary what they do over there," said a former manager. "Hardly anyone on the line can take it for long. They load you in and they load you out."[45] He said that when he finally decided to leave, "it was like getting out of prison." He said that he's getting less salary now than when he worked at Monfort, but that he feels more human. "After ConAgra took over, they instituted these programs where the supervisors have to go to classes to learn how to listen to employees, but it's all a joke. Nobody's listening to them!" He said that the company has become more vigilant than before about employees using drugs — marijuana, cocaine, amphetamines. "But they're really just looking for bodies out there. You dehumanize people, you're going to get a lot of drug abuse." Richard Lee Harris, a former health services director, said, "They use and abuse people as long as they can and then get rid of them." He said that the drug testing program is completely arbitrary. Some people are hired even though they test positive initially. Others are fired for testing positive rather than being treated or given compensation for injuries. "It all depends on who you are."

One way that workers are motivated to work as long as they can is through the profit-sharing program. But many say that they are cheated out of bonuses anyway. According to Marvin Smith:

> When it's right before profit-sharing time, they start writing people up for every little thing that happens. And you know, if you get written up for so many things, you get fired. . . . It seems like a lot more people get fired right before profit-sharing time. Seems like they put up with a lot before profit sharing, but when profit sharing's getting close, they don't put up with nothin'.

Profit sharing occurs only once a year. It is not guaranteed, and the timing is often confusing. A man who had planned to get his bonus and then quit was told that he had quit two days before he was eligible. He felt as if he had been misled and said: "I think they wanted a big turnover rate so they wouldn't have to pay the profit sharing."[46] Another worker, who had had a flat tire on the way to work and called in late, was fired anyway, a few days before profit-sharing time.[47] In the summer of 1991, hundreds of employees were fired or quit when Monfort invited the U.S. Immigration and Naturalization Service to the Greeley slaughterhouse (see Chapter 7). Those who left are bitter that they could not claim bonuses, which, in some cases, would have amounted to nearly $2,000. Others say that the line is deliberately speeded up off and on during the last month before bonus time, in an effort to "shake out" the workforce.

One would think that criminal laws would be more than justified against meatpacking barons who systematically violate the basic rights of workers to dignity and protection on the job. However, it is the workers who are made to feel like criminals when they seek even minimal rights to compensation for illnesses and injuries sustained in workplaces. Monfort workers are made to feel that they have themselves commited a crime when they apply for workers' compensation payments.

Because a majority of Monfort workers are recent immigrants to the United States, they either do not know about the minimum protections that they are guaranteed by law — such as workers' compensation — or they feel powerless to seek justice. A large number have never done any kind of wage work before, either because they are very young or because they have come to Greeley directly from rural areas in Mexico, where their families traditionally engaged in subsistence farming. They do not know English and they are made to feel as if they should expect to work harder for less, without any "special privileges," so long as they are "outsiders." For many, all the deductions from their paycheck are simply a rebate to government agencies or employers, because they do not dare to make any claims for tax returns, social security, or other benefits due them. Nor do employers explain to workers how they can make such claims. If they go to the union organizing office for information or assistance, they risk immediate dismissal from their jobs. Even though U.S. law protects workers' rights to safe workplaces, to workers' compensation, to legal representation, and to union representation — regardless of citizenship status — workers are often unaware of these rights. When they do seek legal help, many say that they have a hard time finding lawyers who will represent them.

In spite of these problems, an estimated one thousand workers' compensation cases are disputed with Monfort in Greeley every year. The company is self-insured but is subject to state law regulating enforcement. Employees who refuse out-of-court settlements are subjected to lengthy litigation and harassment. At workers' compensation hearings, injury victims sometimes are interrogated extensively by Monfort lawyers regarding the exact circumstances of their injuries, even though workers' compensation covers all injuries sustained in the workplace, regardless of cause. The company makes every attempt to implicate the workers in some wrongdoing or to reveal aspects of their personal lives that would cause them embarrassment. Monfort attorneys will delay proceedings through endless cross-examinations, then request that the hearing be prolonged to introduce another witness. In such cases, a worker who has returned to Greeley from out of state to defend a claim may have to come back again six months later, at his or her own expense, so that the hearing can continue.[48]

Nearly all the claims brought before the court are sustained, regardless of the effort made by the company to refute them. In fact, lawyers do not take up claims unlikely to be sustained in court. Nevertheless, because making a claim is so problematic for employees, and because the company routinely appeals decisions in an effort to wear down applicants, a majority of workers who are severely disabled from occupational diseases are eventually supported by family members or friends or by tax-supported programs, rather than by workers' compensation. Typically, workers use up their own and family members' savings before turning to public and private social service agencies for assistance. Even where workers' compensation claims are successfully processed, payments are delayed, on the average, at least a year.[49]

Kay Norton, vice president in charge of legal and government affairs at Monfort/ConAgra, has taken a public role in criticizing Colorado's workers' compensation system for allegedly over-compensating workers and lawyers at the expense of companies (including insurance carriers). In speeches before business groups, she emphasizes increasing health costs rather than emphasizing increasing injury and illness incidence. When forced to acknowledge that work-related illnesses and injuries are at an all-time high, she cites worker carelessness. Increased insurance costs are blamed on opportunism by employees and their lawyers. Among the remedies that she proposes are: establishing ceilings for coverage of certain kinds of illnesses and disabilities, increasing vigilance against unnecessary claims, and prohibiting legal representation for workers.

In March, 1991, Kay Norton's husband, Senator Tom Norton, a Republican member of the Colorado State Legislature, introduced a workers' compensation bill that included her proposed provisions. Lobbying by businesses for the bill was so intense that, for the first time, legislators threatened to outline restrictions on lobbying to curtail instances of "unethical conduct" by "certain businesses." Community organizations were forced to resort to demonstrations outside the state capitol to gain the attention of legislators. By the time the bill passed the Senate it had been amended enough that Senator Norton himself voted against it. However, it weakened workers' rights by providing a formula for the amount of compensation possible for certain medical impairments, which must be identified by "approved medical care providers" (that is, company doctors). Loss of future wages because of a worker's inability to re-enter the workforce is not compensated. Instead, the bill limits or bans re-employment after workers' compensation awards are made, restricts workers' rights to legal representation, and penalizes workers who seek to expedite claims.

Since the law went into effect, insurance providers complain that costs have gone up and workers complain that their rights have been severely curtailed. Colorado businesses are planning to introduce new legislation that will further undermine workers' rights to compensation for job-related injuries and illnesses. A voter initiative sponsored by attorneys challenges the right of businesses to shield themselves from lawsuits. Media attention to the issue focuses on individuals who have been able to "beat the system" and live off fraudulent claims. Needless to say, these individuals did not work at Monfort, Inc.

The Greeley–Weld County Chamber of Commerce and the Colorado Association of Commerce and Industry (CACI) are both heavily involved in the Workers' Compensation Coalition, which lobbied hard to push business interests in the legislature. CACI also advises manufacturers how to get low penalties for OSHA violations. Myra Monfort was elected to head CACI in October 1991. The job of CACI's president is to monitor legislation at the state level and to oversee lobbying for business interests.

A top priority for CACI, according to Myra Monfort, is revamping the state's educational system. "Are we producing graduates we want? Who can determine that best if not business?"[50] Business-school "partnerships" are being established as a complement to cuts in state funding for educational institutions. Industry enthusiasts say that business must be involved in education "from the cradle to the grave" in order to "bolster the economic, educational and social well-being of the United States."[51] At a time when corruption in high places is rampant, corporations are seeking to consolidate control of educational institutions, pressing for a public mandate to silence criticism of business-government collusion and to undermine workplace organizing efforts and the political rights of workers.

All of Weld County's representatives to the Colorado State Legislature are Republicans. Greeley's representative, David Owen, serves on state agricultural committees and on the Business Affairs and Labor Committee. Owen received an award from fellow Republicans for introducing an anti-union, right-to-work bill in 1991. The bill did not pass, but Owen's office says that a new version of it will be introduced.

Businesses lobby against workers' rights based on the premise that workers' demands hinder industrial development. They claim that the state cannot attract new industry if wages are high, worker insurance programs are expensive, and corporations are expected to pay for the services they exact from communities. Even liberal legislators, hungry for campaign support from businesses, succumb to the idea that whatever is good for the corporation is good for the people. Corporations threaten legislators with plant relocations if their demands are not met. ConAgra's president, Charles Harper, told Nebraska legislators that if tax codes were not revised, "Some Friday night we turn out the lights, click, click, click . . . back up the trucks, and we'll be gone by Monday morning."[52]

Small towns are particularly vulnerable. Residents of Windsor, a small Weld County town between Greeley and Fort Collins, are reportedly suffering from the effects of toxic poisoning from smokestack emissions at the Kodak company. These emissions affect everyone, not only workers at the plant, yet residents are hesitant to complain. They fear that the plant will move elsewhere, property values will decline, and local businesses will suffer. At Monfort and other meatpacking plants, issues such as worker safety, which do not affect everyone equally, generally do not come under public scrutiny at all. Because most meatpacking plants are now located in small towns, the public conscience is influenced by the fact that entire communities are effectively held hostage.

At the national level, legislators also claim that they are serving their constituencies by representing corporate interests. One of ConAgra's most dedicated private envoys in Washington, D.C., is Greeley's Republican Representative Wayne Allard, a veterinarian who was elected to Congress in November 1990. In his first year in Congress, he became a member of the House Agriculture Committee. He sits on subcommittees concerning livestock, dairy, and poultry; conservation, credit, and rural development; and department operations, research, and foreign agriculture. As a member of the House Interior and Insular Affairs Committee, Allard serves on the Water, Power, and Offshore Energy Resources Subcommittee and the Subcommittee on Energy and the Environment. He is also a member of the House Small Business Committee, serving on subcommittees for antitrust, impact of deregulation and ecology, and general economy and minority enterprise development.

In 1991 approximately one-half of the bills sponsored or cosponsored by Wayne Allard appeared to bear directly on the interests of ConAgra, including bills on product liability, food quality protection, workers' rights, ecology, development incentives for rural industry, and regulatory relief for agricultural enterprises. Allard received a rating of zero in a survey by the League of Conservation Voters for his 1991 voting record. Ken Monfort praises Allard warmly in his newspaper columns and congratulates other Colorado representatives who support Allard's inititatives, holding out to them the promise of future support.

Patronage of this sort is clearly at work in congressional scuttling of environmental initiatives. A recent United Nations study cites overgrazing as a major source of environmental destruction in the United States.[53] Federal land is particularly susceptible to overgrazing. In summer 1991, Colorado members of Congress fought diligently against increases in grazing fees charged to cattle ranchers for the use of government land.Current fees do not even cover the cost of land management, and grazing fees on private land are much higher than those on public land. Typically, ranchers move cattle seasonally between private and public lands. Proponents of the bill were accused by ranchers of having a hidden agenda, putting environmental considerations above "human needs." Former Monfort executive Senator Hank Brown, consistently takes environmentalists to task for their "insistence that nature is good and man is bad." In October 1991, he began hosting a cable TV show, at the expense of taxpayers, to "educate" constituents about such legislative issues. His attitude toward consumer and environmental issues is demonstrated in this comment about groundwater testing: "If we did not implement the new tests, it is estimated that four-tenths of one person out of the entire population of the country might catch cancer."[54]

Much of the legislation Brown that sponsors or co-sponsors never reaches public attention. For instance, while he was a member of the House of Representatives in 1989, he pushed through an amendment to the Food Security Act of 1985, making criminal the "disruption" of a farm animal facility, and authorized a study that temporarily removed anhydrous ammonia (a highly poisonous gas used in the refrigeration of meat) from the list of substances subject to regulation in the Hazardous Materials Transportation Act.

Senator Brown currently sits on the Committee on the Judiciary, which is mandated to oversee "protection of trade and commerce against unlawful restraints and monopolies." Because ownership of the meat industry is more concentrated than at any other time in history and the industry is currently under scrutiny for price-fixing and insider manipulation of sales (see Chapter 6), Brown's position on this committee is a classic case of the fox guarding the chicken coop.

As a state representative in 1973, Brown opposed the establishment of the Colorado Occupational Safety and Health Administration (COSHA), a counterpart to OSHA, which was established at the federal level in 1972. At the time, he had recently joined Monfort as director of development. After Brown went to Washington, D.C., Ken Monfort was so confident of his loyalty that he wrote in a June 13, 1990 *Greeley Tribune* column: "I would vote for Hank if his opponent were me."

As a new Colorado senator, Hank Brown's primary concerns were to support President George Bush's foreign policy initiatives. Before Monfort, Inc., merged with ConAgra, and before the company became determined to make a major push into foreign markets and to develop foreign operations, Ken Monfort had been an advocate of demilitarization. He and Brown had differed somewhat on foreign policy issues. Yet, by 1991, Monfort praised both Brown and Bush for having the "guts" to do anything necessary to protect U.S. business interests abroad.

In October 1989, Monfort wrote: "We spent the Soviets into chaos and bankruptcy. We must get our own house in order before we do it to ourselves."[55] By July 1991 he wrote: "I am not sure we are providing enough help in the right places to our new friends the Russians and East Europeans." ConAgra's first quarter report to stockholders in 1992 included the following statement: "It's very possible the United States will take substantial steps to help the Soviet people feed themselves this winter. If so, ConAgra's diversified food base makes our company well-positioned to participate and benefit."

Monfort praised the military buildup in the Persian Gulf on behalf of U.S. oil interests and hinted that the use of nuclear weapons might be a wise choice:

> We are there to protect "friendly" governments, our oil supply, and in the long run, Israel. Since I am a 60-plus-year-old with sons probably too old for the military and grandsons too young, I evaluate our position as being worthwhile. . . . So how do we go about it? . . . In the long run, we Americans will have a hard time tolerating television pictures of starving Iraqi kids or American male hostages. Will our government have the guts to tell the press and the TV cameramen that they cannot go to Iraq to report? . . . The question gets to be how do we value them [the Iraqis] versus ourselves. No one has mentioned the possibility of using atomic weapons, but if you were George Bush or Colin Powell or Dick Cheney, and you knew that you were about to lose 100,000 Americans without the use of tactical atomic weapons versus 5000 with the use . . . how would you vote?"[56]

In foreign policy, as in business operations, those of "lesser value" (not coincidentally, those who are racially or ethnically different, both in the case of the Iraqis and in the case of Monfort's ill-paid and ill-treated workers) are exempt from enjoying the benefits of political democracy. They are, if corporate interests dictate, expendable.

Monfort chided members of Congress who insisted on debating foreign policy. In business, he said, the person who is ultimately responsible for the operation has the final say on policy. "The question of war and peace seems to me to deserve the same type of decision making and understanding."[57]

Ken Monfort's son, Charlie, who is now in charge of the international divisions of Monfort, Inc., said in the fall of 1991: "I think we are headed toward a world marketing system someday where everything will be bought and sold on a world basis."[58] Early in fiscal year 1991, ConAgra and the U.S.S.R. State Commission for Food and Food Procurement reached an agreement for ConAgra to be involved in managing of poultry and hog operations in the U.S.S.R. ConAgra Eastern Europe and ConAgra Soviet Union were established before this agreement was made. The company was seeking global deregulation through the General Agreement on Tariffs and Trade (GATT) to make U.S. investment in foreign countries more profitable. At the same time, U.S. corporations were pressuring foreign competitors in the meat industry to accept limitations on sales and investments in the United States.

The government of Australia bowed to U.S. pressure in September 1991 to reduce beef exports to the United States by 28,000 tons (from 337,000 tons in 1991). Reduction of Australian beef imports to the United States increases competition for the Japanese market, which is dominated by Australia and the United States. ConAgra is the principal U.S. exporter of red meat to Japan[59] and is seeking to secure its interests against all possible contingencies by making major investments in red meat operations in Australia. Ultimately, if ConAgra is successful, such maneuvering threatens the food security of many countries and gives the United States a powerful political weapon to use against those who challenge this country's New World Order.[60]

Whenever the U.S. economy enters a period of stagnation, corporations externalize the problems of internal decay by turning toward the power and pressure of the state to "force open markets that the private sector cannot."[61] However, U.S.–based corporations are not the only ones playing this game, and economic stagnation on a world scale places severe limits on such manipulative practices. Capitalist development cannot sustain "border-hopping" forever. Heavily indebted countries are the first to fall under the pressure to remove protective barriers that safeguard against unequal trade. When their economies fail, banks and corporations that have investments in these countries are affected as well. The likely outcome is that nation-states will eventually have to reconstruct their own economies based on domestic considerations.

Because of the contraction of U.S. red meat markets, the drive to increase the profitability of meat production in the United States, the concentration of the meatpacking industry, and corporate expansion on a global scale, meatpackers are expected to give up their claim to stable employment. They endure continual pressure to speed up production, risking their lives in dangerous workplaces. They do not receive wages commensurate with the gains made from their labor, nor are they allowed democratic rights to organization and representation. Meatpackers are held hostage, as are the communities in which they live, by corporate elites.

Competition in attracting industries to communities, states, and countries enhances corporate control over workers. Within the United States, workers who are not U.S. citizens suffer the most, but sooner or later, all workers' rights are undermined. Employers know that their strategies can backfire if foreign and native-born workers join forces to oppose corporate control, so companies do everything possible to prevent the internationalization of workers' movements and the growth of solidarity among workers, farmers, and consumers.

Lessons from a Century of Struggle   6

This chapter attempts to place unfolding events at the Monfort plants in a wider context, both historically and in terms of conflicts and social movements that impinge directly on issues discussed earlier. Solutions to the problems described are necessarily part of a much larger undertaking, of which popular protest is an integral part. Nevertheless, by acquiring a deeper understanding of contradictions in any area of social life, we can assure that our actions become part of the solution rather than part of the problem.

In the 1990s, U.S. farmers and ranchers continue to suffer from the effects of an economy linked precariously with government-supported expansion of U.S. corporate activity abroad. Subsidies and incentives given to big corporations by local, state, and national governments contribute to the concentration of land ownership as well as the concentration of power in meatpacking and related industries. By the beginning of this decade, 1 percent of the U.S. population owned 50 percent of the privately held land. Food production was even more concentrated than land ownership.[1] Farm owners and ranchers who had escaped bankruptcy or foreclosure were faced with increasingly restricted outlets for their products. Some livestock producers who had not survived were conducting lawsuits against meatpacking companies for price-fixing and other fraudulent practices and were calling for a stop to the concentration of power by a handful of corporations. Iowa State University professor John Helmuth wrote:

> When an industry drives its best small and medium sized companies into bankruptcy, when cattle producers and farmers are driven into bankruptcy by lower and lower prices, when workers are treated like

animals and injured and maimed for life, and consumers are charged higher and higher prices for minimum quality, often unsafe meat, something is wrong.[2]

In a critique of industry concentration, agro-economist A. V. Krebs wrote: "The history of American agriculture . . . has been characterized by a continual restructuring of rural society aimed not toward meeting its own worthwhile community needs, but rather at satisfying the needs of remote and self-serving 'communities of economic interests'."[3] A recent report on legislation affecting the meatpacking industry and immigrant labor concludes: "Meat packers and poultry processors [that is, companies] have been able to entrench themselves in their host communities and regions much more deeply than was possible earlier in this century, when poultry was primarily a family farmyard business and meatpacking was largely separated from the feed and livestock raising regions."[4]

An economist at the University of Wisconsin, Bruce W. Marion, says that the rate of concentration in the meatpacking industry is unprecedented: "There is no parallel in any of the industries — food and non-food — that I am aware of."[5] He calculates that cattle feeders lose some $50 million each year from the loss of competitive markets. Meatpackers that have taken over the industry are able to stop buying cattle for days or weeks at a time, thus driving down prices and forcing feeders out of business.

In 1991, while reports to stockholders indicated that meatpackers' profits were soaring, the Big Three (Monfort, Excel, and IBP) were cutting back production on select days in all the major cattle-producing states, complaining that cattle prices were inflated. Workers would have hours cut back one week and be subjected to speed-up the next. In effect, companies could afford to take temporary losses, if necessary, in order to bring about further control of meat production from farm to table, forcing suppliers to sell at lower prices.

A federal probe into pricing patterns was finally prompted in mid-1991 when the gap between wholesale prices for red meat and prices at the supermarket reached unprecedented levels for the sixth month in a row. The probe was conducted by the U.S. Department of Agriculture's Packers and Stockyards Administration, which had been established in 1921 to enforce federal legislation prohibiting price-fixing and other unfair and deceptive practices in the livestock industry. It initially focused on the manipulation of cattle-pricing reports by Monfort, Inc. The company did not report sales from its own feedlots and was allegedly under-reporting high prices paid for cattle elsewhere in order to project a deceptively low market price. This had the effect of driving prices down.

Government investigation was handicapped by weak enforcement provisions of federal legislation that allow cattle buyers to provide price information on a voluntary basis. In the late 1970s, the head of the Packers and Stockyards Administration suppressed the results of studies of price-fixing in the meat industry and was subsequently rewarded with an executive position with IBP.[6] In August 1991, Monfort attempted to foil investigations by withholding information altogether.[7] Federal investigators then shifted attention to the lag in retail price adjustments, retail prices began to come down, and public concern abated.

In the present context, it appears that companies have found ways to fix prices without risking criminal prosecution or government intervention of any kind. Asked to comment on a call for Justice Department intervention — initiated by two senators from Nebraska at the urging of cattle feeders' legal action groups throughout the country — Monfort's Gene Meakins said: "It's a free-enterprise system, and that's the way it works. . . . I don't know exactly what that means unless they're going to investigate the free-enterprise system."[8]

The philosophy that all is fair under free enterprise was the defense of the meat industry at the end of the nineteenth century when public outcry against price-fixing prevented the formalization of a "meat trust" and the establishment of a gigantic holding company by Morris, Armour, and Swift.[9] The companies instead created the National Packing Company, which enabled them to "retain their independence yet collude, and perhaps collude more effectively than in the days of the pools."[10] By the early twentieth century, the large packers seldom engaged in either outright conspiracy or price competition, practicing "price leadership" instead. "By this time, all knew each other's costs, and all understood that only mutual trouble would flow from 'rocking the boat.' "[11]

Monopoly in the meatpacking industry was averted by the development of "oligopoly," an arrangement that enabled the principle players to cooperate just enough to further their common interests — and avoid government intervention. In 1903 packers in the state of Illinois, which was the center of meatpacking activity at that time, were ordered not to

> combine with respect to bidding in the purchase of livestock, fixing the prices at which meats are to be sold, establishing and maintaining rules for credit, imposing uniform cartage charges, and monopolizing or attempting to monopolize trade by means of railroad rebates or discrimination, or to use "any other method or device, the purpose and effect of which is to restrain commerce."[12]

The force of the order was weakened, however, by an additional clause: "Nothing herein shall be construed to prohibit the said defendants . . . from curtailing the quantity of meats shipped to a given market where the purpose of such arrangement in good faith is to prevent the over-accumulation of meat as perishable articles in such markets."[13]

The court left the big meatpackers free, after all, to pursue their mutual interests — at the expense of workers, consumers, and smaller businesses — without the serious threat of government intervention. The National Packing Company was dissolved voluntarily, but meatpackers continued to practice "price leadership" and expanded their power by diversifying business activities.

The creation and collapse of meat cartels in the early part of this century paralleled forays into international markets. National legislation calling for meat inspection was brought about because the industry needed to create confidence in meat products to further foreign trade. Enforcement came only in the wake of protracted workers' struggles and exposés such as that of Upton Sinclair, who not only defended meatpackers' right to live with dignity but also described the dirt and disease that affected the quality of meat products prepared under unsafe conditions.[14] Similarly, in the 1990s, revelations about the declining quality of meat, and bans on the importation of U.S. beef by other countries (especially the European Common Market),[15] have caused a flurry of concern about certification. But in many instances government agencies are less powerful than corporations. Surveillance and enforcement can be undermined at every level of government, including the international level.

Unless countervailing power is developed by grassroots movements, agreements of any kind that are made between governments and corporations are likely to be ineffective in preventing abusive practices by business. The potential for developing such movements depends to a great extent on the kind of power available to those affected by business-government collusion.

Once corporate conglomerates gain effective control of land and water resources, individual farmers, ranchers, and feedlot owners are no longer essential actors in the process of production. Because of the crisis-oriented nature of their organizations, they have limited power to defend against price manipulation, speculative activity, and contract arrangements with corporations. Lawsuits are often initiated only when many farmers unite in a desperate struggle that is made visible to the public. Suits are typically dismissed on appeal after farmers have been demobilized and driven back into individual struggles for survival. Large farmers who have been able to profit from the situation then emerge as spokespersons for "rural America."

Meatpacking giants, whose own success has been built on the defense of free enterprise, demonstrate disdain for the "losers." They claim that big businesses are the true defenders of the nation's values. Financially successful businesses use the rhetoric of competition to destroy those who seek to balance profit seeking with concern for the survival and well-being of communities and societies. When ideological arguments fail, outright bribery and corruption are used to assure that their own interests prevail. Sometimes they get caught: IBP's president was eventually convicted in 1981 of bribing New York's mafia in order to gain access to New York City's beef market. But the company's ascendancy was already assured by then. Cargill's cozy relationship with President Richard Nixon allowed the company to reap enormous benefit from grain sales to the Soviet Union. Cargill was enabled to expand beef operations while other companies were hurt by inflationary trends that followed. Like ConAgra today, Cargill proclaimed abhorrence for government intervention and controls, yet it would have been "virtually impossible for the world's largest grain trader to operate without the continued support of many governmental institutions and organizations."[16] Ruthlessness and hypocrisy are endemic to business success. Yet, all of this is rationalized as the price we must pay in order to enjoy the benefits of an "efficient" economic system.

Ken Monfort's absorption with his own personal and ideological transformation (as expressed in his *Greeley Tribune* columns), brought about by the competitive process is instructive to us for what it says about the political economy of capitalism. What should concern us is not an appraisal of Ken Monfort's character but an assessment of the effect that business-government collusion has on society as a whole.

As testimony in this book reveals, and as numerous other studies have shown, the concentration of power in the hands of corporations, and collusion between government and business, are not necessarily efficient. They are not efficient, for instance, in assuring the quality of meat or in assuring that natural resources will continue to be available. Human and other resources can be damaged or used up, and investments can be transferred elsewhere. The public can be assaulted with information produced by corporate-influenced research and corporate-financed "public interest groups" intended to convince them that they don't have to be concerned about water depletion and contamination, soil depletion, and disease.[17] Contrary to what industry spokespersons say, exposés of corporate crime do not get instant publicity and generous financial backing. They are generally made public only at great risk to people who have nothing tangible to gain from antagonizing industry giants. Critics of big business can be silenced at will unless they are able to build coalitions that include large sectors of the public.

Even consumer boycotts, unless they are combined with support for workers' struggles, do not produce structural change. In the face of reduced demand, corporations can shift exploitive activity to other areas. (For example, reducing consumer demand for beef increases the production of dairy products, poultry, fish, vegetables, or grains, but it does not necessarily reduce the power of corporations in public life. In fact, as beef industry advocates correctly point out, a reduction in consumer demand tends to favor big corporations over small businesses.)

Eventually, the well-being of consumers, workers, and communities affected by the growth of industry becomes a point of contention in which power struggles over production processes take center stage. Because cost efficiency in the labor process is essential to maximize profit, corporations are, above all, determined to retain control of the production process, fighting government regulation and efforts by employees to gain some control of the workplace.

It is in the area of labor-management relations that the abusive power of corporations can be challenged most effectively. Wageworkers can be replaced as individuals, even more easily than farmers, but as a group they have more potential power to challenge the political hegemony of corporate giants than do ranchers, farmers, or feedlot operators. Attempts to cut back work forces by introducing labor-saving technologies provide only temporary advantages to companies, because other companies can duplicate technology. The development of new markets or new market niches also inevitably leads to increased competition from other companies. The volume of production must increase in order for corporations to stay ahead of the competition. Sooner or later, employers must expand their operations — and their work forces — in order to survive. This is why meat production is at the same time highly competitive and highly profitable. The margin of profit may be low, but high rewards are assured for those who can maintain volume of production in a labor-intensive, low-wage industry. Struggle over labor relations is therefore essential to accomplishing structural change in political economy.

Meatpackers have been among the most militant in their organizing efforts historically. Within a system where free enterprise is sacrosanct, workers' struggles to defend their rights have been considered "subversive." Meatpackers' so-called subversiveness — their unwillingness to forsake visions of a more humane society — has contributed strategically to the overall advancement of workers' rights in the United States. Whenever labor leaders have urged accommodation to companies, especially on issues of workplace control, the overall advancement of workers' interests has been threatened.

The first labor struggles in the meatpacking industry were won without achieving union recognition. They happened in the nineteenth century when railroads were locked in disputes with the meat industry over transportation rates. Residents of Chicago's Packingtown forced fertilizer companies to move out of the city because of the stench caused by rendering operations. In the midst of these struggles — and protests by ranchers, growers, and retailers about the price of cattle and the quality and cost of chilled beef — meatpackers waged their battles. Employees who filed suit against companies for injuries sustained at work often won their cases, but there was no guarantee that companies would pay. Packinghouse workers rioted as the depression of the 1870s ended and the cost of living rose.

Women were hired in meat canneries and some were hired to do "light" trimming in slaughterhouses. More than half the workers were foreign-born. Ethnic organizations in Chicago carried arms to labor meetings to protect themselves from company repression. Finally, workers went on strike and were able to win wage increases by keeping scabs or would-be strikebreakers from taking over their jobs. In the 1880s packinghouse workers were among the first to win 8-hour workdays, but this gain had to be constantly defended. Some two hundred thousand workers were involved in strikes and demonstrations demanding legislation to enforce 8-hour agreements.

On May 1, 1886, when workers declared a national strike to support demands for the 8-hour workday, union leaders in Chicago were framed by undercover agents and were hanged. They were executed not for any crime they had committed but because they were accused of harboring "dangerous utopian visions" that threatened the capitalist system. These events, subsequently known as the Haymarket Affair, helped to bring about worldwide solidarity in workers' struggles.[18]

In September 1886 meatpackers were prominent in organizing a United Labor Party, which called for a ban on private detective agencies, enforcement of 8-hour provisions in workplaces, government ownership of all means of transportation and communication, state inspection of factories and penal and charitable institutions, compulsory school attendance, and an employers' liability law. Industry owners fought back by waging an aggressive campaign against Anarchists and Communists. Chicago police threatened that "every lamp-post in Chicago will be decorated with a communistic carcass if necessary" to prevent workers from organizing. The Knights of Labor, which had been most involved in workers' struggles for the 8-hour workday, retreated from conflict, distancing itself from the "headstrong packinghouse workers." Subsequent struggles were weakened by the betrayal of union leaders and by ethnic conflict between Irish workers and more recent immigrants.[19]

Chicago meatpackers went on strike in 1917 to challenge a wage differential between workers of European descent and black workers from the South, who had been hired to undercut wage structures. Inspired by the Russian Revolution, meatpackers organized a Stockyards Labor Council (SLC), which included some twenty thousand African American workers among a membership of thirty-five to forty thousand. Tens of thousands of stockyard workers massed in a public parade to demand the withdrawal of government troops from black communities following race riots that broke out in 1919.

The SLC was chartered by the Chicago Federation of Labor and was the first industry-wide workers' organization to challenge company power in a "mass-production, trustified industry."[20] The organization did not survive the 1920s, largely because of recurring antagonism between black and white workers.[21] Progressive leadership was decimated when thousands of foreign-born workers were deported or jailed as communists or subversives. However, many SLC members were among those who separated from the American Federation of Labor (AFL) to form the Congress of Industrial Organizations (CIO) in the 1930s. Packinghouse workers in Minnesota, North and South Dakota, and Iowa, influenced by the "Wobbly" movement (Industrial Workers of the World) — which had been conducting organizing drives among farmworkers, miners, and lumberjacks throughout the Midwest — also joined the CIO, which set up a Packinghouse Workers Organizing Committee in the fall of 1937. Former Wobblies insisted that the development of class consciousness was more important than "winning a few more pennies an hour."[22]

The CIO was beset by conflict between radical and conservative unionists from the outset. When Austin, Minnesota, meatpackers engaged in a sit-down strike, their leaders were forced out of the Packinghouse Workers Organizing Committee. Members in several states withheld dues in protest. Meatpackers waged battles within the CIO until they were granted the first international union charter in 1943.

Many unionists in the United States signed no-strike pledges when World War II began, but immediately after the war ended one hundred and twenty-five thousand members of the CIO's United Packinghouse Workers and ninety thousand of the AFL's Amalgamated Meat Cutters and Butcher Workmen of North America went on strike against Armour, Swift, Wilson, Cudahy, and Morrell. The two unions agreed not to return to work until both had settled. Their action was followed by a wave of strikes by an estimated five million workers in the United States, which also gave impetus and support to struggles for political freedom in the former colonies of governments that had been engaged in the war.

As post–World War II inflation threatened to undermine the economic gains that workers had made in labor struggles of the 1930s, unions began to demand cost-of-living adjustments (COLAs) in wage agreements. The United Packinghouse Workers demanded a cost-of-living bonus to be paid weekly or monthly. In the midst of an "orgy of price-gouging by companies," Chicago and Milwaukee meatpacking workers passed resolutions in 1946 demanding that the government take over and nationalize the entire meat industry. The government did introduce price controls on meat, but as the New York Stock Exchange went into a steep decline, President Harry S. Truman lifted price controls, and the market rebounded.[23]

As the Cold War began to dominate U.S. foreign policy, unions were subjected to a new wave of anti-Communist witch-hunting. The civil liberties of foreigners and Communists were undermined by law. Radical labor leaders were expelled from the CIO, and many workers were fired for political reasons. Union halls were invaded by police. Although profits from meatpacking doubled between 1947 and 1948, workers' wage demands were undercut by a government "fact-finding board." Passage of the Taft-Hartley Act in 1947 limited labor's power to act as a countervailing force to capital. The act limited by law the boundaries of labor disputes to encompass only an immediate employer and employee, thus hurting workers in geographically isolated circumstances more than those whose power was already well established.[24]

In 1955 the CIO's United Packinghouse Workers Boston local was decertified after a long and bitter strike. By 1956 preparations were being completed for a merger between the AFL and the CIO, and in 1968 the United Packinghouse Workers were absorbed by the AFL's Amalgamated Meat Cutters and Butcher Workmen.

The top six meatpacking companies in the United States had become diversified companies, or conglomerates, by the early 1970s. Some had been bought out.[25] Several had divested themselves of distribution companies as the new boxed beef technology was developing. Emerging meatpackers such as Monfort and IBP were able to begin the process of undermining pattern agreements that had been established at Swift & Company, Armour and Company, Wilson Foods, John Morrell, Cudahy Company, and Hy Grade Foods. Hormel, which had not been bought out, began entering into marketing agreements in South Africa.

The newly merged AFL–CIO was slow to respond to these changes, and to the Teamsters union's willingness to make sweetheart deals with companies. Industrial unionism among meatpackers was weakened further when the meatpackers' union merged with the larger and more bureaucratically structured Retail Clerks International in 1979 to form the United Food and Commercial Workers Union (UFCW) (see Chapter 3). Nevertheless, beef slaughterhouse workers rallied in the mid-1980s, waging militant strikes against a Cudahy plant in Wisconsin, an IBP plant in Dakota City, Nebraska, and a John Morrell plant in Sioux City, Iowa. Because contracts in these plants expire at different times, the battles waged against concessions did not lead to a defense of meatpackers throughout the industry. Union locals were left to negotiate without the assurance that they would be backed up by solidarity from other workers whose contracts were also due to be renegotiated. Union organizers in Greeley were cautioned not to wage an attack on ConAgra that might jeopardize negotiations being conducted with ConAgra subsidiaries elsewhere. All were vulnerable to new recessionary trends in the economy and in the meat industry.

In the 1980s both unions and management increasingly courted the power of the government to bolster their own side in disputes, a practice encouraged by developments in labor law.

Conservative labor leaders were especially prone to rely on legal maneuvers rather than on rank-and-file militancy.

Rank-and-file unionists have made sporadic attempts to challenge conservative leaders' hegemony within unions. The P-9 UFCW local in Austin, Minnesota, which was expelled from the UFCW in 1986 for refusing to end a strike and grant concessions to Hormel, attempted to recertify itself under a new name, the North American Meatpackers Union (NAMPU); organizers attempted to recruit other militant locals in the UFCW to their new union.[26] Subject to charges of dual unionism, NAMPU was short-lived as an organization, but its leadership continued to wage battles within the UFCW to foster democratic decision-making processes, to encourage unionization of unorganized plants, and to reach out through networking to workers in plants where the Teamsters union had contracts.

The question of the need for new workers' organizations continues to surface among those who are committed to greater democracy and a return to the concept of unionism as a social movement rather than a bureaucratic establishment with a self-serving leadership. But controversy and debate within unions has found a new focus that also has historical precedents — the need to rethink union positions with regard to U.S. foreign policy.

The U.S. labor movement has always been divided between those who support U.S. business expansion abroad (represented in early years by the AFL) and those who promote the international organization of workers to oppose the penetration of U.S. capital in foreign countries. "Business unionism" holds that U.S. workers benefit from corporate expansion, which is said to enable workers to demand higher wages from successful companies. There was some truth to this argument, especially during the early post–World War II period, during which U.S. corporations sought new markets overseas through expanded trade relations and through the establishment of factories in foreign countries for producing commodities that could be sold in those same countries. Increasingly, however, as U.S. corporations seek new sources of raw material and cheap labor abroad, factories in the United States are closed down and relocated elsewhere. Commodities produced abroad are then transported back to the United States. Production costs are lower outside the United States, and transportation costs to U.S. markets can easily be covered by the difference. Under these conditions, workers in both countries have an obvious stake — not only morally, but also in terms of immediate practical interests — in supporting each other during labor disputes rather than in support-ing the uncontrolled expansion of corporations. Instead of allowing employers to play workers off against each other, employees have much to gain from developing a strategy to defend their common interests.

In the long run, workers have always had more to gain from defending their class interests as workers than from supporting the interests of their employers. But compromises have been made in the interest of immediate survival. In the wake of the economic crisis that followed post–World War II expansionism, the AFL and the CIO reached agreements to accommodate the interests of business in exchange for union recognition and economic conces-sions.[27] U.S. foreign policy was increasingly oriented toward pre-venting labor movements in other countries from challenging U.S. business expansion abroad.

In the 1960s, the AFL–CIO began cooperating with the U.S. government in supporting the establishment of covert operations abroad to undermine democratic unions and to set up business unions, often with the aim of overthrowing governments that were not allied with the United States in the Cold War. Funding and control of "labor organizations" that served as fronts for U.S. busi-ness expansion came mostly from U.S. corporations and from the U.S. government.[28] Elected governments were sometimes over-thrown with the cooperation of the "free trade unions" established by the U.S. government at the urging of U.S. corporations. Every time extraordinary repression against grassroots labor movements occurred overseas, opposition surfaced within the AFL–CIO against its support for business unionism and for U.S. political intervention abroad.[29]

By the early 1980s the U.S. government was undermining implicit accords that had been established earlier between labor organizations and corporations in the United States by intervening directly in labor-management conflict, effectively undermining workers' right to strike.[30] At the same time, the U.S. government, under the Reagan administration, was escalating military aid to the El Salvador government in Central America. The El Salvador government not only repressed grassroots peasant and labor union movements, but it also condoned the murder of U.S. government agents who had been sent to El Salvador as labor organizers.

A group of labor union officials in the United States met in 1981 to form a National Labor Committee in Support of Democracy in El Salvador. At 1983 and 1985 AFL–CIO conventions, dissenting forces were able to challenge, in small ways, the authority of labor's "old guard" leadership. AFL–CIO monetary support for CIA–controlled international operations was cut, but the promotion of support for U.S. foreign policy among unionists was taken up by organizations such as the National Endowment for Democracy and Social Democrats–USA. These groups were heavily funded but had no solid base among workers. The identification of these groups with "social democracy" belied the fact that they were guided solely by the needs of transnational corporations.

In spite of overwhelming evidence that the exportation of U.S. capital is increasingly harmful to U.S. workers as well as to foreign workers,[31] the AFL–CIO still officially supports corporate interests over international worker solidarity. Protection for U.S. workers is sought primarily by discouraging imports, promoting nationalism, and opposing "free production zones" outside the United States.[32] Little is done to educate workers about the realities of "global sourcing" for labor, natural resources, and weak governmental regulation.

Although top officials of union federations in the United States are allied with business interests, union members, many union locals, and an increasing number of union officials support international labor solidarity as the appropriate response to the globalization of a capitalist economy. Sugar workers, auto workers, communications workers, textile workers, soft drink bottlers, and other victims of border hopping by transnational companies have been organizing internationally for more than a decade. Because of international boycott campaigns and the refusal of workers to go along with the diversion of production during strikes, decisive victories have been won in some local struggles. In the United States and in other countries, alliances are also being made among factory workers, environmentalists, progressive farmers, incipient student movements, and ecumenical church groups.[33]

For many reasons, these movements and alliances are still weak, but the direction toward unity is clear. The current situation in the meatpacking industry could provide a focal point for united action across a broad spectrum of social forces, if meatpackers themselves lead the way. The prospects for this depend, to a great extent, on the vision and commitment of those who live and work in meatpacking communities.

The UFCW has been attempting to organize undocumented workers in red meat plants such as those owned by Monfort, Excel, and IBP. However, the AFL–CIO (to which the UFCW belongs) initially supported the 1986 Immigration Reform and Control Act, which provides sanctions against the hiring of undocumented workers in the United States. Obviously, many immigrants may feel that the union is not their best defense against company abuse. The AFL–CIO did oppose the "fast-tracking" through Congress of a free trade initiative sought by the Bush administration to further open up opportunities for U.S. corporate expansion in Mexico, but it did little to inform workers of the dangers of this initiative. The Mexican government led workers to believe that the agreement would relieve repression against them at the border. Although it is widely assumed that the initiative will accelerate plant closings in the United States, workers in the United States have not mobilized effectively to oppose the initiative.

Already, Mexico's northern state of Chihuahua is being "sourced" as a site for meatpacking operations by U.S.-based companies. Cargill has reportedly purchased a beef and chicken plant in Saltillo, in anticipation of a free trade accord. Both Tyson and ConAgra are reportedly building new plants or buying existing plants in Mexico.[34] The Mexican government's threat to place protective tariffs on imported meat will most likely encourage this trend.

Workers who have suffered the effects of company border hopping from one state to another, which forces wages down by playing off local and state governments against each other, must now face the consequences of border hopping from country to country. Unions lobby against plant relocations but are slow to mobilize workers in actions of solidarity across state and national borders. Efforts to organize the half-million workers employed by U.S. companies in Mexico as part of the Border Industrialization Program (a model for the Free Trade Initiative currently under negotiation) are hampered by the fact that these workers can leave their $5 per day jobs in Mexico for work in the United States. As more U.S. factories move south, repression at the border is not likely to abate, and the need for worker solidarity will become even more apparent.[35]

On both sides of the border, industrial workers are drawn largely from the ranks of farmworkers. While the meatpacking giants assess opportunities for the super-exploitation of workers in Mexico, agribusiness in general has already taken over much of northern Mexico for the production of winter vegetables and other food products for the U.S. market. Farmworkers' struggles on both sides of the border have been hampered by an absence of coordinated activity to defend workers' rights.

The United Farm Workers of America (UFWA), under the leadership of Cesar Chavez, made its greatest gains when the organization championed the cause of farmworkers regardless of their legal status while working in the United States. During the height of the farmworkers' movement in the late 1960s and early 1970s, leaders also shared a revolutionary vision. Socialism, or grassroots democracy — a society governed by working people, not by profit-making corporations, was the driving force of the farmworkers' movement. This vision enabled union members to overcome ethnic barriers and to reach out to large segments of the U.S. population that had never before shown concern for the plight of farmworkers.

The farmworkers' union was weakened ideologically when the AFL–CIO embraced its cause. Although farmworkers in California made some concrete gains from "mainstreaming" their struggle, the overall farmworkers' cause suffered when radical organizers were purged.

Today, organized farmworkers cannot rely upon the union's support if they are undocumented. In fact, the union has campaigned for the exclusion of immigrant labor. Most farmworkers are not being actively recruited by the UFWA, which has limited its organizing efforts, for the most part, to southern and central California. The union conducts boycotts against grape growers in an effort to restrict the use of harmful pesticides, but workers are inhibited from striking.[36]

In Colorado, labor on industrialized farms is done mostly by seasonal migrant workers, most of whom are Spanish-speaking and all of whom are unorganized. Small farmers who have been driven out of business sometimes work alongside former migrant workers in meatpacking or other food-processing industries. Union organizers say that former farm owners are slow to promote union organization. Some are vulnerable to racist manipulation by employers. This holds back workers' struggles. As the recession deepens, however, workers laid off from urban industries, young people escaping urban ghettos, and aspiring college students are being attracted to work in small-town meatpacking plants. Their presence may help workers break out of their isolation and has the potential to give new impetus to organizing efforts.

The growing power of corporations and the growing impoverishment of workers and small entrepreneurs in our society as a whole can contribute to building unity within popular organizations. Meatpackers can play a central role in pushing union and community organizations to take a more militant stance against corporate greed. In order to succeed, they will have to regain some of the vision lost through decades of compromise and concessions.

Whether established union organizations can meet this challenge will depend in part on their willingness to encourage and accept grassroots leadership. Progressive community organizations, such as *Al Frente de Lucha* in Greeley, can also play a positive role by allying themselves with workers and by supporting workers' demands for democracy and accountability within unions. Workers will have to fight hard against the denigration of women and recent immigrants. In small towns, cultural contact can be facilitated more readily than in large cities. The parochial attitudes of educators, retail merchants, and church members can be challenged by the special efforts of groups that have links with organizations outside local boundaries, in order to build larger communities of interest.

Historically, women have often been more effective than men in overcoming prejudices and promoting grassroots leadership. Although they are slower to mobilize, they are steadfast once they make a commitment to struggle. They are less likely to be driven by personal career goals and more likely to be community oriented. The 1987–1988 Portion Foods strike in Greeley demonstrated the capabilities of women whose potential for leadership is often underestimated by both union and company officials.

Few of the obstacles that workers face are new. In the past, people in the most degrading and desperate circumstances have eventually overcome their fears and have demonstrated a willingness to make personal sacrifices — including risking their own lives — for the common good. They were able to do this most effectively when guided by a determination to challenge the political subordination of workers as a basis for societal organization.

The vision of a society that holds workers' welfare to be more important than the personal profit of entrepreneurs is as old as the factory system itself. It is not out-dated, however. What is out-dated is a so-called free enterprise system where corporate greed far outweighs any sense of social responsibility. The American Dream espoused by corporate officials and their political allies — the naked pursuit of profit — is what needs to be exposed and repudiated.

Almost 150 years ago, when Karl Marx declared that socialism was the natural solution to the problems of capitalism, he was not espousing an abstract idea. He said that the majority of the population — the workers — would have to dictate the rules and regulations of society. This is the famous "dictatorship of the proletariat," in which personal profit and the accumulation of capital in private hands is no longer the goal of production. In this popular democracy (as opposed to bourgeois democracy) the real needs of people could be served. Marx theorized that socialism would pave the way for a less contentious stage of societal development — communism — in which social classes, and the state itself, would "wither away." The common yearnings of human beings, espoused from time immemorial, could then be realized: "From each according to ability, to each according to need."[37]

Rather than fearing the vision of a just and democratic society, which is the only basis upon which a stable economic order can be built, we should be striving to better understand the conditions under which such a vision can be realized. The urgency of finding a solution to the problems of capitalism has never been greater (whether capitalism is based on private ownership, as in the United

States, or on state capitalism, as developed elsewhere). The eroding of workers' rights and the aggressive campaign being waged to mobilize the entire planet to march to the tune of transnational corporations has created an economic crisis of unprecedented magnitude.

For more than a century, capitalist elites have mobilized all of their resources to prevent the ideals of socialism and communism from taking root. The internationalization of capital has undermined every possibility for the real empowerment of workers wherever the ideals themselves have prevailed. Capitalists are now gloating over the "demise of communism," robbing workers of a vision that has grounded them and helped to sustain them when their struggles for democracy, peace, and prosperity were met with repression and hostility.

Decades ago, when one-third of the workers in the United States were organized in unions, the alienation of workers could be disputed, as could the prediction that capitalism would inevitably lead to increasing misery and poverty among workers and increasing power and wealth for capitalists. In the post–World War II period, politicized workers were able to set an example for others, questioning the premise that workers were destined to lead lives of quiet desperation. For a short period of time, workers dictated, to a certain extent, the terms of their employment.

Capitalists, however, driven by market forces, were able to regain the upper hand by extending their economic and political domain outside the United States and by entrenching domestic control through racism, sexism, and nationalism. Any obstacle in their path was considered subversive of "American values." By 1990 only about 12 percent of U.S. private sector workers were unionized,[38] and unionized workers' power was weakened by bureaucratic leadership. Gains that had been made through decades of struggle in combatting sexism and racism were under attack. Profiteering at the expense of workers, consumers, and the natural environment grew, while challenges to business's right to rule were labeled "un-American."

The "American Way," as defined by the present-day barons of capitalism, is to provide certain limited opportunities for individual advancement while denying the basic human needs of the majority of employees. Employers rationalize exploitive practices by permitting or encouraging the advancement of a few "qualified" members of a minority population. Such actions obscure the reality that the "un-qualifiedness" of the pool of workers from which they are recruiting — in the current situation, their vulnerability as illegals, their language handicap, their desperate economic situation (especially that of single mothers) — is in fact a super-qualification on which rests the entire edifice of competitive production. This assures an "enthusiastic" workforce, willing — at least for a time — to tolerate horrendous conditions.[39]

In many ways, Greeley, Colorado, is a microcosm of what is happening everywhere. When I asked Jim Kadlecek, the outgoing director of Greeley's Economic Development Action Project, what he thought would be necessary to turn things around in Greeley, he said that a strong leader would have to emerge among the poor. I think that many workers are waiting for just such a leader and that they are likely to be disappointed. Workers will have to lose their fear of powerful elites and develop collective leadership among themselves. Women will have to assume prerogatives that challenge male dominance in workplace organizing.[40] No "strongman" can save us in the long run. In this respect, the followers of Marx have certainly erred, deifying leaders who give focus to their aspirations, giving rise to bureaucratic structures that encourage the emergence of new forms of capitalism and imperialism.

There is no single way that grassroots democracy can be advanced. Spontaneous demonstrations of workers' power are no doubt necessary as a catalyst to organization, and workers do need organizations to represent their particular interests, but in some cases broad community support for marginalized citizens may have to be developed before effective unionization can occur. In Colorado, churches and other community groups are taking a stand on the side of workers and their families. Work-injured citizens groups realize that they must reach out beyond the big cities. In communities of the south, anti-racist coalitions and women's organizations have been spurred to action on behalf of injured and displaced poultry workers.

Although workers need unions to represent their interests, unions should not be relying on donations to electoral candidates as a way to further their objectives. Rather, unions should oppose the whole idea of political patronage as a form of government. It is also clear that workers cannot rely on lawsuits, or laws, to protect their rights. They must struggle to make the legal system responsive to democratic control.

The lessons of history are as much the lessons of failure and defeat as they are of victory in waging war against oppressive elites. In Mexico, hundreds of thousands died in order to assure that the land and its resources would be returned to the people. Yet, much of the land and resources have been lost to them again. Many of the grandchildren of the Mexican Revolution are held hostage in factories, fields, or wherever they can find work. Agribusiness expansion has deprived them of land and livelihood.

In the United States, farmers and workers organized cooperatives in the 1930s and 1940s and passed laws restricting corporate control of rural areas. Many believed that the cooperative movement would bring about socialism without bloodshed. They have been sorely disappointed. The cooperatives they organized, which included meatpacking operations such as Farmland Industries and Land-O'-Lakes, functioned within capitalist market structures. They became ruthless competitors themselves or were bought out by others in the 1980s.

The fundamental problems engendered by capitalism, and possible solutions to them, have been debated and struggled over for more than a century. Despite the euphoric response by capitalists to the demise of the U.S.S.R. and other postrevolutionary governments, the problems of capitalism have not been resolved and the struggle is not over.

Instead of accepting as eternal the "triumph of free enterprise" and the "failure of communism," we must ask ourselves, What can be done to revive the struggle for human dignity? What can be done to build solidarity across national and state borders? How can workers reclaim control over their lives and belief in the possibility of a just and peaceful world?

Capitalism's triumph is a catastrophic event. Nevertheless, because the globalization of a capitalist economy has brought us closer together, there is some hope in the current crisis. Workers and their allies are faced with a new challenge to unite in a larger-than-ever struggle for life and liberty. This will require a sober assessment of the past and a serious and sustained commitment to the future. Some who are engaged in this struggle believe that we will have no future at all unless we are able to regain common control over productive processes, respect for individual dignity and worth, and democracy for all.

Epilogue

The Center for the Study of Responsible Law in Washington, D.C., published a report in 1983 titled *Return to the Jungle: How the Reagan Administration is Imperiling the Nation's Meat and Poultry Inspection Program.*[1] Production speed in meat-processing plants, which is officially regulated by the need to assure quality control of meat products (not to assure worker safety), was at an all-time high. Accidents and injuries in meatpacking were soaring, while the American Meat Institute was lobbying to loosen enforcement standards and sanctions and to place a curtain of secrecy over damaging inspection reports. Occupational Health and Safety Administration (OSHA) inspectors had been cut back, and companies were exerting pressure on the Department of Agriculture to allow businesses to police themselves. Workers were reportedly taking stimulants to avoid "line-hypnosis" due to speed-up. Yet, government officials were under intense pressure to remove all barriers to the industry "restructuring" that was the cause of such problems.

Five years later, when the Streamlined Inspection System (SIS) was introduced as a U.S. government–funded pilot program, Iowa Beef Processors (IBP), the nation's largest producer of boxed beef, declined to participate. The company had already been cited by OSHA for massive health and safety violations and was unwilling to risk further attention. Monfort, Inc., was among the favored candidates for participation in the SIS.

When Monfort was charged with 197 egregious and willful violations of health and safety regulations in April 1991, the SIS program had been in place for four years.[2] Litigation that had begun in May 1991 to determine the status of OSHA's proposed $1.1 million fine against the company, was still in the "discovery stage" over a year later. The company was using procedural grounds to dispute the fine. In a now-familiar pattern, Monfort hired someone who was particularly well placed to maneuver within the government regulatory system. The company's lawyer was Robert Moran, former head of OSHA's review commission. In an eleventh-hour

move by the Bush administration, Monfort Vice President Kay
Norton was appointed to an OSHA national advisory committee.[3]

As OSHA litigation continued, "streamlined" production continued as well. In the summer of 1992, the SIS program had begun
to founder in the midst of scandals over unhealthy meat. Ken
Monfort, who had retired as president of ConAgra Red Meat Cos. in
1989, came to the company's defense, implying that the SIS had
been of no particular benefit to the company financially: "We
listened to their proposal and agreed to the test — although we
knew it would cost us some extra money." He failed to mention that
production had increased dramatically in plants where the govern-
ment-funded, self-monitoring program had been instituted.[4]

According to Edward Murphy, safety director for Monfort's
Grand Island plant from August 1986 to April 1991, any "extra
money" paid out by the company as a result of the SIS could only
have been that incurred from workers compensation costs for
injuries and illnesses due to line speed-up. In testimony given
before the House Education and Labor Subcommittee on Labor
Management Relations, August 5, 1992, Murphy said that plant
officials "made it falsely appear that more resources were dedicated
to food safety in order to comply with the requirements of the
inspection program." When officials from Washington came to
review the SIS cattle inspection program, he said, supervisors were
ordered to slow down the lines and call in additional staff. In
shocking testimony, Murphy revealed various mechanisms by
which the company had made it impossible for safety engineers to
carry out their mandate. For example, supervisors were under
severe pressure to keep the line moving at break-neck speed no
matter what the cost to workers or consumers, and health and
safety records were habitually falsified or destroyed. (*Rocky Mountain News*, August 6, 1992. Murphy's testimony appears in Appendix
A of this book. The company declined to comment to reporters on
this testimony except to make a general denial of the allegations.
It may be that Murphy's dismissal was prompted by the need to
find a scapegoat for charges brought by the OSHA commission.
However, Murphy says that he was fired because he cooperated
with OSHA and that he had had some success in reducing injuries
at the plant before he was fired. The company's Fiscal 1990 Annual
Report mentions money spent at the Nebraska beef plant to "im-

prove working conditions by making jobs less stressful and less repetitive." Murphy's testimony must be taken seriously because it complements that of line workers to a remarkable degree.)

A government veterinarian involved in designing the SIS said to one investigator that Monfort's Greeley plant has "the fastest kill floor in the world," but insisted that "chances of diseases are not that great" and that "if the line is too fast, time-study people come in and identify just what a person can do"[5] (referring, evidently, to the pace-setting devices described by workers elsewhere in this book). Workers told reporters that the head Department of Agriculture (USDA) inspector at the Greeley plant constantly tells employees that stopping the line to check carcasses or heads "costs the company four hundred dollars a minute."[6]

Monfort's public defense against opponents of the SIS was to accuse whistleblowers of having personal axes to grind. Richard Monfort, president of the company since 1989, also called attention to "pioneering research" being carried out in Greeley to detect the bacterial content in meat.[7] He did not mention that consumer advocates have been demanding for decades that meat inspection include bacteria counts. Far from being pioneers in promoting attention to this issue, Monfort was anticipating the day when industry influence in the USDA would no longer be sufficient to ward off consumer demand for such protection. The Colorado Beef Council also put Monfort's vice president for marketing in charge of "myth busting." He was provided with "a lot of information and a lot of scientific data that we can present the public through the media to respond to all the myths as they come along."[8]

An outbreak of new "myths" was soon to follow. In January/February 1993, several hundred people became seriously ill and two children died after consuming hamburgers at a Jack-in-the-Box restaurant in Seattle, Washington. Beef used at the restaurant reportedly originated in Michigan, Colorado, and California. The source of contamination was thought to be animal feces, through which the bacteria E. coli was spread.[9]

Richard Monfort asserted that ConAgra "runs thousands of tests a week trying to detect bacteria. That's why we have the cleanest meat in the industry." The company also said that it applies "light acetic acid carcass washes" to fresh meat.[10] As pressure built up for the government to establish new rules for meat inspection, other industry spokespersons and their allies, such as Elizabeth M. Whelan, president of the American Council on Science and Health, argued that regulation was not the answer:

> There is no way under our current system that we are going to eliminate bacteria, even potentially life-threatening kinds, from our meat supply. . . . The primary responsibility for avoiding food-borne illness lies with the consumer and the commercial food preparer, not the government. . . . Our technophobic society must take part of the blame for the continued threat posed by natural food pathogens, because we have not yet embraced the most cost-effective way of keeping our meat supply free of all pathogens, including E. coli: irradiation of fresh meat and poultry products.[11]

Other industry proposals included using chemicals to remove the hair on cattle. Monfort reportedly plans to apply the chemicals in booths to avoid causing loss of workers' hair.

Speed of production lines in slaughterhouses was not even discussed in media accounts of the problem. When Congress finally voted to cut off funds for the SIS, a *Greeley Tribune* editor commented: "Both consumers and the meat industry will benefit if the USDA can devise a means of reinstating the SIS program and defending it from its opponents."[13] A USDA official said: "I haven't read the language of the bill, but probably it will mean juggling of resources and maybe some people." He declared that the whole program was likely to be renamed, with many of the same functions retained under a newly titled meat inspection system.[14]

Among those who voted against the bill that required phasing out the SIS as of October 1, 1992, were Colorado's Senator Hank Brown and Representative Wayne Allard, both unwavering allies of Monfort, Inc. Another ardent defender of the SIS was the Bush administration's assistant secretary of agriculture, Jo Ann Smith. Smith is a cattle rancher herself and is also past president of the National Cattlemen's Association and former chair of the Cattlemen's Beef Promotion and Research Board. The conflict of interest between her role as a promoter of beef and her role as regulator of the beef industry was not, apparently, a major issue in debate over the program.

Speed-up in the production of meat has obviously engendered multiple problems for workers and consumers. Congress's withdrawal of funding for the SIS does provide evidence of public concern for the regulation of food production to protect consumers. Corporate response, besides increased emphasis on marketing (paid for by higher prices to consumers), is to compensate for consumer health problems caused by high-speed production of meat by shifting the blame to consumers and food handlers and by inventing new methods of "sterilizing" meat. Consumers certainly cannot be assured that appropriate solutions will be found, however, so long as congressional watchdog committees and the USDA itself are staffed with beef industry magnates and their friends.

Problems for workers are even less amenable to simple solutions. After conducting hearings on the under-reporting of injuries to meatpackers in 1988, the Committee on Government operations concluded: "Meatpacking plants today have machines that can grind 1000 pounds of meat per minute. But far too little has been done to improve the safety and working conditions in this industry which continues to grind up its workers like the product it produces."[15] Meatpacking workers are no better off today than they were when that statement was made. Nevertheless, there has been a resurgence of activism among those who are suffering from work-related illnesses and injuries. The relatives of those killed at Monfort's Grand Island plant organized a petition drive in order to bring pressure to bear on OSHA and to force an investigation at the plant.[16] Work-injured citizens, organizing either independently or in conjunction with unions, are winning small victories in state legislatures in Louisiana, Georgia, and New Mexico.[17]

It is possible that such groups will become a major political force throughout the nation in the 1990s. In Colorado, the Work Injured Citizens' Coalition (WICC) has not yet effectively reached many of those in need of representation — such as Spanish-speaking workers and ex-workers at Monfort, Inc. However, WICC, together with another organization called Safe Workplace Colorado![18] has worked with unions to oppose new legislation sought by industry. The legislation seeks to repeal a state law prohibiting employers from charging employees for any part of workers' compensation insurance. Greeley attorney Richard Blundell says of the repeal effort: "Not even antebellum slaves had to pay their masters for the 'privilege' of working for slave wages under unsafe and debilitating conditions."[19]

Senator Tom Norton is one of the authors of the bill that is opposed by workers. He says that if employees could be required to pay the company for their own insurance, they "would help create safer workplaces."[20] Norton is now president of the Colorado Senate and has been named "legislator of the year" by the Economic Developers' Council of Colorado. He has declared an interest in running for governorship of the state.[21] An aide to U.S. Representative Wayne Allard wrote in praise of Norton's efforts to prevent a workers' compensation amendment "that would have had disastrous consequences for Colorado businesses and economic development in the state had it become law."[22] He pointed out that every member of the Weld County delegation to the state legislature is either a committee chairman, a member of the Joint Budget Committee or in an elected leadership position in either the House or Senate. "Do I hear the cries of 'break up the Weld County delegation' in the halls of the Capitol? Not yet, but if the next Speaker of the House comes from Weld County, look out."[23]

Government economists said at the end of 1992 that there had been a "spurt in the growth of worker productivity over the last eighteen months" without adding jobs or work hours and without improved technology. Growth in worker productivity was attributed to "correcting sloppy management" and was hailed as a sign that economic recovery was underway.[24] Such a "recovery" holds little promise for those who toil daily in the nation's industrial plants, certainly not for those in the food-processing industry or in other jobs characterized by repetitive motion.

The inability to find a solution to health and safety problems in meat production is directly related to the search for captive labor. In spite of recession, there is an absolute increase in the demand for labor in Greeley and in other places where work conditions have become more dangerous and difficult. High turnover, and the decline of the white male labor force, stimulate recruitment of immigrant and female workers, but turnover remains high and labor shortages continue.[25]

The availability of foreign workers during a period of economic recession is generally viewed by displaced workers and farmers as an "invasion" of foreign and minority workers rather than as a crisis created in part by the penetration of big business in subsistence economies internationally. Peasants and wage-workers have little choice but to become part of a floating labor force. As we have seen, U.S. government policy both facilitates and sanctions migration from farms to cities and the flow of workers across boundaries.

Debates on the North American Free Trade Agreement (NAFTA) — an agreement that Senator Hank Brown says is the "best thing for the United States since the Louisiana Purchase"[26] — focus in part on NAFTA's probable impact on Mexican labor. A study conducted by the International Trade Commission predicts that such an agreement will create more landless laborers and will accelerate out-migration from Mexico.[27]

Even without NAFTA, sanctions imposed on companies and workers have done nothing to stem the tide.[28] The Mexican government is under pressure from its citizens to push for a more open border.[29] The U.S. government is under pressure to improve enforcement of restrictions on immigrant labor; at the same time, it is under pressure to help companies lower production costs so as to be competitive in the global marketplace. Implementation of a free trade initiative will make these contradictions more apparent than ever. By mid-February 1993, ConAgra had already joined other major meatpackers who were buying or building plants in Mexico.[30]

On September 24, 1992, Monfort, Inc.'s Grand Island plant was the scene of what one official characterized as the largest Immigration and Naturalization Service (INS) raid in several decades. Two hundred armed agents from all over the United States shut down the plant at 6:30 p.m. With a helicopter hovering overhead, and with eighty vehicles waiting outside, the entire work force was subjected to a lengthy process of identification, matching documents presented with names that the agency had gathered in a pre-raid investigation. At least 307 suspected illegals, most of them Hispanic, were arrested. Most agreed to voluntary deportation and were taken to a nearby National Guard Armory to await further processing. Twenty-two asked for deportation hearings.

The Nebraska Mexican-American Commission criticized the way the raid was carried out. The commission said that workers had been threatened, shoved, and shouted at; cars had been illegally searched; and native-born citizens had been required to produce documents proving citizenship. Workers could only take with them what could be carried in a shoebox. Many were unable to contact family members before deportation.

The Grand Island raid took place only a few days before workers were to have received annual bonuses. Although company spokespersons expressed willingness to pay those affected, no mechanisms for doing so were indicated. In addition to the night shift workers deported by the INS, UFCW union organizers estimated that at least 160 day shift workers were fired the next day. Hundreds more reportedly failed to show up for work.

As a result of the raid at Grand Island, many Greeley workers left their jobs, hoping to avoid arrest or deportation. Line workers said that about one-third of their fellow production workers were gone. White, English-speaking and black workers were being hired, but most reportedly left after a few hours or a few days. The plant was then run on short hours.

INS officials said that they planned no new raid at the Greeley plant, where they believed that the hiring situation had improved after the agency's 1991 investigations. Workers say, however, that recruitment of undocumented Mexicans, Salvadorans, Guatemalans, and Hondurans continued after the investigations and that the sale of jobs continued after the INS raids of summer 1991.

Monfort executives claimed that the raid was a "publicity-generated event," that the company had never knowingly hired illegals, and that Monfort notified INS after hearing rumors that illegal aliens were working at the slaughterhouse, and cooperated with authorities in "weeding them out."[31] According to newspaper reports, the long-time personnel manager at the Grand Island plant was himself a former employee of the U.S. Border Patrol. He reportedly died of a heart attack two weeks before the INS raid. The *Grand Island Independent* editor delared: "Monfort officials were not naive. . . . Monfort wasn't innocently lured into an immigration service trap, but don't make the giant meatpacking company into a sinister monster, either. Monfort is a valued part of the Grand Island area. With a slight change in attitude and hiring practices, it can become a respected part, too."[32] At present — months after the raid — no fines have been levied against the company and no criminal charges have been filed.

The most obvious outcome of the INS raids on the Monfort plants has been an increase in racism and hostility to foreigners. Letters to local newspapers express comments such as the following: "The illegal immigrants are just like illegal drugs. They are a festering boil on our society and it is time we lance that boil." A worker who is a U.S. citizen wrote: "We were all treated like criminals. What happened to our rights as United States citizens?"[33]

Following the Grand Island raid, public attention focused on the problems of businesses that were left with unpaid debts or of family members left behind when Monfort workers were deported. Although only U.S. citizens or legal residents who have been in the United States for a number of years can apply for welfare, many residents assumed that Mexicans and others who stayed in the United States when relatives were deported would be a tax burden on the community. In general, the marginalized status of Mexicans and Mexican Americans was exacerbated by the INS raids. One inevitable consequence of such marginalization is workers' increased vulnerability to exploitation at the hands of employers. Those who continued to work for Monfort were more pressed than ever to show loyalty to the company in return for job security.

Issues of worker exploitation were not addressed in the public dialogue that followed the INS crackdown. The Grand Island plant had been purchased by Monfort in 1979, and its capacity doubled, at the same time that the unionized Greeley plant was closed. Unions at both places were broken, wages were reduced, and benefits were cut. This history, certainly known to many of those who expressed satisfaction or outrage at the INS raids, was conveniently overlooked.

On August 16, 1992, after more than ten years of litigation, the National Labor Relations Board (NLRB) ordered Monfort, Inc., to make restitution to those who had been affected by discrimination against former employees when the Greeley slaughterhouse reopened in 1982. The company was also ordered to reinstate those who had been fired for engaging in union organizing activities and to provide guarantees that such activities would be protected in the future. Because of the flagrant nature of Monfort's violations of labor law, the NLRB order (which appears in Appendix B of this book as an order of compliance) was published several times in local newspapers. The NLRB also ordered that it be posted in the plant and read aloud to employees. It is signed by Charles E. Sykes, the lawyer whom Ken Monfort had contracted to supervise breaking of the union at the slaughterhouse in 1982 and again, at Greeley's Portion Foods plant, in 1987. Sykes is now working full-time for Monfort, Inc.

The NLRB ruling affects some 260 former union workers. Others who did not apply for work in 1982, but who should have been notified when the plant reopened, are not included in the final version of the decision handed down by the U.S. 10th Circuit Court of Appeals. In any case, many former employees have left the area. The burden of locating them falls on the union.

Francisco Cortez, who was a member of the rank-and-file Strike Committee that pushed for more militancy and more organizing in the community to prevent scabs from entering the plant during the 1979 strike, says that he is not interested in getting any money from Monfort, Inc. He thinks that the company and the union are both getting off too easily. Cortez, who works on his own doing house repairs in Greeley, says: "I wouldn't take their money. . . . I've still got my pride."[34] He says that the restitution order is a small price for the company to pay in return for the profit made during all these years. "Many of those who lost their jobs also lost their homes, their families, and their self-respect." He blames the union for letting the case drag on so long and for doing little to organize meatpacking workers in the meantime.

The rank-and-file Strike Committee in which Cortez participated met regularly during the 1979 strike. Its members organized a dance to collect funds and to build up community support. They were accused by union representatives of being "wildcatters" when they called a special meeting to propose blocking the plant gates. "We were all getting arrested for petty stuff," says Cortez. "We thought it would be better to get arrested for real stuff." He's glad that the UFCW — including former union leaders quoted extensively in this book — are now taking stronger lines. But he thinks that the main push for all workers will have to be the promotion of internationalism and support for revolutionary struggles wherever these are occurring. "I think most workers are socialists at heart," he says. "Both the companies and the unions are beating the 'death of communism' theme. We can't afford to buy into that. . . . The companies think they have the right to make all the rules, and the unions don't really believe in workers' power." Cortez feels that rank-and-file meatpacking workers must network among themselves in different cities and states in order to confront the many obstacles that must be overcome before workers can begin to reclaim their rights.

~

A major setback for organized labor in the United States came in June 1992 with the U.S. Senate's failure to pass the Workplace Fairness Act. A similar bill passed in the House, but without enough votes to prevent a presidential veto. It would have prohibited employers from hiring permanent workers to replace striking union members. Opponents of the bill claimed that the need for U.S. competitiveness in world markets makes it necessary to discourage strikes by workers.

According to some analysts, Congress has been moving toward support for government-supervised mediation of major labor disputes while unions have been moving toward seeking legitimacy in exchange for weak contracts. The AFL–CIO is looking for ways to cooperate with business. Businesses, on the other hand, are lobbying *against* even such concessions to labor as mandatory employee safety committees. The choice for labor is being posed, in official circles, as that between company unions (once outlawed in the United States) or no unions at all.[35]

In 1992, the National Right to Work Committee, a business lobby group, gave Greeley's state representative, Republican Dave Owen, its Statesman of the Year Award for his renewed attempt to enact anti-union legislation in Colorado (which failed to pass the House by only one vote in 1992). The Colorado Association of Commerce and Industry selected Owen as Legislator of the Year.[36]

In public debate over union representation for workers, the voices of rank-and-file workers are rarely heard. Women and men who work in places like Greeley's beef slaughterhouse or the Portion Foods plant do not even enjoy the status of a special interest group in our society. Displaced workers also remain unorganized.

A leaflet that was prepared by the Monfort workers' rank-and-file organizing committee in December,1979, read: "We say that the union is a good thing as long as we the workers are the union. But right now we feel that our voices aren't being heard. Are we going to wait until we lose everything (including our union) before we react to these injustices?" Workers protested their contract's no-strike clause, which made it impossible to enforce contract agreements except at the time that negotiations were underway. They also protested proposed cuts in rest periods and holidays.

Years later, when rank-and-file workers' worst fears had become reality, an immigrant worker in Monfort's restructured work force sounded an even more urgent theme:

> Just now the company is mailing Christmas cards to all "their workers," those who contribute to their riches. But that is a psychological trick. I wonder about those who suffer from the work there, can they really have a Merry Christmas? . . . with deformed hands, with pain in their backs, with their bones close to arthritis and many with advanced cases of nerve disease? What about the many who are no longer working because they were hurt in accidents there, those who were let go without the company admitting their rights? Economic necessity obligates you to keep going, sometimes even to deny the exploitation. But there are many who are fighting from within to get recognition of their time of work and all their pains. I believe that if a call went out to all people that still hurt and were hurt at Monfort, that many would come forth.[37]

Although the exploitation of immigrant workers is symptomatic of larger problems that plague our society and our world, it is all too easy to blame the immigrants themselves for somehow failing to make the grade. A study conducted at Chicago's Loyola University concluded that the workers most affected by unsafe workplaces are Hispanic immigrants, "many of whom are young and inexperienced, do not understand their rights, have little formal education and knowledge of English."[38]

A careful examination of situations existing in towns such as Greeley shows that it is not the workers who have brought miserable working conditions upon themselves. Rather, it is businesspeople who thrive on workers' ignorance, inexperience, and lack of education. And it is an economic and political system that justifies and facilitates the victimization of minorities.

Hispanics in Greeley who have been silent in the past about abuses in the meatpacking industry have begun to speak out locally. The *Greeley Tribune* has been obliged to print some of their comments. One who called himself "Ben Bunfort" wrote about "Good Hispanics" who "praise the opportunities afforded to them by Bunfort Inc's generosity, while the 'Bad Hispanics' continuously whine about losing parts of their bodies on the kill floor here at Bunfort's."[39] Ken Monfort declared, in his *Tribune* column of September 16, 1992, that he would retire from writing for the newspaper, saying: "I was always considered a friend and advocate of Hispanics, but no longer. Something changed. Was it me, or their spokespersons?" One of his critics responded: "I'm sorry to see that he is retiring from writing a column. He taught me a lot about state and local government." An admirer wrote that "in an era with outbreaks of greed from meatpacker workers to top executives . . . Ken Monfort is truly a legend of our times."[40] On November 28, 1992, the Monforts reportedly attended a banquet at which Ken Monfort was inducted into the Colorado Agriculture Hall of Fame.[41]

Although I am aware that corporate elites are generally unavailable to talk with those who have been or are likely to be critical of company policies, I attempted several times to secure an interview with Ken and Myra Monfort, both of whom continue to play important public and private roles on behalf of Monfort/ConAgra. In September 1992, I wrote to Myra Monfort:

> I am a teacher of Women's Studies, Sociology of Minorities, and Social Change at the University of Northern Colorado. I helped initiate a group research project in Greeley several years ago, dealing primarily with labor conditions in the meatpacking industry, and based primarily on conversations with workers and former workers at the Monfort plants. The research also deals with related issues such as legislation and community responses to the growth of the meatpacking industry in Greeley. It would be helpful if we could talk with you and your husband about the issues raised by our research.

Eventually, Myra Monfort sent a letter in which she indicated that, although she retains the title of "consulting attorney" for the company, she and her husband were preparing to winter in Florida. "Were I still involved and present at the office," she wrote, "the very press of everyday business would preclude the luxury of such conversations."[42]

Greeley continues to be a company town, where conversations about workers' rights, corporate accountability, and democratic decision making are regarded by many people as a "luxury." Even those who work at one of the most dangerous and dehumanizing industrial plants in the country may exhibit a stiff upper lip to the public. A Monfort worker who lost his arm recently when it was caught under a large metal folder that rammed down on the box he was spraying with silicone told reporters that it was all his own fault: "First of all, I called my mother and asked her to cancel my appointment with my chiropractor — I got rid of the tendonitis in my arm."[43]

Fragile alliances still exist in places such as Greeley, in order to keep the situation from erupting. But residents are not immune from the larger currents of revolt and conflict occurring in the nation's cities and around the world. People grumble about paying high fees for ambulance and health services or about huge write-offs by such services due to unpaid bills. City council members debate about a controversial new privately run prison to be built on the North Side. Although Colorado voters have passed an "Official English" initiative and have restricted the power of the state to levy taxes, Spanish-speaking residents are organizing to demand bilingual education and bilingual representation in the court system.

The ongoing problems of minority workers cannot be wished away by efforts to further marginalize or silence them. Given the tense situation that has developed among different sectors of Greeley's population, many members of the community are fearful for the future of their children. At the university, a new generation of students is caught between personal ambition and social responsibility in a rapidly changing world. The awakening of public awareness brings with it the possibility of rekindling the fires of protest, of joining together manual workers and other exploited or concerned people in an effort to create a more humane society.

~

Addendum - July 1993:

The UFCW conducted an election at the Greeley beef slaughterhouse April 29, 1993. In spite of widespread fear that the plant will close down if workers are unionized, the union won (by a margin of less than one hundred votes). UFCW organizers say that before the election, in blatant violation of the 1992 court order (see Appendix A), which states that the company shall "not threaten employees that the plant will be closed if the employees selected the union to represent them" and shall "not threaten an employee that the employees would lose their profit sharing benefits if the employees selected the union as their collective-bargaining representative," workers were given videos of the plant closing that took place in 1980 and received leaflets that said "Protect Your Bonus. Vote No!"[44]

Monfort contested the election results, charging a union organizer with using coercion against several employees. The NLRB refused to overturn the election, saying: "While impolite and rude in some cases, this conduct merely reflects the high emotions of a long, highly contested partisan election campaign."[45] Gene Meakins said that the company plans to appeal the decision,[46] which leaves workers in limbo — and vulnerable to being fired arbitrarily — only a few months before profit-sharing bonuses are due.[47]

APPENDIX A

Testimony of Edward Murphy Before the House Education and Labor Subcommittee on Labor Management Relations Concerning Corporate Whistleblower Protection, August 5, 1992 (H.R. 1664, Representative Barbara Boxer)

MR. CHAIRMAN:

Thank you for inviting my testimony. My name is Edward Murphy. For nearly five years, from August 1986 until April 1991, I served as the Safety Director for the Monfort, Incorporated meat processing plant in Grand Island, Nebraska. I have been in the safety field since 1981. Since February 1985 I have been a member of the American Society of Safety Engineers, and served as the local ASSE section chief. During my term I never had a negative performance appraisal and, to my knowledge, lasted in this position longer than any other Monfort safety manager.

On April 18, 1991, however, without any prior counseling or warnings I was fired, effective April 17. The termination was despite management's repeated denials of any problems when I asked if my job was in jeopardy. It occurred after I had received the maximum permissible merit raise in September, 1990. It came immediately after a six month program in which I had successfully reduced accident injury rates to record low levels at Grand Island.

There was much more to do, however. Less than a month before my termination, the Department of Labor's Occupational

Safety and Health Administration (OSHA) proposed a $1.1 million fine against Monfort, which the company planned to appeal.

My job was a real life Ph.D. program for the facts of life on corporate accountability. Monfort is one of the nation's largest meat packing companies and a participant in the U.S. Department of Agriculture's Streamlined Inspection System — Cattle (SIS–C), an honor system in which companies inspect themselves to earn the USDA wholesome seal for their meat.

Unfortunately, the primary lesson I learned is that truth is a four letter word at Monfort. Without legal protection for workers, corporate integrity exists at the whims of its leaders. It always was a struggle to do my job, but before the retirement of Ken Monfort as the firm's president and his wife Myra as general counsel, I received corporate headquarters support in challenges to the most dangerous abuses. I proceeded at my own risk when disclosing any bad news to company officials.

THE TEN COMMANDMENTS

Ten commandments summarize the company's code of conduct in practice:

1. The first commandment is that only production counts. Everything takes a back seat to getting the product out the door. The philosophy was to maximize output by getting away with as much as we could.
2. The law takes a back seat, if it is on the bus at all. The employee's duty is to follow orders. Period. As I was repeatedly told, "Do what I tell you, even if it is illegal."
3. Behead the messenger. Disclosing bad news — anything that could threaten perceived sacred cows and short term profits, even within the company, was asking for retribution.
4. Don't get caught. Frequently company officials took the position that there shouldn't be any record of a problem. Reports simply were not prepared, regardless of legal requirements or corporate policy. Those that existed on occasion were falsified. Otherwise, the truth could come back to haunt the company if there were trouble later.

5. Solemn lip service should always be paid to safety. But do not allow the responsible professionals to do their job and make safety a reality, instead of an empty word.
6. Do not cooperate with OSHA, which is perceived as an enemy. Do not have extended discussions with an OSHA inspector. Never volunteer any information. Never admit to a violation. Never admit that you were aware of a problem.
7. Keep the plant safety manager ignorant. Supervisors and workers repeatedly were told not to talk with me.
8. The company cannot afford to invest money correcting illegal, dangerous safety hazards.
9. Social Darwinism is the rule. Injuries to production workers occur because of "wimps," and will continue unless and until managers succeed in "weeding out the wimps." That's the solution.
10. Bully, harass and intimidate employees until they either leave, or give up on their values.

Another way to summarize reality at this company is that cheating became a way of life. It did not only extend to occupational safety. The National Labor Relations Board cited Monfort for repeated egregious violations. Plant management cheated foreign customers on exports. For example, Canada does not want its meat imports washed in chlorinated water. Monfort did it regularly, anyway, and turned off the chlorination system just before Canadian export inspections.

The firm regularly cheated American consumers in the Streamlined Inspection System for Cattle (SIS–C) meat inspection program. For example, knives are supposed to be routinely cleaned after cuts. This prevents cross contamination form filth and disease. But most of the knife rinsing stations in fabrication were inoperative or too far away from the worker to be used. In slaughter, the combination of low staffing levels and too fast chain speeds meant that even those rinsers that worked could not be used. On one occasion the fabrication plant manager attempted to fire the whole quality control (QC) staff when they challenged production for tampering with already approved products.

OCCUPATIONAL SAFETY VIOLATIONS

I took my position as safety director seriously, because my job could make the difference between life and death, or between workers losing arms and fingers and workers returning home each day with limbs intact. The company took the safety director position seriously, too, as a threat to productivity. That explains why it took a tough safety manager to last a year at Monfort's Grand Island plant. Examples of the most crude safety violations are summarized below:

- *Ergonomics and repetitive motion disorders.* Monfort employees had an unacceptable risk of becoming functionally crippled from any number of repetitive motion disorders, because the company ignored and refused to implement basic steps to prevent them. For example, a job rotation program existed, but workers were sent to different high risk jobs using the same muscle groups for similar tasks. Management was hostile to reducing body stress by redesigning equipment. I was able to do this once, and ordered not to do it again.

- *Lockout controls.* This OSHA requirement means employees cannot start working with a piece of equipment until it is at a zero energy state. Lockout controls guarantee that the machinery has been de-energized. That way it cannot move and hurt them, instead of leaving it to chance. There was no management commitment to this kindergarten principle of safety. One key to the program was for each employee to have a personal identified lock necessary for equipment to be turned on and off. During one of my audits, fabrication maintenance officials falsely told me the lockout numbers were complete and up to date. The truth is that some of the workers had not been issued lockout numbers at all, others had the same one, and a significant number of others had not been educated on the lockout program. Fabrication officials commonly hovered around employees and remarked that there was no time for lockouts.
    Two workers died because of violations — one who was sucked into a hole in a moving conveyor that was supposed

to be turned off, and another whose head was crushed when he was installing a shield on a machine that removes fat and manure from beef hides.

- *Inadequate access.* Lockout sloppiness was even more danger-ous, because workers had no choice but to crawl all over the equipment like monkeys. For example, just to reach their work areas some employees had to crawl under chain driven conveyors. In an area known as the "race track," for a while employees had to sit on a moving conveyor and roll over to reach their work areas.

- *Guards.* Further aggravating the hazards, machine guards were missing or inadequate in areas throughout the plant. This means, for example, that chains were exposed or not fully covered. Monfort did not make a serious effort to fix un-guarded sprocket chains, although there were widespread violations. The result was often broken bones and finger amputations.

- *Ventilation.* Although some fans existed, they were inade-quate. For example, after following up on employee com-plaints about one fabrication shop, I learned that our exhaust system failed to remove potentially harmful welding fumes. Fabrication management did not take sustained, effective corrective action.

- *Exposure to chemicals.* I was particularly disturbed by unnec-essary exposure to gases like ammonia, which burns the eyes, skin and lungs. Our refrigeration system continued to leak. Fabrication officials sometimes had normal work continue in areas where they knew unidentified, irritating substances were present. Management issued dust masks to "protect" the workers, although these masks are useless for controlling hazardous vapors.

- *Improper maintenance.* Management officials also pressured maintenance employees to hurry up. A good example of the results involved fork lifts and pallet jacks, used to haul car-casses and other loads up to 2,000 pounds. One in particular was noted for starting and running on its own, because of shorts due to condensation. A morbid joke among workers was not to turn your back on a pallet jack. The brakes were deficient on many of them. I went to the mat about one particular forklift, because it was around an ammonia accumulator in an area with no exit path. The fabrication production manager dismissed the problem, saying that brakes were not necessary. Yet several holes punched by this same forklift in walls and doors proved him wrong. When I persisted, he threatened first to fire me and second to cut off the brake pedal so there would be nothing left to fix.

Maintenance employees frequently complained to me that production supervision harassed them while they were repairing equipment. As late as April 8, 1991, just before my termination, a production superintendent pried a large chain back onto a sprocket, because he didn't want to wait a minute or two for maintenance to lock it out.

- *Emergency exits.* Even under the best operation, a meat packing plant is a dangerous place, full of life threatening machinery. As illustrated by the fire in the chicken processing plant in Hamlet, North Carolina, workers must have a safe way out if something goes wrong. We did not have an adequate escape system in the packaging area for these type disasters.

  I used to lie awake at night worrying about what could happen. For example, overexposure to ammonia functionally blinds the worker by creating watery, burning eyes. It becomes impossible to find one's direction. Workers would have to crawl over boxes and conveyors to reach exit doors in the packaging area, and some of the equipment might still be operating. With a large number of plant employees who could be trapped or mutilated, in my professional judgement the consequences could dwarf those of the Hamlet tragedy.

  Management simply did not share this commitment in practice. There was little or no safety training for supervisors. The fabrication manager canceled my training courses for his supervisors, on grounds that they were of "no value." It all depends whether you place a value on human beings. I conducted analogous training for slaughter supervisors over a three year period, and slaughter injuries decreased approximately 50%.

After the second employee death, I recommended 15 reforms. The company chief executive officer and the general counsel told me that, at most, perhaps one would be acted on.

Even without consistent procedures, training or enforcement, I was able to make progress through persistence and raw determination. During my last six months I was able to design and implement two separate safety incentive plans: one for supervisors through cash awards and another for all personnel which gave gift certificates based on safety knowledge. The overall injury rate dropped from 40%, from around 65 incidents per month to 35. I believe that with an effective system we could have prevented both fatalities at Monfort Grand Island, 60–70% of the traumatic injuries and 40–50% of repetitive motion disorders. Most frustrating, the program would more than have paid for itself by reducing workers compensation costs by 40–50%.

HARASSMENT AND INTIMIDATION

Unfortunately, my successful safety offensive in 1990–1991 may have been my downfall. It occurred almost simultaneously with the OSHA inspection that led to the $1.09 million proposed fine in March 1991. Due to the combination, I was a marked man who represented potentially threatening testimony against the company. Moreover, due to the OSHA regulatory sanctions, I was about to gain a mandate for further unwelcome reforms. My termination was no surprise. Rather, it was the culmination of retaliation that company officials had been pursuing for years in an effort to gain my resignation. I simply was not willing to quit and abandon my duties. I have discussed the harassment campaign with lawyers from the Government Accountability Project, who told me that the tactics covered most classic reprisal techniques that they have encountered. Examples are summarized below:

1. *Make the whistleblowers, instead of their message, the issue.* The point of this tactic is to obfuscate the dissent by

attacking the source's motives, professional competence, sanity, economic credibility, sexuality or virtually anything else that will work to cloud the issue. On numerous occasions a fabrication manager called me a "sissy" and a "wimp" while the corporate Safety Engineer called me a "dumb son of a bitch" for wanting to comply with emergency response standards for release of hazardous substances.

The beginning of the end for me was in 1989 when I told Monfort's general counsel that a production manager had lied to OSHA by claiming that all forklifts/pallet jacks were properly maintained, when in fact they were not. I warned that the truth would come out and make matters worse. The general counsel responded: "I don't want to hear it and you're just out to get" the manager. I eventually was fired for creating an atmosphere of "hostility, distrust and negativism," among other allegations.

The company informally reported that I was mentally unbalanced, and also attempted to obtain a negative psychiatric evaluation of me. In early 1991 I agreed to see a therapist for stress, after Monfort said it would cover the medical expenses. I thought maybe our disagreements had been in good faith and the company wanted to help. But the company then tried to feed derogatory information about me to the therapist, and to learn what was in his files. After he protested, a corporate vice president wrote that they only wanted to help me, because Monfort was "concerned" that I was a danger to myself or others, possibly even suicidal. Two days after this letter the company completed their help by firing me without warning.

2. *Isolate the whistleblower.* Here the idea is to isolate the employee to make an example of him or her, as well as to block access to information. I was excluded from meetings on ideas for which I had been an advocate. For years, supervisors who were seen talking with me were called into the plant manager's office and interrogated about the discussions. When maintenance employees wanted to speak to me they made sure that the door was locked so that no one could enter the shop. The company had made it clear

that any employee or supervisor spoke to me at his or her own risk.

3. *Gag them.* The most direct, crude way to retaliate is by flatly forbidding an employee to communicate. If you don't keep your mouth shut, you're guilty of insubordination and can be fired. I was ordered not to communicate with OSHA, even for advice on technical interpretations of the law. I was even prevented from pursuing subjects with my own managers, who just didn't want to hear it. For example, before the fabrication manager "solved" the problem of the brakeless fork lift by saying he'd cut off the brake pedal, he threatened to fire me if I didn't drop the subject.

4. *Reorganize.* This approach strips the employee of responsibilities without a formal demotion or other forthright action that would have to be defended. In October 1990 the company executive personally redefined my job. Contrary to the previous four years, I no longer was to write policies or procedures on safety, I was only to be a monitor.

5. *Put them on a pedestal of cards.* This tactic is just the opposite of reorganizing a whistleblower into irrelevance. It involves appointing the whistleblower to solve the problem and then making the job impossible through a wide range of obstacles undercutting any realistic possibility of achieving reform. If that works, the finale is then to fire the employee for incompetence when the problem is not solved. Amazingly, a few months after I was functionally reduced to being a monitor, Monfort ordered me to write 13 safety procedures for the entire corporation. At first I thought this was an opportunity. Then I learned that corporate officials were ordering safety directors at other plants not to speak with me. Further, I was denied access to basic information necessary for my assignment.

6. *Discriminate.* In addition to obvious tactics like favoritism, bureaucracies will use a double standard in enforcing laws or rules. What is acceptable for management or "team players" is a serious offense if committed by a whistleblower. Monfort selectively enforced the lockout rules to fire those who were out of favor, while winking at repeated

management violations or limiting discipline to verbal counseling.

7. *Display chutzpa in selecting charges.* One principle is that it is important to go beyond merely defeating the whistle-blower. In order to prove to others that no one is safe, the goal is to make stick the most outrageous charges possible. A self-effacing, soft-spoken individual will be fired for being an insufferable, loud-mouthed egomaniac. In my case, I had been outspoken about inconsistent enforcement of safety rules. Correspondingly, the last of the charges for my dismissal was that I had created an atmosphere of "inconsistency."

8. *Hire someone else to do the dirty work.* Here the idea is to purchase a blue chip, "expert" buffer for the retaliation. In 1991 Monfort retained the Jefferson Group, which included a former OSHA official, to do a thorough review of the company's safety program. Unfortunately, it soon became clear they were investigating me rather than Monfort's program. They did not cooperate at all with my attempts to go over regulatory compliance. However, the former OSHA official told me point blank to get another job.

9. *Hit them with a Catch 22.* This form of harassment requires little explanation. Management simply puts the dissenter in an impossible situation: You have two choices, and you are "damned if you do and damned if you don't." Often the order is to violate the law, which illustrates how the corporate whistleblower bill would help by protecting an employee who refuses to obey such an order. In practice, the company used its occupational safety rules as weapons against those who were out of favor, instead of policies to protect its labor force during operations.

To illustrate, when I reported complaints of ammonia releases, the corporate Safety Director told me that I would be fired if I responded. He also told me that if I did not respond to the leaks, I would be fired. I am aware of many other instances where Monfort management disciplined or terminated employees for just that — following orders to violate its own rules.

10. *Attack them physically.* When all else fails, try physical intimidation: beat up the whistleblower. One production official repeatedly threatened me, pounded his finger into my chest and attempted to back me up against the wall. Bruises remained on my sternum for several days.

To say this harassment caused unhealthy stress is an understatement. I could not sleep at night, and during 1991 gained 30 pounds in a matter of weeks. There was extreme strain on what had been and again is an extremely strong marriage. I found the strength not to collapse under the pressure due to my faith. Sometimes I would pray at length just for the courage to go to work.

FALSE AND INCOMPLETE RECORDS

The intensive harassment of me and others was understandable. Monfort had a lot to hide. As summarized above, things went from bad to worse for me after I refused to cooperate with lying to OSHA. When intimidation failed, the company tried more direct coverups — destroying information or making sure that information never got written down in the first place. Illustrative examples from my experience are listed below:

- There were repeated reports that the company was maintaining two sets of OSHA logs — one for the government and one for Monfort that was more accurate. Personnel resigned in protest over orders to carry out this program. In my experience, the OSHA log kept getting erased from the computer and had to be "reconstructed" by others.

- There was a tradition of lying to OSHA. To illustrate, in 1989 a worker broke his ankle in three places due to a pallet jack operating without brakes. The fabrication manager told OSHA he was unaware of the accident, although he had initiated the report. He denied any knowledge of the pallet jack brake problems, although I had been protesting for years about the problem. He further reassured OSHA that the standard procedure was to repair any known defects, although that was not the case.

- When OSHA subpoenaed records for an investigation, I was ordered to shred many of the documents that they had requested.

- Plant supervisors falsified counseling cards in Safety Training Observation Program (STOP), to make it appear they had been providing on-the-job assistance when they had not. I was suspicious, because supervisors would turn in cards indicating extra, intensive safety counseling at the same time injuries were increasing. Later, some supervisors told me that the fabrication plant manager had ordered them to do so.

- Toward the end of my stay we were ordered not to write up accident investigative reports, in violation of the corporate loss control manual. The reason? Corporate counsel said they could become "smoking guns." The records could prove that we were aware of violations and intentionally allowed them to continue.

- Monfort had a tradition of incomplete records. As early as September 1987 I had complained that investigative reports were being filed for less than one third of the cases.

- The company also declined to regularly prepare written performance evaluations. In my four years and eight months at Monfort, I only saw one in writing about myself. (I was told that another good evaluation also existed.) Monfort's general counsel explained that performance evaluations documenting good work made it harder to get rid of employees.

- The deception extended beyond occupational safety. When USDA officials came from Washington to review the SIS Cattle inspection program, Monfort slowed the lines down from normal rates of operation. Extra employees were called in from other shifts to staff the lines. This made it falsely appear that more resources were dedicated to food safety in order to comply with the requirements of the inspection program.

OSHA EMPLOYEE PROTECTION PROGRAM

The OSHA employee protection program is a bad joke. In February 1991 I filed a discrimination complaint, because I could see the handwriting on the wall and wanted to prevent my termination by acting first. Although you are legally entitled to a ruling in 90 days, there wasn't a decision until that fall. By that point I had already been fired and found another job.

The agency ruled against me due to a lack of voluntary witnesses. The problem is that they had only interviewed two management witnesses, although I gave them a list of numerous names. Some witnesses told me that they would testify if they were subpoenaed. Although I passed that information along, OSHA did not bother.

In November, I appealed the OSHA decision and am still waiting to hear the results. In the meantime, I have filed a tort suit for damages due to wrongful discharge. But even if I win, I will not get my job back and nothing will be done to prevent the disasters waiting to happen at Monfort.

For me the lessons learned are disillusioning. I would not voluntarily talk to OSHA again, and am not willing to ever again be in that situation without any genuine legal rights. My dissent had nothing to do with labor-management disputes. For a while I was a top target of labor organizers, because my efforts undercut the need for the union. I stayed as long as I did because employees told me they had no one else to turn to, because I cared, and because I was stubborn. But never again.

This is exactly the wrong kind of message for corporate employees who want to do the right thing. The right message is the one sent by the corporate whistleblower protection bill: you cannot challenge life threatening misconduct without committing professional suicide.

Not all employers are like Monfort. I believe that the vast majority of businesses are law-abiding. But for those companies that have no respect for the law, ethical workers have no chance for survival. Until the enactment of genuine protections for whistleblowers in the private sector, employees will have to choose between their jobs and their conscience.

APPENDIX B

Notice to Employees Posted Pursuant to a Judgment of the United States Court of Appeals Enforcing an Order of the National Labor Relations Board August 16, 1992

The National Labor Relations Board has found that we violated the National Labor Relations Act and has ordered us to post, mail, publish, read, and abide by this notice.

Section 7 of the Act gives employees these rights.

> To organize
> To form, join, or assist any union
> To bargain collectively through representatives of their own choice
> To act together for other mutual aid or protection
> To choose not to engage in any of these protected concerted activities

All our employees have the right to join the United Food and Commercial Workers International Union, AFL–CIO, or any other labor organization, or to refrain from doing so.

We will not threaten employees that, if the United Food and Commercial Workers International Union, AFL–CIO, Local Union No. 7 wins a representation election, our Company would settle an unfair labor practice case, fire our present employees, and rehire our former employees.

We will not tell employees that if the Union lost the representation election our Company would vigorously fight an unfair labor practice case, even if it took years to do so, before our Company would fire even one present employee in order to rehire a former employee.

We will not threaten employees that the plant will be closed if the employees selected the union to represent them.

We will not threaten an employee by telling him that the employees' selection of the Union as their collective-bargaining representative will cause the Greeley plant to be closed again, and suggest to the employee in the same conversation that the employees should form their own organization to bargain with our Company instead of selecting the union to represent them.

We will not unlawfully interrogate employees concerning their union sympathies.

We will not tell an employee that employees who voted for the Union were a bunch of troublemakers and ought to be fired.

We will not threaten an employee that the employee would lose their profit sharing benefits if the employees selected the Union as their collective-bargaining representative.

We will not threaten an employee with retaliation for revealing statements made by a supervisor of our Company, which had resulted in the Union's filing of unfair labor practice charges against our Company.

We will not tell an employee that an employee who would testify against our Company in a NLRB hearing ought to be shot or abandoned on some island.

We will not promise an employee free work gloves if the employee votes against the Union.

We will not tell an employee to solicit other company employees to sign a petition against the Union, in the context of telling the same employee that he will be sure to get a promotion to a leadman's job.

We will not create the impression of surveillance by taking notes behind employees wearing union insignia.

We will not disparately apply our work rules to permit employees to engage in antiunion activities in the plant while refusing to permit employees to engage in prounion activities.

We will not fail to rehire or delay in rehiring, because of past union membership and activities, former employees of our Company after they have filed Monfort applications for employment concerning production jobs and our Company's Greeley plant.

We will not refuse to rehire an employee because the Union has filed an unfair labor practice charge with the NLRB against our Company concerning our Company's termination of that employee.

We will not unlawfully discharge any of our employees or discriminate against them in any manner because of their union affiliation or because they engage in union activities.

We will not in any other manner interfere with, restrain, or coerce employees in the exercise of the rights guaranteed them by Section 7 of the Act.

We will offer James Little immediate and full reinstatement to his former job or, if that job no longer exists, to a substantially equivalent position, without prejudice to his seniority or any other rights or privileges previously enjoyed, and we will make him whole with interest for any loss of earnings and other benefits suffered as a result of the discrimination against him.

We will offer to Ruth DeVargas and to all former employees who filed Monfort applications but were not rehired because of their past union membership and activities immediate and full reemployment in the positions for which they would have been hired but for the Respondent's unlawful discrimination or, if those positions no longer exist, to substantially equivalent positions at our Company's Greeley plant, without the loss of their seniority or any other benefits dating from the time we should have hired them, dismissing, if necessary, any and all persons hired to fill such positions, and we will place on a preferential hiring list all remaining individuals who would have been hired but for the lack of available jobs.

We will make whole Ruth DeVargas and each of those former employees whom we unlawfully failed to hire or delayed in rehiring for any loss of earnings and other benefits resulting from our discrimination against them, less any interim earnings, plus interest.

We will mail copies of this notice to all our employees and to the discriminatees mentioned above; we will publish copies of this notice in local newspapers, and we will read this notice to all of our employees, or we will permit an agent of the NLRB to read this notice to all of our employees.

We will, on request of the Union made within 1 year of the issuance of the Board's Decision, Order, and Direction of Second Election, make available to the Union without delay a list of names and addresses of all employees employed at the Greeley, Colorado plant at the time of the request.

We will, immediately on request of the Union, for a period of 2 years from the date on which this notice is posted or until the Regional Director of the NLRB certifies the results of a fair and free election, whichever comes first, grant the Union and its representatives reasonable access to our bulletin boards and all places where notices to employees are customarily posted.

We will, immediately on request of the Union, for a period of 2 years from the date on which this notice is posted or until the Regional Director certifies the results of a fair and free election, whichever comes first, permit a reasonable number of union representatives access for reasonable periods of time to our plant in nonwork areas during employees' nonworktime so that the Union may present its views on unionization to employees, orally and in writing.

We will, for a period of 2 years from the date on which this notice is posted or until the Regional Director certifies the results of a fair and free election, whichever comes first, give the Union reasonable notice and give two union representatives a reasonable opportunity to be present if we gather together any group of our employees on worktime at our plant and speak to them on the question of union representation, and we will, on request, give one of the Union's representatives equal time and facilities also to speak to you on the question of union representation.

We will, in any election which the NLRB may schedule at our Greeley plant within 2 years of the posting of this notice and in which the Union is a participant, permit, on request by the Union, at least two union representatives access to the plant and appropriate facilities to speak to you for 30 minutes on working time. This speech will take place not more than 10 working days, but not less than 48 hours, prior to the election.

MONFORT OF COLORADO, INC. (employer)
Dated September 1, 1992
Signed by Charles E. Sykes, Attorney

Notes

PREFACE

1. Water use statistics source: Worldwatch Paper No. 103: 14 (Washington, D.C.: Worldwatch Institute). Land use statistics sources: Worldwatch Paper No. 103: 17; A. V. Krebs, 1992, *Corporate Reapers: The Book of Agribusiness* (Washington, D.C.: Essential Books): 362.
2. "Boxed beef" refers to meat that is cut up and packaged at the factory instead of being shipped as whole carcasses.

INTRODUCTION

1. Upton Sinclair, 1906; 1946, *The Jungle* (New York: Signet Classics): 31.
2. *Greeley Tribune,* August 19, 1990.
3. *Greeley Tribune,* April 28, 1991. ConAgra report on fiscal 1992, annual meeting of stockholders.
4. Michael Wilbur, 1990, "Monopoly Power in the Meatpacking Industry," *Reap News and Views,* December.
5. *Denver Post,* July 21, 1990; September 19, 1991. *Greeley Tribune,* December 8, 1991.
6. *Greeley Tribune,* April 28, 1991.
7. Peggy Campbell, *Greeley Tribune,* May n.d., 1991.

CHAPTER 1

1. Ora B. Peake (Colorado State College of Education, Greeley), 1937, *The Colorado Range Cattle Industry* (Glendale, Calif.: Arthur H. Clark): 40.
2. *Al Frente de Lucha,* March 1991. (Subsequent comments by Salazar were taken from this source unless identified otherwise.
3. Sarah Deutsch, 1987, *No Separate Refuge: Culture, Class, and Gender on an Anglo-Hispanic Frontier in the American Southwest, 1880–1940* (New York: Oxford University Press): 174. Among those driven out of northeastern Colorado at this time were a colony of African American workers who had come from Chicago (*Greeley Tribune,* December 14, 1991).
4. *Greeley Tribune,* January 28, 1990.

5. Sarah Deutsch, 1987: 134, 173–176. Mario Barrera, 1979, *Race and Class in the Southwest: A Theory of Racial Inequality* (Notre Dame, Ind.: University of Notre Dame Press): 63–73.
6. *Al Frente de Lucha,* March 1991.
7. *Al Frente de Lucha,* April/May 1991.
8. Rodolfo Acuna, 1988, *Occupied America: A History of Chicanos,* 3d ed. (New York: Harper and Row): 260–266.
9. The word *bracero* means "arm" or, in this case, "workhand."
10. Irving Davis, Jr,. and William H. Metzler, 1958, *Sugar Beet Labor in Northern Colorado,* Technical bulletin no. 63 (Fort Collins, Colo.: Colorado State University Experiment Station): 61.
11. *Ibid.,* 63.
12. *Al Frente de Lucha,* October/November 1991.
13. Conversation with Joaquina Rodriguez, summer 1991
14. *The Mirror,* April 24, 1991; May 1, 1991.
15. Work contractors, who usually also provide transportation to the worksite, are known as "coyotes."
16. It is unlikely that Monfort administrators were unaware of the victimizing of undocumented workers in this way, because rumors had been rampant for at least a year. The press and police were also informed and could easily have conducted a sting operation to expose such a blatant form of what is usually called indentured slavery. However, action was only taken after the theater audition occurred, and then only when the "responsible" employee was on vacation. No one was ever arrested or fined.
17. *Al Frente de Lucha,* February 1991.
18. *Greeley Tribune,* June 30, 1991.
19. Letter written by Pete Longoria, *Greeley Tribune,* summer 1991 (undated clipping in author's possession).
20. *Greeley Tribune,* May 10, 1991.
21. *Greeley Tribune,* May 2, 1991.
22. Men who were deported said that they were kept outside Denver for a month and then were taken in buses, shackled, for a 14-hour ride to the Mexican border. During that time they were given two sandwiches and one cup of water. Although the bus driver stopped frequently, he allowed them outside the bus to relieve themselves only once. Women who were deported were taken to Mexico by plane.
23. Telephone conversation with Lourdes Gouveia, summer 1991.
24. *Greeley Tribune,* June 11, 1991.
25. *Greeley Tribune,* May 29, 1991.
26. *Greeley Tribune,* May 10, 1991.
27. Conversation with confidential source, June 11, 1991.
28. *Greeley Tribune,* August 26, 1990.
29. Although Monfort receives reimbursement for 50 percent of a trainee's salary for eight to sixteen weeks (*Greeley Tribune,* July 4, 1991; September 8, 1991), one of the workers' consistent complaints is that they do not get any training and must struggle on their own to learn the skills necessary to perform their jobs (see Chapters 4 and 5).

30. *Greeley Tribune,* June 14, 1991. (Subsequent comments in this paragraph by Father Urban were taken from this source.)
31. Mario Barrera, 1979: 82, quoting a 1929 study by Paul Taylor, *Mexican Labor in the United States: Valley of the South Platte, Colorado* (Berkeley: University of California Publications in Economics) 6 (5).
32. *Greeley Tribune,* July 18, 1990.
33. *Greeley Tribune,* October 3, 1990.
34. Study conducted by Tom Deen, UNC health and human services graduate student, November 1991.
35. A special program initiated by volunteers from the University of Northern Colorado offers English classes to selected employees at the plant, who take these classes on their own time. Although this is helpful to individuals who can participate, it also gives the company a rationale for not providing interpreters or Spanish-speaking supervisors on the disassembly line.
36. *Greeley Tribune,* October 3, 1990.
37. *Denver Post,* January 6, 1991. The city of Greeley annexed a large area north of the city so that Anheuser Busch could build a plant there. A mineral rights dispute ensued, and the company located in Fort Collins instead. Some complained that Monfort had an interest in preventing the beer company, which hires at a base rate much higher than that of the meatpacking plant, from locating in Greeley. Competition for the use of water also appeared to be a factor in the dispute (*Greeley Tribune,* November 8, 1989).
38. Sources for these statistics are the Colorado Department of Labor and Employment and the U.S. Department of Commerce, Bureau of the Census. See also U.S. Geological Survey data as reported in the *Greely Tribune,* December 10, 1989.
39. *Greeley Tribune,* January 21, 1991.
40. See *Greeley Tribune,* November 19, 1989; December 23, 1990.
41. *Greeley Tribune,* March 22, 1991.
42. Conversation with Fahti Imami, October 1991. The property manager was Jack Cochran. The housing situation has since worsened for low-income residents in Greeley (*Greeley Tribune,* July 18, 1993).
43. Interview with Lucy Zamora, fall 1992.

CHAPTER 2

1. *Greeley Tribune,* April 28, 1991.
2. *Ibid.*
3. "A Congregation of the First Rank, " *Greeley Tribune* supplement, October 2, 1988.
4. *Playing the Game: How Power and Influence Work in Greeley, Greeley Tribune* special issue, October 1988.
5. *Ibid.,* 24.
6. *Ibid.,* 22.
7. *Ibid.,* 11.
8. *Greeley Tribune,* October 2, 1988: 3.

9. *Greeley Tribune,* October 21, 1988.
10. *Greeley Style Magazine,* winter 1989.
11. *Greeley Tribune,* October 2, 1988.
12. *Greeley Style Magazine,* winter 1989.
13. Report of January 1991, from a study by Ann Garrison, University of Northern Colorado economist, commenting on trends in the preceding decade.
14. Monfort of Colorado newsletter, summer 1979.
15. An Associated Press report of April 18, 1980 (*Denver Post,* April 17, 1980), showed Monfort to be "by far the biggest violator" of DES regulations, in a scandal that rocked the entire industry. "Ken's Comments" on DES appeared in a summer 1979 Monfort of Colorado newsletter.
16. *Colorado Business,* May 1985.
17. *Colorado Business,* May 1985. ABC News, *20/20* segment, January 5, 1990.
18. *Colorado Business,* May 1985.
19. *Ibid.*
20. ConAgra, Fiscal 1990 Annual Report. *Greeley Tribune,* August 19, 1990.
21. *Greeley Tribune,* November 16, 1988.
22. Most of those employed at Portion Foods received a starting wage of $4.50 per hour in 1984, although some of the men employed there received up to $5.70 per hour. Starting wages at the main packing plant were $6.00 to $7.20 per hour. See Greeley Museum Monfort file, study by George Kandel, Jr., and Tim Ewing.
23. The Monfort sewage plant was built at a cost of $1,100,000 in 1972. In 1988, Monfort, Inc., bought the plant for $436,000 in order to meet legal requirements for opening a new lamb slaughtering facility. Ken Monfort commented: "I'm not real sure what the problem with that has been in the past, but now we won't have to argue that any longer" (*Greeley Tribune,* November 21, 1988). Greeley's mayor, Robert Markley, said: "The opening of the plant was in jeopardy and I think we showed Monfort we believed in the importance of that facility." The advantage to the city was that they were relieved of liabilities for damages or fines for running the sewage plant (*Greeley Tribune,* November 21, 1988).
24. See House Journal, Labor Peace Act of 1965 (HB 1461). An interview with Sal Salazar, June 15, 1991, included discussion of union issues prior to the 1970s.
25. Jimmy M. Skaggs, 1986, *Prime Cut: Livestock Raising and Meatpacking in the United States, 1607–1983* (College Station, Tex.: Texas A&M Press): 181.
26. Philip Agee wrote in his "CIA Diary" of December 18, 1964:

> A new victory for the station at Georgetown, British Guiana, in its efforts to throw out the leftist-nationalist Prime Minister and professed Marxist, Cheddi Jagan. In elections a few days ago Jagan's Indian-based party lost parliamentary control to a coalition of the black-based party and a splinter group. The new Prime Minister, Forbes Burnham, is considered to be a moderate and his ascension to power finally removes the fear Jagan would turn British Guiana into another Cuba. The victory is largely due to CIA operations over the past five years to strengthen the anti-Jagan trade unions, principally through the Public Service International which provided the cover for financing public employees strikes. Jagan is protesting fraud; earlier this year he expelled Gene Meakins, one of our main labor

agents in the operation, but it was no use. (Philip Agee, 1975; 1989, *CIA Diary: Inside the Company* [New York: Bantam Books]: 634.)

Cheddi Jagan himself described this whole affair in a book titled *The West on Trial: The Fight for Guyana's Freedom* (Berlin: Seven Seas Books, 1966; 1975). Detailing how antigovernment riots sparked by police brutality under British rule served to discredit Jagan's political party, he concluded: "They made of our small country a sacrificial offering to the 'Almighty Dollar.' " Undercutting wages of the emancipated Africans by cheap Indian immigrant workers was the source of early conflict, which was exacerbated by CIA-backed company unions, resulting in claims that "Guiana, torn by racial strife, was not ready for independence" (341–342).

27. *Colorado Business,* May 1985.
28. *Greeley Tribune,* August 18, 1979; April 4, 1984. Interview with Steve Thomas, August 10, 1990. At the time of this writing, there was no union representing the workers at the Grand Island plant.
29. *Greeley Tribune,* December 27, 1989.
30. *Greeley Tribune,* October 4, 1989.
31. Before the plant closure, Monfort packing plant workers received a starting wage of $7.98 to $9.18 per hour. When the plant reopened, the starting rate was $5 to $6 per hour. (*Rocky Mountain News,* January 6, 1980; *Denver Post,* July 21, 1990). The average for the industry in 1982 was $10.50 to $11.50 per hour, although several other plants were paying as low as $6.50 (*Business Week,* August 1982).
32. *Denver Post,* September 28, 1982.
33. *Ibid.*
34. This statement by Arden Walker, made before the National Labor Relations Board, was cited in testimony before a Subcommittee of the Committee on Government Operations, U.S. House of Representatives, May 6, 1987, "Underreporting of Occupational Injuries and Its Impact on Workers' Safety," Part 2, p. 42. Testimony indicated that Walker had worked for Iowa Beef Processors before he worked for Monfort.
35. *Greeley Tribune,* September 5, 1982.
36. *Greeley Tribune,* March 7, 1986.
37. *Greeley Tribune,* January 26, 1989.
38. *Greeley Tribune,* February 1, 1989.
39. Greeley Museum Monfort file.
40. Douglas H. Constance and William D. Heffernan, 1991, "The Global Food System: Joint Ventures in the U.S.S.R., Eastern Europe, and the People's Republic of China," Paper presented at the Midwest Sociological Society meetings, Des Moines, Iowa.
41. A. V. Krebs, 1992, *Corporate Reapers: The Book of Agribusiness* (Washington, D.C.: Essential Books): 378, 379.
42. IBP's problems in maintaining its lead are outlined in Douglas H. Constance, and William Heffernan, 1989, "IBP's Rise to Dominance in the Meatpacking Industry: Boxed beef and busted unions," Paper presented at meetings of the Agriculture, Food and Human Values Society, Little Rock, Arkansas, 22.
43. See ConAgra report on fiscal 1992 first quarter and annual meeting of stockholders and *Business Week,* November 11, 1991.

44. See William D. Heffernan, 1989, "Confidence and Courage in the Next 50 Years," *Rural Sociology,* 54 (2): 155.

45. One of those whose interests rivaled those of the Monforts was Robert Tointon, who was for many years president of Hensel Phelps Construction Company and who later became president of Phelps-Tointon, Inc., and numerous other firms associated with construction and financial services. Tointon also has a history of repudiating union contracts and has been embroiled in lawsuits and controversies regarding discrimination and over-charging for work done at Denver's International Airport, convention centers, and other construction projects in Colorado and elsewhere. Tointon is chair-man of the Board of the University of Northern Colorado in Greeley. His most recent dispute with the Monforts was over a proposed move of Weld County offices from downtown Greeley to a site north of the city which was purchased from the Monforts by the county. (*Greeley Tribune,* November 22, 1987; February 19, 1991; April 5, 1991; August 7, 1991.)

46. Interview with Christine Johnson, June 25, 1990.

47. A new ambulance service building is being located near the Monfort slaugh-terhouse. The county's finance director said: "The site in North Greeley will provide better access to areas with the highest needs for ambulance service" (*Greeley Tribune,* November 13, 1992).

48. *Greeley Tribune,* June 8, 1986.

49. *Colorado Business,* July 1989.

50. *Greeley Style Magazine,* winter 1989.

51. *Colorado Business,* May 1985.

52. William D. Heffernan, 1989: 158.

53. *Greeley Tribune,* February 4, 1986.

54. "The Monfort Story," Company publication, late 1970s.

55. A. V. Krebs, 1990, *Heading Toward the Last Roundup: The Big Three's Prime Cut* (Washington, D.C.: Corporate Agribusiness Project): 8.

56. *Denver Post,* March 8, 1987.

57. *Ibid.*

58. *Denver Post,* April 19, 1990.

59. The article was written by Sheryl Jimenez. It appeared in the original edition of *Hispanic Horizons,* September 13, 1989.

60. Frank Lucero, *The Mirror,* September 22, 1989.

61. Claude Johns, *The Mirror,* September 22, 1989.

62. *Greeley Tribune,* April 7, 1991.

63. Before the fundraising campaign was over, the university also received a $150,000 gift from ConAgra Red Meat Companies and United Agri Products of Greeley (also a ConAgra company). The gift was received in the midst of a controversy between residents in a student/family housing complex and a United Agri Products chemical plant located nearby. Student residents were demanding an investigation of air and water pollution created by the plant, and the university had taken little action.

64. *The Mirror,* September 29, 1989.

65. Russ Bellant, 1992, *The Coors Connection* (Boston: South End Press).

66. *Hispanic Horizons,* March 1991.

67. *Denver Post,* March 30, 1990. *Greeley Tribune,* September 24, 1991.

68. Senate Bill 1738, first introduced in the U.S. Senate in November 1991 by Colorado Senator Tim Wirth, would ban beef imports from European Common Market countries in retaliation for the ban on U.S. beef. Manufacturers of growth-promoting implants cite corporate-sponsored research defending the use of such implants, which nearly double the rate of growth of cattle in feedlots (*Greeley Tribune*, November 10, 1991).

69. *Greeley Tribune*, June 20, 1988.

70. Affidavit signed by David Carney and notarized by Stephen F. Parmenter, included with a Council on Economic Priorities Press Release of April 4, 1991.

71. Letter dated April 6, 1990.

72. David Carney affidavit.

73. *Greeley Tribune*, May 17, 1992.

74. Telephone conversations with Dale Gorman, June 1993.

75. *Greeley Tribune*, May 3, 1992.

76. *Greeley Tribune*, January 24, 1992.

77. *Greeley Tribune*, April 19, 1992.

78. *Greeley Tribune*, April 18, 1992.

79. *Greeley Tribune*, February 21, 1990.

80. Interview with Ford Cleere, March 8, 1990. Cleere told me that he had met Monfort only once and was chagrined. Cleere was retired at the time and has since died.

81. Such labels were common in Monfort's columns in late 1989 and early 1990.

82. *Chicago Tribune*, October 23, 1988.

83. *Greeley Tribune*, July 25, 1990.

84. Interview with Ron Bush, October 6, 1990.

85. *Greeley Tribune*, March 19, 1990.

86. Interview with Ira Tropp, January 8, 1991.

87. See footnotes 63 and 95 this chapter. Controversies over groundwater pollution are also discussed in the following newspaper articles: *Westword*, January 29–February 4, 1992; *Greeley Tribune*, March 28, 1991; *Greeley Tribune*, May 4, 1991; *Greeley Tribune*, May 31, 1992.

88. Conversation with Elaine Schmidt and Carol Andreas in Wes Potter's office, summer 1990.

89. After the Associated Press reported that Monfort was planning to use "fruit scents" to battle odors emananting from its Grand Island, Nebraska, operation (*Greeley Tribune*, July 2, 1993), a *Greeley Tribune* columnist wrote a satire about the situation in Greeley, saying that he had been told by "the local Cow Factory people" that the scent wasn't needed in Greeley because they had already spent millions of dollars to correct the problem. (*Greeley Tribune*, July 10, 1993.)

90. *Greeley Tribune*, August 12, 1990.

91. *Greeley Tribune*, February 14, 1991.

92. Wes Potter, *Greeley Tribune*, February 14, 1991.

93. *Greeley Tribune*, April 5, 1972. *Denver Post*, September 5, 1990; October 7, 1987.

94. *Greeley Tribune*, February 5, 1993.

95. Although dumping of raw waste from meat-processing plants is more likely to be immediately detected, water pollution from feedlots is a more consistent problem. The disposal of waste from feedlots threatens underground water

sources as well as rivers and streams. Regular monitoring of wells in the Greeley area began in 1992. Because state agencies are too understaffed to undertake such a major testing program, the task falls mainly to county officials. Colorado State Senator Tom Norton, whose wife is vice president for legal and political affairs for Monfort, Inc., has been pushing for elimination of the Water Quality Control Division of the State Department of Health. He has been accused of using his influence as a legislator to intervene on Monfort's behalf to secure a waiver of water tests in 1987, when his engineering firm was also working for the Monfort company (*Greeley Tribune,* September 29, 1992).

96. See the Epilogue for further discussion of the Streamlined Inspection System (SIS) and of controversies regarding tainted meat.
97. *Grille Tribune,* March 25, 1989.

CHAPTER 3

1. *Greeley Tribune,* April 8, 1980.
2. Greeley Museum Monfort File, *Greeley Tribune,* (n.d.) 1982.
3. The grievances mentioned also appeared in testimony used in an NLRB suit that the union eventually won against the company. (See Appendix B for findings of the suit.)
4. *Greeley Tribune,* March 25, 1982.
5. *Colorado Business,* May 1985.
6. Interview with Jim Spohr, June 22, 1990. (Subsequent comments by Spohr were taken from this interview unless identified otherwise.)
7. *Greeley Tribune,* November 4, 1979.
8. *Rocky Mountain News,* January 6, 1980.
9. Interview with Joe Benevidez, July 26, 1990. (Subsequent comments by Benevidez were taken from this interview unless identified otherwise.)
10. Interview with Steve Thomas, August 10, 1990. (Subsequent comments by Thomas were taken from this interview unless identified otherwise.)
11. A documentary film titled *Meat,* made at the Monfort plant in 1976 by Fred Wiseman, shows a manager explaining to subordinates plans for speeding up a particular operation. The manager appears stoney-faced and inflexible when told by supervisors that new requirements would be impossible to enforce. He insists calmly but stubbornly that supervisors implement the new plan no matter what the cost, that nobody should be permitted to "waste any time down there."
12. *Greeley Tribune,* November 13, 14, 15, 16, 20, 29, 1979. (Some of the articles on these dates did not appear in the Greeley Museum's Monfort file.)
13. Although this is a widely circulated supposition in Greeley, repeated by workers, I have never seen allegations in a published source.
14. Steve Thomas, "Monfort and Big Business Day" speech given April 17, 1980.
15. *Colorado Business,* May 1985.
16. *Ibid.*
17. *Greeley Tribune,* March 29, 1980.

18. *Rocky Mountain News,* January 6, 1980. Retaliation was especially feared by those who refused to go back to work without a contract in January 1980.
19. Thomas speech April 17, 1980.
20. *Rocky Mountain News,* January 6, 1980.
21. *Rocky Mountain News,* April 1, 1980.
22. Monfort of Colorado newsletter, winter 1978–1979.
23. *Greeley Tribune,* November 3, 1979.
24. Steve Thomas, recalling the trajectory of the strike in a "Monfort and Big Business Day" speech, April 17, 1980.
25. Inequities in meat pricing nationally were the subject of hearings before a Small Business Committee in 1978, in which it was charged that U.S. Department of Agriculture (USDA) officials were helping big meat companies conspire to fix prices paid for live cattle. See A. V. Krebs, 1990, *Heading Toward the Last Roundup: The Big Three's Prime Cut* (Washington, D.C.: Corporate Agribusiness Project). Lawsuits initiated by feedlot operators at this time took thirteen years to go through the courts and were recently dismissed, after many of the plaintiffs were no longer in business. Charles Jennings, the USDA official who was supposed to be watchdogging the industry, resigned his post when the controversy broke and became vice president in charge of public relations at IBP. Congressional inquiries about price-fixing in the red meat industry were renewed in the fall of 1991 (see Chapter 5).
26. *Progressive Grocer,* April 1982.
27. *Business Week,* March 15, 1982.
28. *Business Week,* August 1982.
29. A. V. Krebs, 1990: 52. In 1987, ConAgra agreed to a financial settlement with eight hundred of the employees who had been laid off at the time of the takeover.
30. See Donald D. Stull, 1990, " 'I come to the garden': Changing Ethnic Relations in Garden City, Kansas," *Urban Anthropology,* 19 (4): 303–320; and Michael Broadway, 1990, "Meatpacking and Its Social and Economic Consequences for Garden City, Kansas in the 1980's," *Urban Anthropology,* 19 (4); 321–343.
31. See A. V. Krebs, 1990: 51.
32. Lewie G. Anderson, 1991, *Reform Needed Within the United Food and Commercial Workers International Union* (Gaithersburg, Md.: REAP): 21.
33. Douglas Constance, and William Heffernan, 1989, "IBP's Rise to Dominance in the Meatpacking Industry: Boxed Beef and Busted Unions," Paper presented at the Agriculture, Food and Human Values Society meetings, Little Rock, Arkansas, 20.
34. A. V. Krebs, 1990; 13.
35. *Reap News and Views,* September/October 1992.
36. In 1991, REAP reported that UFCW International President William Wynn received an annual salary of $250,000 and that twenty-four other UFCW officials received salaries of over $100,000.
37. When referring to the decision by Monfort to fine all of its workers, then to rehire them at lower wages in Marshalltown, Iowa, UFCW International spokesman Allen Zack said: "This is not something new for Charlie Sykes, this gimmick of shutting down plants and opening them under another

company is something he's been doing for some time" (as quoted by Gene
Erb, *Des Moines Register,* August 20, 1989).

38. *Greeley Tribune,* April 11, 1990; August 16, 1992; September 14, 1992. *Denver Post,* April 11, 1990. (See Notice to Employees, Appendix B.) Subsequent quotations in this paragraph are taken from these sources and from original court papers on file with the author.

39. The NLRB decision in this case was announced November 22, 1985. Her testimony appears in 298 NLRB No. 16, Ruth de Vargas, 154–163. We interviewed Ruth de Vargas and her family December 13, 1990.

40. *Greeley Tribune,* April 30, 1992.

41. A. V. Krebs, 1990: 54.

CHAPTER 4

1. Confidential source, Our Lady of Peace Catholic Church (Greeley) public hearing, November 19, 1987.

2. Public hearing, November 19, 1987.

3. Ruth de Vargas, public hearing, November 19, 1987.

4. Jesus M. Briones, public hearing, November 19, 1987.

5. Martha Valencia, public hearing, November 19, 1987.

6. Interview with Father Gary Lauenstein, Our Lady of Peace Catholic Church, April 26, 1990. Subsequent comments by Father Lauenstein were taken from this interview.

7. *Greeley Tribune,* April 29, 1987. Interview with Christine Johnson, June 25, 1990. (Subsequent comments by Johnson were taken from this interview unless identified otherwise.)

8. Interview with Steve Clasen, June 19, 1990. (Subsequent comments by Clasen were taken from this interview.)

9. Interview with Sharon Hill, July 21, 1990. (Subsequent comments by Hill were taken from this interview unless identified otherwise.)

10. Weld County Court, Greeley, Colorado, July 1990.

11. Letter from Pete Cohneg to the *Greeley Tribune,* December 18, 1987.

12. Interview with Ron Bush, October 6, 1990. (Subsequent comments by Bush were taken from this interview.)

13. Interview with Martha Valencia, July 19, 1990. (Subsequent comments by Valencia were taken from this interview.)

14. Interview with Paul Apodaca, August 3, 1990. (Subsequent comments by Apodaca were taken from this interview.)

15. Undocumented workers are disparaged as "wetbacks" because Mexicans cross the Rio Grande River to get into the United States.

16. Testimony from public hearings, November 19, 1987.

17. See *Des Moines Register,* August 2, 22, and September 2, 1989. During this controversy, Charlie Sykes resigned from the MSP Board of Directors when news reports indicated that he had organized similar union-busting schemes for IBP and for Monfort in Nebraska. As a result of the Marshalltown situation,

the State of Iowa passed a workers' protection law in 1990 aimed at curtailing exploitive industry recruitment practices. According to members of Prairie-Fire Rural Action, which lobbied for enactment of the law, Monfort was not in compliance with any of its provisions a year later. See *Shattered Promises: The Plight of Non-English Speaking Workers in Iowa's Meatpacking Industry* (Des Moines, Iowa: PrairieFire Rural Action, 1991).

18. Interview with Al Gollas, April 28, 1991.
19. Confidential source.
20. Interview with Rosa Morado, summer 1990. (Subsequent comments by Morado were taken from this interview.)
21. Interview with Robert Muck, summer 1991. (Subsequent comments by Muck were taken from this interview.)
22. Interview with Viviano Torres, August 23, 1990. (Subsequent comments by Torres were taken from this interview.)
23. Interview with Guadalupe Valdez, July 3, 1990.
24. Interview with Kenneth Warembourg, January 12, 1991. (Subsequent comments by Warembourg were taken from this interview.)
25. Interview with Marvin Smith, summer 1990.
26. Interview with Gilberto Maldonado, summer 1990.

CHAPTER 5

1. Telephone conversations with Pamela Nelson, summer 1991.
2. Pamela Nelson left Monfort in March 1986 to work full-time for the UFCW.
3. *Omaha World Herald,* November 6, 1991.
4. OSHA: USDL 91138. Press release, March 27, 1991. U.S. Department of Labor Office of Information and Public Affairs VIII, Denver, Colorado.
5. Patty Stander testimony in the OSHA case that concluded March 27, 1991.
6. Alexander Rhoads, *Dollars and Sense,* March 1992.
7. Interview with Marvin Smith, summer 1990. (Subsequent comments by Smith were taken from this interview.)
8. Interview with Viviano Torres, August 23, 1990. (Subsequent comments by Torres were taken from this interview.)
9. George Villa, member of *Al Frente de Lucha.*
10. Interview with Josie Martinez, July 13, 1990.
11. Report obtained from OSHA's Denver area office through the Freedom of Information Act. Testimony of Phillip L. Immesote, international vice president and director, Food Processing, Packing, and Manufacturing Division, United Food and Commeracial Workers Union, accompanied by Deborah Berkowitz, director of health and safety, March 20, 1991, hearing before the Employment and Housing Subcommittee of the Committee on Government Operations, House of Representatives.
12. Interview with Christine Johnson, June 25, 1990.
13. Interview with Rudy Gonzales, December 13, 1990.
14. Interview with Lorenzo Leyba, June 21, 1990.

15. Conversation with Cecelia Vialpando, December 1992.
16. The case cited is no doubt representative of many situations where employees are made to feel that they must perform physical labor according to a standard set by the strongest men — or suffer the consequences. In our interviews, men complained as much as did women that work expectations were not adjusted to individual differences. However, a study done at an unidentified meatpacking plant showed that the most severe injuries were to women who attempted to do heavy laborers' jobs beyond their physical strength. "Women's lesser physical strength was considered to be their own fault, about which nothing could be done. Whereas men had machines adjusted down to their abilities, women were expected to keep up with the full speed." (Dorothy Remy and Larry Sawers, "Economic Stagnation and Discrimination," in Karen Sacks and Dorothy Remy, eds., 1984, *My Troubles Are Going to Have Trouble With Me: Everyday Trials and Triumphs of Women Workers* [New Brunswick, N.J.: Rutgers University Press]: 95–112.)
17. Interview with Guadelup Valdez, July 3, 1990.
18. Interview with Julie Lujan, June 21, 1990.
19. *Greeley Tribune,* August 15, 1989.
20. *Los Angeles Times,* March 31, 1991.
21. Sharon Cohen, "Danger at Work," October 1989, Associated Press report (unpublished report in author's possession).
22. "A Chain of Setbacks for Meat Workers," *Chicago Tribune,* October 25, 1988.
23. *Greeley Tribune,* April 28, 1991.
24. Testimony given June 6, 1989, issued in Government Document LC 89-602906, *Dramatic Rise in Repetitive Motion Injuries and OSHA's Response,* 127.
25. *Chicago Tribune,* October 26, 1988.
26. *Occupational Hazards,* May 1989.
27. Richard Lee Harris, who was Monfort's health services director for four years (until February 1992), said that the ergonomics program would help a lot if its main features were implemented, but that the company is unwilling to hire more people, implement job pairing (rotation), or make needed mechanical changes. Interview of July 22, 1993. (Subsequent comments by Harris were taken from this interview.) OSHA issued a fine of $10,000 against Monfort August 5, 1993, for failure to implement a strategy against cumulative trauma disorder in its ergonomics program at the Greeley slaughterhouse. Inspection was carried out in response to a specific complaint. A company spokesperson said the fine would be appealed. See *Greeley Tribune,* August 5, 1993.
28. *Denver Post,* February 26, 1990.
29. Interview with Rosa Morado, summer 1990. (Subsequent comments by Morado were taken from this interview.)
30. U.S. Department of Labor Occupational Safety and Health Administration, 1990, *Ergonomics Program Management Guidelines for Meatpacking Plants,* OSHA 3123.
31. Information obtained from OSHA under the Freedom of Information Act indicates that during the 1980s, Monfort was cited fifteen times for specific health and safety violations at its Greeley plants. In eleven of these cases, no penalty was exacted. Penalties for the other four citations totaled $1,500.

32. Richard Lee Harris said that he was instructed by the corporate executive in charge of risk management to submit modified reports. (Interview, July 22, 1993.)

33. *Greeley Tribune,* March 20, 1991. Meakins's comment may not have been gratuitous. A UFCW handbook informs workers that "in cases where employers violate the employee's rights, the government can order the company to bargain with the union." UFCW reformists say that such back-door agreements often lead to sweetheart contracts that do not give workers real protection.

34. *Greeley Tribune,* April 28, 1991.

35. *Ibid.*

36. *Greeley Tribune,* April 28, 1991. David Algeo, the *Tribune* reporter who made public the massive abuse of workers at Monfort, Inc.'s Greeley plants, left town a few months later. *Tribune* employees say that he had met with increasing resistance in investigating worker-management relations at the Monfort/ConAgra plants and felt unduly restricted by the newspaper's cautious approach in reporting on business affairs.

37. Conversation with Julie Vonk, May 26, 1993.

38. According to workers' compensation lawyer Richard Blundell, Groves did not diagnose illnesses as CTDs, which would have been an admission that they were occupationally caused. Instead, he diagnosed these as bursitis, arthritis, or tendonitis. (Interview with Richard Blundell, July 21, 1993.) Since Groves left the Greeley Medical Clinic to assume an executive position at Monfort, most of the company's workers' compensation claims have been handled by Dr. Richard Steig of the Colorado Rehabilitation Institute (CRI). Dr. Steig is the husband of Monfort's risk management director, Lucille Gallagher.

39. For example, Myra Monfort was on the Board of Directors of Greeley's Northern Colorado Medical Center at the time that this testimony was received. The head nurse at Greeley's Sunrise Clinic was married to the safety engineer at the meatpacking plant. (She has since been hired at the Monfort plant herself.) Several health workers in Greeley said that kidney infections, most likely caused by working long hours at Monfort plants without bathroom breaks, were routinely attributed in medical reports to other causes. Tom Deen, a UNC graduate student who had worked twelve years at the Sunrise Clinic was denied entry at the Monfort plant when he attempted to conduct a study of new safety measures reportedly being introduced there.

40. Interview with Marvin Smith, summer 1991. (Subsequent comments by Smith were taken from this interview.)

41. *Chicago Tribune,* October 23, 1988.

42. The tour took place on the day shift August 1, 1991, and was guided by fabrication supervisor Steve Pifs. I toured the plant with a cousin from Minnesota, Stan Pankratz, who had sold cattle to Monfort.

43. Interview with Viviano Torres, August 23, 1990. (Subsequent comments by Torres were taken from this interview.) Several suits have been brought against the company on overtime issues. Monfort received a fine of $30,000 on one of these Another is pending. See *Greeley Tribune,* December 18, 1992; April 2, 1993.

44. Interview with Robert Muck, summer 1991.

45. Interview with Ira Tropp, January 8, 1991. (Subsequent comments by Tropp were taken from this interview.)

46. Interview with Manuel Marquez, summer 1991.

47. Interview with Rudy Gonzales, December 13, 1990.

48. With the permission of those affected, the judge allowed me to tape proceedings held September 12, 1990, in Greeley.

49. Even in situations where workers are not so vulnerable as they are at Monfort, Inc., workers' compensation does not necessarily serve the purposes for which it was established. In Santa Clara County, California, a 1987 study showed that out of 7,214 cases of carpal tunnel syndrome reported by insurance providers, about half of which were work-related, only seventy-one received workers' compensation payments. (Testimony given before a Subcommittee on Employment and Housing, U.S. Congress, June 6, 1989.) Another study showed that those who begin new jobs after applying for compensation earn, on the average, less than half of their previous income. See Victoria V. Buchan, 1989, "Delay in Worker's Compensation Claim Processing: Lifestyle Effects for Worker and Family," *Employee Assistance Quarterly* 5 (2).

50. *Greeley Tribune,* October 20, 1991.

51. *Greeley Tribune,* October 30, 1991.

52. Robert Reich, 1991, "Who Is Them?" *Harvard Business Review* (March/April).

53. The study has not been made public but is discussed in *Cattle Country News,* September 16, 1991.

54. *Greeley Tribune,* October 21, 1992.

55. *Greeley Tribune,* October 4, 1989.

56. *Greeley Tribune,* September 12, 1990.

57. *Greeley Tribune,* December 12, 1990.

58. *Greeley Tribune,* September 29, 1991.

59. As of spring 1992, nearly 10 percent of ConAgra's red meat sales went to foreign markets. Japan bought 42 percent, followed by South Korea (29%) and Mexico (8%). In April 1992, the U.S. government opened an agricultural trade office in Japan. In June 1992, Colorado's Governor Romer led a move to establish a U.S. governors' association office in Moscow to help U.S. businesses take advantage of the "windows of opportunity" in Russia, especially in agribusiness. A push was also on to get the U.S. government to subsidize the sale of meat to Russian farmers. By June 1993, Charlie Monfort said that he was planning to send a representative to China (*Greeley Tribune,* June 6, 1993).

60. Food security is a major issue for "developing" countries, which are forced to export labor-intensive agricultural commodities while importing grains and other basic food supplies. Industrialized countries are also vulnerable to political and economic instability when transnational corporations promote both exports and imports of meat, grains, and other food commodities rather than promoting national self-sufficiency.

61. The current impetus for this practice is discussed by James Petras, January 27, 1990, "The World Market: Battleground for the 1990's," *Economic and Political Weekly.*

CHAPTER 6

1. Department of Agriculture and Department of Commerce sources, as cited by William D. Heffernan, 1989, "Confidence and Courage in the Next 50 Years," *Rural Sociology,* 54 (2): 153.
2. John W. Helmuth, from the introduction to A. V. Krebs, 1990, *Heading Toward the Last Roundup: The Big Three's Prime Cut* (Washington, D.C.: Corporate Agribusiness Project).
3. A. V. Krebs, 1992, *Corporate Reapers: The Book of Agribusiness* (Washington, D.C.: Essential Books): 17.
4. David Griffith, with the research assistance of Vernon Kelly, 1990, *The Impact of the Immigration Reform and Control Act's (IRCA) Employer Sanctions on the U.S. Meat and Poultry Processing Industries* (State University of New York, Binghamton: Institute for Multiculturalism and International Labor).
5. Bruce W. Marion, quoted in Lewie G. Anderson, 1989, *Return to the Jungle: An Examination of Concentration of Power in Meat Packing* (Gaithersburg, Md.: UFCW).
6. A. V. Krebs, 1990: 30.
7. *Wall Street Journal,* August 16, 1991.
8. *Greeley Tribune,* August 13, 1991.
9. Government threats to dismantle the Northern Securities Company aborted a merger agreement between Morris, Armour, and Swift, which had been inititated in May 1902.
10. Mary Yeager, 1981, *Competition and Regulation: The Development of Oligopoly in the Meat Packing Industry* (Greenwich, Conn.: Jai Press): 151.
11. *Ibid.,* 158.
12. *Ibid.,* 183–184.
13. *Ibid.,* 184.
14. Upton Sinclair's novel, *The Jungle,* was first published in 1906. It established the author as a leading advocate of socialism, not only in the United States but throughout the world. Sinclair's contemporary, Jack London, also a socialist, wrote: "What *Uncle Tom's Cabin* did for the black slaves, *The Jungle* has a large chance to do for the white slaves of today." Sinclair himself wrote: "I aimed at the public's heart and by accident I hit it in the stomach."
15. *Greeley Tribune,* October 28, 1990.
16. Roger Burbach and Patricia Flynn, 1980, Agribusiness in the Americas (New York: Monthly Review Press and NACLA): 248.
17. For environmental critiques of the meatpacking industry see Alan B. Durning and Holly B. Brough, 1991, *Taking Stock: Animal Farming and the Environment,* Worldwatch Paper No. 103 (Washington, D.C.: Worldwatch Institute); and Andrew Johnson, 1991, *Factory Farming* (Cambridge, Mass.: Basil Blackwell).
18. At an international meeting of socialists in 1890, May 1 was declared a workers' holiday to commemorate the 8-hour struggle worldwide.
19. See Richard O. Boyer and Herbert M. Morais, 1955, *Labor's Untold Story* (New York: United Electrical, Radio and Machine Workers of America): 91–92.
20. *Ibid.,* 208, quoted from A. Herbst, 1932, *The Negro in the Slaughtering and Meat Industry in Chicago,* Boston.

21. Unpublished paper by Joel Andreas, May 1993: "African-American Workers and the Unions in Chicago's Stockyards: 1917–1919."

22. Melvyn Dubofsky, 1975, *Industrialism and the American Worker, 1865–1920* (New York: Thomas Y. Crowell Co.): 104.

23. See Art Preis, 1964, *Labor's Giant Step: Twenty Years of the CIO* (New York: Pioneer Publishers).

24. Sanford Cohen, 1960;1966, *Labor in the United States,* 2d ed. (Columbus, Ohio: Charles E. Merrill Books) 502.

25. Such brand names as Swift and Armour were retained initially on beef products after companies were bought out. Because IBP entered the meat-packing business by building new plants rather than by engaging in buyouts, and because the IBP name was marred by racketeering charges brought against its owners, IBP still suffers a handicap in marketing. Cargill and ConAgra also had advantages because of earlier experience as transnational corporations.

26. The "P" in "P-9" indicates that the local was formerly a United Packinghouse Workers local, identified with the CIO.

27. See Bennet Harrison and Barry Bluestone, 1988, *The Great U-Turn: Corporate Restructuring and the Polarizing of America* (New York: Basic Books); and Kim Moody, 1988, *An Injury to All: The Decline of American Unionism* (New York: Verso).

28. Kim Moody, 1988: 288–302; Labor Research Review No. 13, 1989, *Solidarity Across Borders: U.S. Labor in a Global Economy* (Chicago: Midwest Center for Labor Research): 63–65. The AFL–CIO's Department of International Affairs (DIA) is funded almost exclusively by U.S. government agencies but is not subject to congressional oversight nor to the Freedom of Information Act. The DIA staff denies links with the Central Intelligence Agency, but close coop-eration has been well documented in a number of sources, including Beth Sims, 1991, *Workers of the World Undermined: American Labor's Role in U.S. Foreign Policy* (Boston: South End Press).

29. Besides supporting antilabor military coups in a number of countries, includ-ing Brazil, Chile, and the Dominican Republic, the AFL–CIO refused to support sanctions against the South African government that were called for by labor unions in that country. The AFL–CIO's Cold War legacy is so strong that the federation has not given support to proposals for national healthcare programs in the United States on the grounds that these pose a danger to the free enterprise system.

30. President Reagan's successful effort to break the air traffic controllers' strike in 1981 is often considered a turning point in the delegitimizing of unions, but the Carter administration had prepared the way by giving the Federal Aviation Administration authority to undermine the authority of air traffic controllers on the job, forcing a showdown with the Professional Air Traffic Controllers Organization (PATCO), and the AFL–CIO turned its back on PATCO. See Kim Moody, 1988: 304–306.

31. See John Cavanagh, et al. 1988, *Trade's Hidden Costs: Worker Rights in a Changing World Economy* (Washington, D.C.: Institute for Policy Studies).

32. Free production zones, which had been established in twenty-one countries by 1991, allow foreign companies to operate outside of prevailing tax laws and

other regulatory structures. These zones foreshadow larger international agreements encompassed in free trade initiatives currently being negotiated.

33. Among these are several organizations in the U.S. Midwest that include meatpacking workers' rights as central to their concerns, including: Prairie-Fire, 550 11th St., Des Moines, Iowa 50309; and Center for Rural Affairs, P.O. Box 405, Walthill, Nebraska 68067.

34. *Dollars and Sense,* March 1992. AP report of February 14, 1993.

35. Maura I. Toro-Morn observes that migration patterns are based on decisions made by corporations and governments, while individual responses are based on family pressure and worker networking opportunities. See "New Theoretical Frontiers: Taking Gender into Account in the Study of Migration," Paper given at the Midwest Sociological Society meetings, Des Moines, Iowa, 1991. Mexican women working in the United States say that they are motivated largely by family goals and opportunities, even though their decisions often contradict cultural prerogatives traditionally accorded women. See Margarita B. Melville, ed., 1988, *Mexicanas at Work in the United States,* Mexican American Studies Monograph No. 5 (Houston, Tex.: Mexican American Studies Program, University of Houston).

36. UFWA affiliates that continued to organize in other parts of the country broke with the union or were expelled. Some of these continued to promote internationalism and socialism.

37. For a concise discussion of these concepts, see Peter Knapp and Alan J. Spector, *Crisis and Change: Basic Questions of Marxist Sociology* (Chicago: Nelson-Hall Publishers, 1991): 225–229.

38. U.S. Department of Labor statistic.

39. See Claudia von Werlhof, "The Proletarian Is Dead: Long Live the Housewife!" in Maria Mies, et al., 1988, *Women: The Last Colony* (London: Zed Books): 168–181. Von Werlhof discusses "un-free" labor that characterizes modern industrial production processes in the global capitalist economy. Her discussion focuses on "femalized," "marginalized," or "houseified" workers who "must demonstrate love even when they do not feel any." The implications of her analysis go far beyond women as workers, because she indicates that any employees recruited from the ranks of small peasants, seasonal agricultural laborers, service workers (including prostitutes), contract and home-workers, and petty traders demonstrate the characteristics sought by world-market manufacturers.

40. At an Excel meatpacking plant 50 miles from Greeley, female workers who had previously demonstrated loyalty to the company were the first to walk off the job in November 1991, when tables were understaffed and supervisors refused to help.

EPILOGUE

1. Kathleen Hughes, 1983, *Return to the Jungle: How the Reagan Administration Is Imperiling the Nation's Meat and Poultry Inspection Program* (Washington, D.C.: Center for the Study of Responsible Law).

2. *Denver Post,* March 28, 1991. "Meat Giant Monfort under Siege," *Denver Post,* July 18, 1993. The amount of the fine is still being disputed.
3. Kay Norton's appointment to the OSHA advisory committee was opposed by residents of Greeley who initiated a petition addressed to newly elected President Bill Clinton and the U.S. Department of Labor, demanding her removal. Six months later Norton and ten other last-minute Bush appointees were taken off the safety board (*Greeley Tribune,* June 2, 1993).
4. *Greeley Tribune,* June 17, 1992. According to one source, production increased by 40 percent. See *Mother Jones,* July/August 1992.
5. *Mother Jones,* July/August 1992.
6. *Ibid.*
7. Patrick Armijo, "Meat Inspection War Brews," *Greeley Tribune,* July 28, 1992.
8. *Greeley Tribune,* July 26, 1992.
9. *New York Times,* January 27 and February 6, 1993. The USDA conducted surprise inspections in ninety beef slaughterhouses in May 1993 and found widespread sanitation problems. The Monfort plant in Greeley was mentioned in AP reports as one where tainted carcasses were found.
10. *Greeley Tribune,* February 5, 1993. USDA meat inspectors say that meat that is washed and not trimmed after contamination prejudices consumers because it embeds harmful bacteria and adds water to the weight of the meat. (April 6, 1990, letter to Clayton Yeutter, secretary of agriculture, USDA.)
11. "Bacteria in the Meat? Just Turn up the Heat, but Not on the Feds," *Greeley Tribune* (reprinted from the *Los Angeles Times*), February 7, 1993.
12. *Greeley Tribune* (AP report), March 2, 1993.
13. Editorial, *Greeley Tribune,* July 29, 1992.
14. "Monfort: USDA Changes Won't Affect Operation," *Greeley Tribune,* July 29, 1992.
15. "Here's the Beef: Underreporting of Injuries, OSHA's Policy of Exempting Companies from Programmed Inspections Based on Injury Records, and Unsafe Conditions in the Meatpacking Industry." 42nd Report by the Committee on Government Operations together with additional views, March 30, 1988, 22.
16. The organizers called themselves Citizens Against the Slaughter of Employees, as testified by Norma Hill in a statement prepared for a March 20, 1991, hearing before the Employment and Housing Subcommittee of the Committee on Government Operations, House of Representatives. Another death at the Grand Island plant occurred November 21, 1992. OSHA proposed a fine of $42,500 for violations of safety rules applicable in the case, as well as for other violations occurring after the previous ruling of March 1991. Monfort is scheduled to challenge the fines July 27, 1993. See AP report, November 22, 1992; *Greeley Tribune,* April 20, 1993.
17. *Labor Notes,* #161 August 1992.
18. Safe Workplace Colorado! is an organization that is attempting to place before voters an initiative that reads: "Anyone who, in the course of business, knowingly maintains an unsafe work environment shall not be immune from suit for a resulting injury or death by a worker and his or her survivors for any and all damages and losses." The group did not secure enough signatures in time for November 1992 elections.

19. Letter to the *Greeley Tribune,* winter (n.d.) 1992.
20. *Greeley Tribune,* January 14, 1992.
21. *Greeley Tribune,* July 18, 1993.
22. *Greeley Tribune,* February 3, 1993.
23. *Ibid.*
24. *New York Times,* November 27, 1992.
25. Kathleen Stanley, 1991, "The Role of Immigrant and Refugee Labor in the Restructuring of the Midwestern Meatpacking Industry," Paper prepared for the Midwest Sociological Society meetings, Des Moines, Iowa.
26. *Greeley Tribune,* October 21, 1992.
27. Center for Rural Affairs Special Report on the North American Free Trade Agreement, October, 1992.Center for Rural Affairs, P.O. Box 406, Walthill, NE 68067–0406.
28. *New York Times,* November 4, 1992.
29. The purchasing power of Mexicans dropped 50 percent in the 1980s. (Labor Notes # 127 [March 1990].)
30. *Grand Island Independent,* October 1, 1992.
31. *Greeley Tribune,* September 24, 1992.
32. *Grand Island Independent,* September 27, 1992.
33. *Labor Notes,* # 160 July 1992.
34. Interview with Francisco Cortez, December 7, 1992. (Subsequent comments by Cortez were taken from this interview.)
35. Associated Press report of February 14, 1993.
36. At the national level, Monfort lobbyists succeeded in winning a $21 million contract for the Mapelli Food Company (owned by Monfort, Inc.) to ship fresh beef to U.S. bases in Europe. (*Greeley Tribune,* July 12, 1993.)
37. *Al Frente de Lucha,* January 1991.
38. "For Hispanic Immigrants, a Higher Job-injury Risk," *New York Times,* February 18, 1992.
39. *Greeley Tribune,* June 14, 1992. The author was Jorge Amaya, outgoing director of the League of United Latin American Citizens (LULAC) and director of the Monfort Learning Center at Rocky Mountain SER.
40. *Greeley Tribune,* June 14, October 4, 1992.
41. Corporations and corporate elites will face new challenges as disabled workers increasingly add their voices to other groups demanding dignity and respect in the workplace. Responding to controversy over the Americans with Disabilities Act of 1991 (ADA) (see *Greeley Tribune,* June 2, 1991), a *Greeley Tribune* reader wrote to the editor:

    > Businesses such as Monfort's, among many others, are users of people. They take an ounce or pound of flesh and when you are no use to them, you are discarded. The ADA will help protect you. A corporation's goal is profit. Corporations only regard their employees when it is advantageous to do so. Corporations do not believe in the humanity and dignity of the individual, just the almighty dollar. When the ADA mandates a little humanity, the complaint, of course, is expense. (*Greeley Tribune,* June 14, 1991)

    The ADA went into effect in July 1992. It defines, among other things, the rights of the disabled in workplaces.

42. Myra Monfort's letter is dated October 12, 1992. Ken Monfort has since resigned from the ConAgra Board of Directors (*Greeley Tribune,* May 7, 1993).
43. "A Big Inconvenience — Severed Arm Healing Nicely," *Greeley Tribune,* October 14, 1992.
44. Interview with UFCW organizer Ed Thompson, July 1, 1993.
45. *Greeley Tribune,* July 22, 1993.
46. *Ibid.*
47. The concerns of workers that the company will not be willing to listen to their complaints — with or without a union — are heightened by the news that ConAgra's income dropped for the fourth quarter of fiscal 1993. The red meat segment of ConAgra saw its profits drop reportedly because of bad weather, which increased the cost of raw materials. (*Greeley Tribune,* July 7, 1993.)

References

Acuna, Rodolfo. 1988. *Occupied America: A History of Chicanos.* 3d ed. New York: Harper and Row.

Anderson, Lewie G. 1989. *Return to the Jungle: An Examination of Concentration of Power in Meat Packing.* Gaithersburg, Md.: UFCW.

Anderson, Lewie G. 1991. *Reform Needed Within the United Food and Commercial Workers International Union.* Gaithersburg, Md.: REAP.

Andreas, Carol. 1991. "Community Issues in Meatpacking." Paper presented at the Midwest Sociological Society meetings, Des Moines, Iowa.

Barkema, Alan D., and Mark Drabenstott. 1990. "A Crossroads for the Cattle Industry." *Economic Review* (July/August).

Barkema, Alan D., Mark Drabenstott, and Julie Stanley. 1990. "Processing Food in Farm States: An Economic Development Strategy for the 1990's." *Economic Review* (November/December).

Barrera, Mario. 1979. *Race and Class in the Southwest: A Theory of Racial Inequality.* Notre Dame, Ind.: University of Notre Dame Press.

Barrett, James R. 1987. *Work and Community in the Jungle: Chicago's Packinghouse Workers, 1894–1922.* Chicago: University of Illinois Press.

Berman, Dan. 1978. *Death on the Job: Occupational Health and Safety Struggles in the United States.* New York: Monthly Review Press.

Bonanno, Alessandro. 1991. "The Globalization of the Agricultural and Food Sector and Theories of the State." Paper presented at the Midwest Sociological Society meetings, Des Moines, Iowa.

Bonanno, Alessandro, et al. 1993. *From Columbus to ConAgra: The Globalization of Agriculture and Food.* Lawrence, Kans.: Kansas University Press.

Boyer, Richard O. and Herbert M. Morais. 1955. *Labor's Untold Story.* New York: United Electrical, Radio and Machine Workers of America.

Brecher, Jeremy, and Tim Costello eds. 1991. *Building Bridges: The Emerging Grassroots Coalition of Labor and Community.* New York: Monthly Review Press.

Broadway, Michael. 1990. "Meatpacking and Its Social and Economic Consequences for Garden City, Kansas in the 1980s." *Urban Anthropology.* 19 (4): 321–343.

Brody, David. 1964. *The Butcher Workmen: A Study of Unionization.* Cambridge, Mass.: Harvard University Press.

Brown, Dennis M. 1991. "Linkages Between Meat Processing and the Economy of Local Communities." Paper presented at the Association of American Geographers meetings, Miami, Florida.

Burbach, Roger, and Patricia Flynn. 1980. *Agribusiness in the Americas.* New York: Monthly Review Press and NACLA.

Cavanagh, John, et al. 1980. *Trade's Hidden Costs: Worker Rights in Changing World Economy.* Washington, D.C.: Institute for Policy Studies.

Center for Rural Affairs Newsletter. P.O. Box 405, Walthill, NE 68067-0405.

Chase-Dunn, Christopher. 1989. *Global Formation: Structures of the World-Economy.* Oxford: Basil Blackwell.

Clorfene-Casten, Liane. 1992. "Unhappy Meals." *Mother Jones.* (July/August).

Cohen, Sanford. 1960; 1966. *Labor in the United States.* 2d ed. Columbus, Ohio: Charles E. Merrill Books.

Constance, Douglas H., and William D. Heffernan. 1989. "IBP's Rise to Dominance in the Meatpacking Industry: Boxed Beef and Busted Unions." Paper presented at the Agriculture, Food and Human Values Society meetings, Little Rock, Arkansas.

Constance, Douglas H., and William D. Heffernan. 1991. "The Global Food System: Joint Ventures in the U.S.S.R., Eastern Europe, and the People's Republic of China." Paper presented at the Midwest Sociological Society meetings, Des Moines, Iowa.

Constance, Douglas H. and William D. Heffernan. 1991. "The Global Poultry Agro/Food Complex." *International Journal of Sociology of Food and Agriculture.* 1 (1).

Davis, Irving F., Jr., and William H. Metzler. 1958. *Sugar Beet Labor in Northern Colorado.* Technical bulletin no. 63. Fort Collins, Colo.: Colorado State University Experiment Station.

Deutsch, Sarah. 1987. *No Separate Refuge: Culture, Class, and Gender on an Anglo-Hispanic Frontier in the American Southwest, 1880–1940.* New York: Oxford University Press.

Dubovsky, Melvyn. 1975. *Industrialism and the American Worker, 1865–1920.* New York: Thomas Y. Crowell.

Durning, Alan B., and Holly B. Brough. 1991. *Taking Stock: Animal Farming and the Environment.* Worldwatch Paper No. 103. Washington, D.C.: Worldwatch Institute.

Gouveia, Lourdes. 1991. "Reaping the Benefits of the Farm Crisis: Meatpacking in Rural Nebraska." Paper presented at the Midwest Sociological Society meetings, Des Moines, Iowa.

Gouveia, Lourdes. 1992. "Dances with Cows: Beefpacking's Impact on Garden City, Kansas and Lexington, Nebraska." Paper prepared for national conference on "New Factory Workers in Old Farming Communities: Costs and Consequences of Relocating Meat Industries." Queenstown, Maryland.

Griffith, David, with the research asistance of Vernon Kelly. 1990. *The Impact of the Immigration Reform and Control Act's (IRCA) Employer Sanctions on the U.S. Meat and Poultry Processing Industries.* State University of New York, Binghamton: Institute for Multiculturalism and International Labor.

Hardy, Green. 1990. *On Strike at Hormel: The Struggle for a Democratic Labor Movement.* Philadelphia: Temple University Press.

Harrison, Bennet, and Barry Bluestone. 1988. *The Great U-Turn: Corporate Restructuring and the Polarizing of America.* New York: Basic Books.

Havens, Eugene A., ed., with Gregory Hooks, Patrick H. Mooney, and Max J. Pfeffer. 1986. *Studies in the Transformation of U.S. Agriculture.* Boulder, Colo.: Westview Press.

Heffernan, William D. 1989. "Confidence and Courage in the Next 50 Years." *Rural Sociology.* 54 (2): 149–168.

Heffernan, William D. 1992. "Restructuring of the U.S. Meat, Poultry, and Fish-Processing Industries in the Global Economy." Paper prepared for national conference on "New Factory Workers in Old Farming Communities: Costs and Consequences of Relocating Meat Industries." Queenstown, Maryland.

Hillman, Jimmye S., and Andrew Schmitz. 1979. *International Trade and Agriculture: Theory and Policy.* Boulder, Colo.: Westview Press.

Hughes, Kathleen. 1983. *Return to the Jungle: How the Reagan Administration Is Imperiling the Nation's Meat and Poultry Inspection Programs.* Washington, D.C.: Center for the Study of Responsible Law.

Johnson, Andrew. 1991. *Factory Farming.* Cambridge, Mass.: Basil Blackwell.

Krebs, A. V. 1990. *Heading Toward the Last Roundup: The Big Three's Prime Cut.* Washington, D.C.: Corporate Agribusiness Project.

Krebs, A. V. 1992. *Corporate Reapers: The Book of Agribusiness.* Washington, D.C.: Essential Books.

Labor Research Review No. 13. 1989. *Solidarity Across Borders: U.S. Labor in a Global Economy.* Chicago: Midwest Center for Labor Research.

LaBotz, Dan. 1992. *Mask of Democracy: Labor Suppression in Mexico Today.* Boston: South End Press.

Lecompte, Janet. 1978. *Pueblo, Hardscrabble, Greenhorn: The Upper Arkansas, 1832–1856.* Norman, Okla.: University of Oklahoma Press.

Limprecht, Jane E. 1989. *ConAgra Who? $15 Billion and Growing: The Story of ConAgra's First 70 Years.* ConAgra, Inc.

Lobao, Linda M. 1990. *Locality and Inequality: Farm and Industry Structure and Socioeconomic Conditions.* Albany, N.Y.: State University of New York Press.

Melville, Margarita B., ed. 1988. *Mexicanas at Work in the United States.* Mexican American Studies Monograph No. 5. Houston, Tex.: Mexican American Studies Program, University of Houston.

Mies, Maria, Veronika Bennholdt-Thomsen, and Claudia Von Werlhof. 1988. *Women: The Last Colony.* London: Zed Books.

Moody, Kim. 1988. *An Injury to All: The Decline of American Unionism.* New York: Verso.

Negrey, Cynthia, and Mary Beth Zickel. 1991. "Industrial Shifts and Uneven Development: Patterns of Growth and Decline in U.S. Metropolitan Areas." Paper presented at the Midwest Sociological Society meetings, Des Moines, Iowa.

Pankratz, Eileen Pembroke Martisko. 1989. *The Rural Crisis: One Woman's Journey from Innocence to a Worldview.* Master's thesis, Mankato State University, Mankato, Minnesota.

Peake, Ora B. 1937. *The Colorado Range Cattle Industry.* Glendale, Calif.: Arthur H. Clark.

Petras, James. 1990. "The World Market: Battleground for the 1990's." *Economic and Political Weekly* (Jan. 27): 35–46.

Platt, LaVonne Godwin, ed. 1987. *Hope for the Family Farm: Trust God and Care for the Land.* Newton, Kans.: Faith and Life Press.

PrairieFire Rural Action. 1991. *Shattered Promises: The Plight of Non-English Speaking Workers in Iowa's Meatpacking Industry.* Des Moines, Iowa: PrairieFire Rural Action.

Preis, Art. 1964. *Labor's Giant Step: Twenty Years of the CIO.* New York: Pioneer Publishers.

Rachleff, Peter. 1993. *Hard-pressed in the Heartland: The Hormel Strike and the Future of the Labor Movement.* Boston: South End Press.

Rifkin, Jeremy. 1992. *Beyond Beef: The Rise and Fall of the Cattle Culture.* New York, New York: Dutton.

Sakai, J. 1983. *Settlers: The Mythology of the White Proletariat.* Chicago: Morningstar Press.

Seiler, Lauren, and Gene Summers. 1979. "Corporate Involvement in Community Affairs." *The Sociological Quarterly* (Summer): 375–386.

Sims, Beth. 1991. *Workers of the World Undermined: American Labor's Role in U.S. Foreign Policy.* Boston: South End Press.

Sinclair, Upton. 1906;1946. *The Jungle.* New York: Signet Classics.

Skaggs, Jimmy M. 1986. *Prime Cut: Livestock Raising and Meatpacking in the United States, 1607–1983.* College Station, Tex.: Texas A&M Press.

Stanley, Kathleen. 1991. "The Role of Immigrant and Refugee Labor in the Restructuring of the Midwestern Meatpacking Industry." Paper prepared for the Midwest Sociological Society meetings, Des Moines, Iowa.

Stull, Donald D. 1990. " 'I come to the garden': Changing Ethnic Relations in Garden City, Kansas." *Urban Anthropology,* 19 (4): 303–320.

Toro-Morn, Maura I. 1991. "New Theoretical Frontiers: Taking Gender into Account in the Study of Migration." Paper presented at the Midwest Sociological Society meetings, Des Moines, Iowa.

United States Government. "Underreporting of Occupational Injuries and Its Impact on Workers' Safety." Part 1 — March 19, 1987.

"Underreporting of Occupational Injuries and Its Impact on Workers' Safety." Part 2 — May 6, 1987.

"Underreporting of Occupational Injuries and Its Impact on Workers' Safety." Part 3 — September 21, 1987.

"Here's the Beef: Underreporting of Injuries, OSHA's Policy of Exempting Companies from Programmed Inspections Based on Injury Records, and Unsafe Conditions in the Meatpacking Industry." March 30, 1988.

"Dramatic Rise in Repetitive Motion Injuries and OSHA's Response." June 6, 1989.

"Ergonomics Program Management Guidelines for Meatpacking Plants." U.S. Department of Labor, 1990.

"OSHA's New Plan to Protect Meatpacking Workers from Repetitive Motion Hazards." March 20, 1991.

"Occupational Injuries and Illnesses in the United States by Industry, 1990." U.S. Department of Labor, April 1992.

Hearing on H.R. 1664, Corporate Whistleblower Protection." August 5, 1992.

Wade, Louise Carroll. 1987. *Chicago's Pride: The Stockyards, Packingtown, and Environs in the Nineteenth Century.* Chicago: University of Illinois Press.

Wilbur, Michael. 1990. "Monopoly Power in the Meatpacking Industry." *Reap News and Views.* December.

Yeager, Mary. 1981. *Competition and Regulation: The Development of Oligopoly in the Meat Packing Industry.* Greenwich, Conn.: Jai Press.

Zipp, John F. 1984. "Plant Closings and the Conflict Between Capital and Labor." *Research in Social Movements, Conflict and Change.* 6: 225–248.

Index

Accidents. *See* Safety and health
Additives. *See* Safety and health
Addoms, Samuel, 39, 61, 71
Adolph Coors Company (Golden, Colorado), 49
AFL. *See* American Federation of Labor
AFL-CIO, 72, 143, 147, 148, 165; foreign policy and, 145, 146, 206(n28), 206(n29)
African-Americans, 107, 141, 191(n3)
Agribusiness. *See* Agroindustry
Agroindustry, 19, 27, 33
Al Frente de Lucha, x, 17, 149
Al Frente de Lucha (bulletin), 18–19
Algeo, David, 203(n36)
Allard, Wayne, 127, 158, 160
Amalgamated Meat Cutters and Butcher Workmen of North America, 37, 72, 142, 143
Amaya, Jorge, 23, 209(n39)
American Council on Science and Health, 158
American Federation of Labor (AFL), 12, 141, 144, 145
American Meat Institute, 45, 46, 50, 53, 114, 155
American Society of Safety Engineers (ASSE), 171
Americans with Disabilities Act, 209(n41)
Anderson, Lewie, 77
Anheuser Busch, 193(n37)
Anschutz, Phillip, 54
Anti-trust: investigations, 47, 128, 135, 205(n9); lawsuits, 42, 76
Apodaca, Paul, 101–102
Aragon, Eddie, 92
Armour and Company, 38, 135, 142, 206(n25); buyouts, 5, 43, 75; master contract with, 73, 143
ASSE. *See* American Society of Safety Engineers
Associated Press, 23

Backhauling, 34
Bankruptcy, 75
Beatrice Foods, 43

Beef production. *See* Meat consumption; Meat processing and packing industry
Benavidez, Joe, 62, 64, 66, 71
Benefits: entitlement, 70, 93, 162 (*see also* Company policies (Monfort)); reduction, 5, 24, 60, 67–68, 75
Beyond Beef: The Rise and Fall of the Cattle Culture, 52
Blundell, Richard, 159, 203(n38)
Border Industrialization Program, 148
Border Patrol (U.S.), 1, 13
Boxed beef, viii, 3, 36, 38, 191(n2)
Boycott, 68
Bracero programs, 15, 22, 192(n9)
Brown, Hank, 38–39, 128, 158, 161
Brown, Rev. Steve, 92
Brown, Rev. Sue, 92
Bush, Ron, 90, 99, 100, 103
Business Week, 74, 75
By-products, 36

CACI. *See* Colorado Association of Commerce and Industry Capitalist development, vii, 34, 131, 138, 153 (*see also* Corporations); opposition to, 151–52; unions and, 144–47
Cargill, 6, 42, 76, 137, 147
Carney, David, 50, 51
Cattlemen's Beef Promotion and Research Board, 158
Cattle ranching. *See* Farming
Center for the Study of Responsible Law, 155
CHAMPS. *See* Corporate Health and Medical Programs, Inc.
Chavez, Cesar, 148
Chemical exposure, 175. *See also* Safety and health
Chicago Federation of Labor, 141
Chicago Tribune, 53
Chicanos. *See* Hispanics
Childcare services, 104
Churches, 20, 24, 25
CIO. *See* Congress of Industrial Organizations
Citizens Against the Slaughter of Employees, 208(n16)

Citizens for Clean Air, 56
Civil Rights Commission, 102
Clasen, Steve, 93, 99
Class divisions, 28–29, 33
Cleanliness. *See* Safety and health
Cleere, Ford, 197(n80)
Clinics, 24
Cole, David, xi
Colonias. See Housing
Colorado Association of Commerce and
    Industry (CACI), 125–26, 165
Colorado Beef Council, 157
Colorado Board of Agriculture, 49
Colorado Cattle Feeders Association, 50
Colorado Cattlemen's Association, 50
Colorado Farm Bureau, 50
Colorado Meat Dealers Association, 71
Colorado Medical Society Workmen's
    Compensation Advisory Committee,
    118
Colorado Occupational Safety and Health
    Act, 128
Colorado Rehabilitation Institute,
    203(n38)
Colorado State University (CSU) (Fort Col-
    lins), 15, 49
Committee, The, 32, 33
Committee, The Other, 33
Communism, 141, 142, 150, 151, 153
Community needs, vii–viii, 134
Company policies (Monfort), xi; bonuses,
    40–41, 119, 120, 122, 162; documenta-
    tion of workers, 19, 21, 192(n16); drug
    use and testing, 122; health benefits,
    24, 67; hiring and firing, 22, 41, 61, 97;
    hours paid, 120; job security, 97; medi-
    cal staff, 85–87, 89, 105, 118, 203(n39);
    medical treatment of workers, 85, 105,
    109, 111–13, 117, 121; profit-sharing
    plan, 38, 40–41, 70, 122–23; retire-
    ment and wage benefits, 38, 60, 67;
    safety incentive plan, 119; sick leave,
    86; whistleblowers, treatment of, 177–
    83
Company records (Monfort): accident re-
    ports, 182; documentation of workers,
    19, 21–22, 192(n16); inaccuracies and
    fabrications, 71, 135, 156, 181–82,
    202(n32), 203(n39); investigative re-
    ports, 182; withholding, 101–11, 135
ConAgra, Inc., viii; asset acquisition, 43,
    76, 77; exports and foreign operations,
    129, 130, 147, 161, 204(n59); inspec-
    tion violations, 51; labor force restruc-
turing, 75; legislation, favorable, 127–
    28, 130; Monfort merger with (*see*
    Merger [Monfort/ConAgra, Inc.]); non-
    meat operations, 47; profitability, 35,
    43, 210(n47); settlements with work-
    ers, 199(n29); size and market power,
    5–6, 42, 43, 47, 206(n25); university
    patronage, 48–50
ConAgra Red Meats, viii, 35, 45, 118; Inter-
    national Sales Corporation, 43–44
Confidentiality, necessity of, x
Congressional Beef Caucus, 39
Congress of Industrial Organizations
    (CIO), 141, 142, 145
Consumer protection regulations, 6, 50–
    52; corporate opposition to, viii, 34
Contracts. *See* Master contracts
Cooperatives, 153
Coors, Joseph, 54
Coors, William, 49
Corporate Health and Medical Programs,
    Inc. (CHAMPS), 118
Corporations: conflict with worker and
    community needs, vii–viii, ix, 6, 56,
    126, 131, 134, 138–39, 150, 151; con-
    trol of communities, 7, 47, 126–27,
    131, 134, 207(n35); economic power,
    47–48, 57, 137; educational institu-
    tions and, 126; governmental assis-
    tance to, 6, 34, 133, 137–38, 161;
    governmental oversight of, 137, 142;
    resources and markets, access to and
    control of, viii, 6, 46–47, 131, 133, 137,
    144; self-protection, 47–48, 57, 138–
    39; transnational policies and needs,
    vii, 146, 151, 204(n60)
Cortez, Francisco, 164–65
Cost-of-living agreements, 38, 67, 75, 142
Council on Economic Priorities (CEP), 51
"Coyotes," 19, 22, 192(n15)
CSU. *See* Colorado State University
Cudahy Company, 38, 73, 142, 143
Cumulative trauma disorders. *See* Repeti-
    tive motion disorders

Deen, Tom, 203(n39)
Department of Agriculture. *See* United
    States Department of Agriculture De-
    partment of Labor; United States De-
    partment of Labor Deportation;
    Mexicans
DES. *See* Diethylstilbesterol
de Vargas, Ruth, 187, 200(n39)
Dickenson, Ruby, xi

Dickeson, Robert, 32, 48
Diethylstilbesterol (DES), 34, 194(n15). *See also* Safety and health, additives
Disassembly lines, 3, 42, 66
Documentation. *See* Company policies (Monfort), documentation of workers; Immigrant workers, documentation

Eastman Kodak, 27, 126–27
Eat Crow Club, 39
Economic Developers' Council of Colorado, 160
E. J. Miller Enterprises (Utah), 77
Employment and Redevelopment Office, 41
Environmental concerns, vii, 6; corporate opposition to regulation, viii, 53, 54; overgrazing, 127–28; pollution (*see* Pollution)
Environmental Monthly, The, 56
Environmental Protection Agency, 36
Equipment. *See* Safety and health, equipment controls and maintenance Ergonomics, 114, 116, 117, 174, 201–202(n16), 202(n27)
Esmark, 74, 75
Excel, 6, 22, 42, 76, 134
Exits, emergency, 176–77
Exporting, viii, 136–37; capital, 146; ConAgra, 130, 204(n59); Monfort disregard of rules, 173; non-U.S. markets, 43, 50, 130, 136, 147

Family of Christ Presbyterian Church (Greeley), 92
Farming: business failures, 33, 47–48, 133, 134; cattle ranching, 9, 46, 134; effects of global economy, 133, 137, 148; exploitation of immigrants, 11, 14, 15; feedcrop contracts, 46
Farmland Industries, 47
Farmworkers: *bracero* programs, 15, 22, 192(n9); exploitation of, 11, 14, 15; union organization of, 12 Farr, W. D., 32
Federal funding: clinics, 24; crop subsidies, 46; economic development office, 41; export efforts, 44; housing subsidies, 28; land acquisition, 10, 133; sewage plant, 36; worker training and recruitment, 24, 39, 41, 192(n29)
Federation for American Immigration Reform, 23
Feedlots, 3, 10, 35, 36; pollution problems, 56, 197–98(n95)

First Congregational Church (Greeley), 32
Food Safety and Inspection Service, 50
Food Security Act of 1985, 128
Food stamp program, 28
Forbes magazine, 42
Foreign policy, effect on labor, 144–47
Fort Lewis College (Durango), 49
Fort Morgan (Colorado), 22
Forward contracting, 46

Gallagher, Lucille, 203(n38)
Gallegos, Christine, 83–84
Garden City (Kansas), 47
Garrison, Ann, x, 33
George Hormel & Company, 73, 77, 143, 144
Gorman, Dale, 51–52
Government Accountability Project, 177
Government regulation, 34, 38, 134–35, 155–58
Grand Island (Nebraska), 171
Grand Island Independent, 162
Grand Island processing plant, 39, 43, 68, 171; inspection abuses, 50–51; INS raid, 161–63; safety abuses in, 31, 110, 117, 156, 172–183, 193(n1); union organization in, 39, 68, 110
Grazing, viii
Great Western Sugar Company, 10–13, 16, 26
Greeley, Horace, 9
Greeley (Colorado), viii, 9–10; anti-union actions, 59–60, 67, 70, 96; churches, 20, 24, 25, 32; civic center, 45; Economic Development Action Project, 152; economic impact of Monfort plant, 5, 6, 33, 59–60, 70; employment statistics, 26; Hispanic community in, 17–19, 20–21, 23, 25, 33, 167; housing in (*see* Housing); Northern Colorado Medical Center, 45, 111, 113, 203(n39); population, 20, 25, 26; political influence of Monfort, 18–19, 44–45, 168; political power and structure, 21, 32; social disparity, 28, 33, 103; social services, 20–21, 24; Sunrise Clinic, 113, 203(n39); transient workforce, 20; UNC, relationship with, 48–49
Greeley Medical Clinic, 113, 118, 203(n38)
Greeley Municipal Museum, ix
Greeley slaughterhouse (Monfort): closure, 39, 40, 59, 70; cutbacks, 60–61; financial records, 61; harassment of workers, 67, 69, 79–80; INS investiga-

tion, 122–23, 162; negotiations, 61–62, 67–68; overtime, 203(n43); production speed-up, 61–66, 69, 105, 114–17, 121, 157; rest periods, 119–20; safety (*see* Safety and health); strikes at, 38, 39, 59–60, 67–69; surveillance in, 72; turnover, 92; union organizing, 59, 78, 163, 203(n33); union presence, 5, 39, 40, 48, 59, 73–74, 169; union strength, 62, 68, 72, 164

Greeley Tribune, 9, 24; articles criticizing Monfort, 55–56, 167, 197(n89); articles supporting Monfort, 40–41, 51, 52, 96; political opinion pieces, 32, 52, 138, 158

Greeley-Weld County Chamber of Commerce, 125

Groves, Dr. Fred B., 118, 203(n38)

Guadalupe House, 20, 21

Guards, machine. *See* Safety and health, equipment controls and maintenance

Hamlet (North Carolina), 176

Harper, Charles M., 97, 126

Harris, Richard Lee, 122, 202(n27), 203(n32)

Haymarket Affair, 140

Hazardous Materials Transportation Act, 128

Health. *See* Safety and health

Helmuth, John, 133

Hensel Phelps Construction Company, 196(n45)

Hill, Norma, 208(n16)

Hill, Sharon, 93, 95, 96, 98

Hispanic Horizons, 48, 49

Hispanics: communities, 10, 11, 13–14 (*see also* Greeley, Hispanic community in); discrimination against, 11–13, 14, 17; Monfort workers, 5, 27, 36, 104

Hormel. *See* George Hormel & Company

Housing: Greeley, 27–28, 193(n42); improvement efforts, 13, 24; subsidized, 28; worker-built *colonias* (Weld County), 11–12, 20

Hubbard, Betty, 95, 99, 103

Hy Grade Foods Corporation, 73, 143

IBP. *See* Iowa Beef Processors

Illness, work-related. *See* Safety and health

Immigrant workers (*see also* Mexicans): alienation of, 26, 28; assistance to, 20–21, 24; communities of, 13, 20;

community attitudes toward, 5, 11–12, 160, 163; competition among groups, 14, 15; conditions in home countries, vii, 5, 19, 148; documentation, 19, 21, 23, 148, 161; farm exploitation of, 11, 14, 15; housing (*see* Housing); incentives for use, 28–29, 160–61, 167; language difficulties, 26, 166; legal rights, knowledge of, 123, 166; meatpacking industry exploitation of, 23, 26, 28, 75, 160, 167; origins, 3, 10, 23; unionization of, 40, 147; work available to, 12, 13, 16, 19, 23–24, 75; workforce percentage, 78

Immigration and Naturalization Service (INS), 21–23; inspections and raids by, 21–22, 122–23, 161–63

Immigration Reform and Control Act (1986), 21–23, 147

Immigration restrictions, 13

Industrial Workers of the World (IWW), 12, 141

Information and Referral Service (Weld County), 41

Injury, work-related. *See* Safety and health

INS. *See* Immigration and Naturalization Service

Inspection. *See* Streamlined Inspection System-Cattle

International Trade Commission, 161

Iowa Beef Processors (IBP), 22, 43, 134, 143; anti-union efforts, 60, 76; Garden City slaughterhouse, 47, 75; injury under-reporting, 109, 115; legal sanctions against, 116, 137, 155, 206(n25); market power, 6, 77, 137, 206(n25); workforce composition, 75 IWW. *See* Industrial Workers of the World

Jackson, Jesse, 103

Jefferson Group, 180

Job competition. *See* Women; World economy, labor competition in Job Service (State of Colorado), 41

John Morrell & Co., 40, 73, 115, 142, 143

Johnson, Christine, 96–97, 98

Johnson, Edwin C., 13

Jones-Costigan Act (1934), 14

Judge, Father Anthony (Tony), 31

Jungle, The, 3, 7

Kadlecek, Jim, 152

Knights of Labor, 141

Krebs, A. V., 75, 134

Labor: as commodity, vii, 139, 160, 207(n39); sources of, 10, 43, 75, 146

Labor relations. *See* Unions

La Colonia, 20

Land ownership, 10, 13, 161; concentration of, 47, 133, 153

Land use, viii

La Raza Unida, 17

Lauenstein, Father Gary, 90–92

Legislation: anti-union, 164; beef imports, 197(n68); corporate interests and, 127; immigrant workers, 28; inspection (*see* Streamlined Inspection System-Cattle); price information, 135; product hazard claims, 50; right-to-work, 37, 72, 126; worker protection, 159, 200–201(n17); workers' compensation, 125, 159

Lexington, Nebraska, 22

Liga Obrera de Hable Espanola, 12

Little, James, 187

Livestock production, viii, 127

Lockout controls, 110, 112, 174–75. *See also* Safety and health, equipment controls and maintenance

Lucero, Ricardo, 24

Mapelli, Roland ("Sonny"), 38, 39, 67, 90–91

Marion, Bruce W., 134

Marshalltown (Iowa), 104

Martial law, 13

Martinez, Delia Anne, 87

Marx, Karl, 150

Master contracts, 73, 143

Meakins, Gene, 38, 48, 69, 103, 194–95(n26); anti-union activities, 93, 117; public announcements, 71, 117, 118, 135, 169

Meat consumption, viii, 39, 42, 52, 72

Meat Cutters union, 72, 74

Meatpackers. *See* Workforce

Meat processing and packing industry: "Big Five" companies, 38; "Big Three" companies, 134; boxed beef (*see* Boxed beef); competition in, 26, 38, 46, 76, 135–36; concentration of power, 6, 46, 52, 61, 75, 76, 128, 133, 143; cost containment, 34, 35; diversification, 136, 143; ergonomic design in, 114, 116, 202(n16); government aid to, 38–39, 137–38; immigrant workers, use of, 15–16, 75, 140; injury rate, 6 (*see also*

Safety and health, injury, work-related); inspection system, 50–52, 136, 155–58; international operations, 147; labor costs, 74, 75, 139; plant closures, 74, 75; plant purchases and sales, 74, 76; plant updating, 74, 75; pricing, 72, 134–35, 142, 199(n25); production process, viii, 3, 18, 36, 40, 74–75, 139, 155; production speed, 4, 76, 114–15, 134, 155, 158–59; product quality (*see* Safety and health, consumers); profitability, 5, 6, 35, 74, 134, 139, 142; size of, viii, 3; unions and (*see* Unions)

Meeker, Nathan, 9

Meilinger, Joel, 91

Merger (Monfort/ConAgra, Inc.), 5–6, 8, 32–33; acquisitions, 77; benefits to company, 42–43, 47; effect on competition, 47

Mexicans. *See also* Hispanics; Immigrant workers: cultural heritage, 17–18; deportation, 21–22, 161, 192(n22); discrimination against, 11–12, 14, 102, 148, 200(n15); military service by, 14; migration by, 19, 161; recruitment for farm work, 15

Military institutions (U.S.), vii

Mirror, The, 49

Monfort, Charlie, 43–44, 130, 204(n59)

Monfort, Edith, 35

Monfort, Inc./Monfort of Colorado, viii; asset acquisition, 61, 77; company policies (*see* Company policies [Monfort]); competition with nonmeat industries, 27; donations and grants, 41; economic conflicts of interests, 35; economic effect in Greeley, 5, 6, 27; environmental violations, 54–56, 197–98(n95); export efforts, 39, 42, 44; feedlot operation, 56, 197–98(n95); government funding for training, 24, 36, 41, 192(n29); Grand Island plant (*see* Grand Island processing plant); Greeley slaughterhouse (*see* Greeley slaughterhouse [Monfort]); illegal aliens, hiring of, 21–23, 161–63; industry competition, 76; injured workers (*see* Safety and health); inspection system in, 50–52, 64, 111, 155–57; intimidation of workers, 22, 59, 62, 68, 101–102; labor law violations, 78–80, 163–64, 169; language barriers at, 26, 193(n35); legal sanctions against, 22,

55, 80, 109, 110, 112, 117, 155, 162, 202(n27), 203(n43), 208(n16); Marshalltown plant, 104; merger with ConAgra (*see* Merger [Monfort/ConAgra, Inc.]); NLRB notice to employees, 185–89; operating costs, 38, 39, 42, 74; political power in Greeley, 18, 25, 54; Portion Foods plant (*see* Portion Foods plant); production capacity, 61, 71; production processes, 36, 42, 45–46, 74, 116, 117, 202(n27); production rate increases, 50, 61–66, 69, 114–117; production rates, 23, 40, 41, 42, 110, 156; profitability, 5, 35, 42, 45, 57, 71, 134; public relations image, 41, 52; records (*see* Company records [Monfort]); restructuring, 18, 34, 39–40, 60; safety (*see* Safety and health); sewage problems, 36–37, 56, 194(n23); shifts, 42; stock sales, 37; supervisor attitudes, 62–64, 67, 97, 102, 107, 111–13, 119, 120, 121, 198(n11); turnover, 20, 22–23, 40, 63, 92, 160; understaffing, 116; unions and (*see* Unions); wages (*see* Wages)

Monfort, Kaye, 44

Monfort, Ken: awards, 31, 49, 56, 167; economic views, 34, 46; foreign policy views, 129–30; industry lobbying, 38–39, 45, 50, 127; minority hiring by, 27; newspaper articles by, xi, 41–42, 52–53, 138, 167; personal and family wealth, 26, 52; political affiliations, 39, 128; political offices, 36; political power, 32, 33, 45, 53, 127; Portion Foods plant meetings, 91–92; as president of American Meat Institute, 45, 46, 50, 53, 114; as president of ConAgra Red Meats, 45, 156; professorship at UNC, 49; public image, 53, 64, 103, 167; retirement, 8, 35, 45, 172; unions and, 93, 96

Monfort, Kyle, 44

Monfort, Myra, xi, 103, 172, 203(n39); as CACI head, 125–26; as corporate legal counsel, 49, 92, 167–68

Monfort, Richard, 37, 43, 44, 157

Monfort, Warren, 35, 37

Monfort Charitable Foundation, 44

Monfort/ConAgra. *See* Monfort of Colorado

Monfort family: charitable projects, 44, 45, 48–49; ownership and wealth, 33, 35–36, 37, 43–44; political power of, 33, 44

Morado, Rosa, 4, 106, 120

Moran, Robert, 155

Morris, 38, 135

MSP Resources, 103–104

Murphy, Edward, 156–57, 171–83

Musick, David, xi

Mutualistas, 13

NAMPU. *See* North American Meatpackers Union

National Agricultural Statistics Service, 47

National Cattlemen's Association, 52, 158

National Endowment for Democracy, 146

National Hog Farms, 54

National Labor Committee in Support of Democracy in El Salvador, 146

National Labor Relations Board, 102; Monfort violation citations, 79, 110, 173; order by, 163–64, 185–89

National Maritime Union, 39, 68

National Packing Company, 135, 136

National Right to Work Committee, 165

Native Americans, 9

Nelson, Pamela, 110–11, 114, 201(n2)

New Mexico, 10–11

New York Tribune, 9

Nixon, Richard M., 137

North American Free Trade Agreement (NAFTA), 147, 161

North American Meatpackers Union (NAMPU), 144

Northern Colorado Brine, 56

Northern Colorado Medical Center, 45, 111, 113, 203(n39)

Norton, Kay, 124–25, 156, 208(n3)

Norton, Tom, 125, 160, 197–98(n95)

Occupational Safety and Health Administration (OSHA), 155, 156; corporate attitude toward, 173, 181–82; employee protection programs, 116, 174, 183; injury log access, 109; proposed actions against Monfort, 110, 117, 172, 177; violations by meatpacking industry, 115, 155–56

Odor pollution and control. (*see* Pollution)

"Official English" initiative, 26, 168

OSHA. *See* Occupational Safety and Health Administration

Our Lady of Peace Church (Greeley), ix, 25, 31; parishioner worker meetings at, 83, 90–91

Owen, David, 126, 165

Packers and Stockyards Administration, 134–35
Packinghouse Workers Organizing Committee, 141, 142
Pattern contracts. *See* Master contracts
Peake, Ora Brookes, 9
Political patronage, 29, 127–29, 135, 152, 158, 159
Pollution: air, 126–27; odor, 54–56; water, 53–54, 197–98(n95)
Portion Foods plant, x, 8; anti-union tactics, 93–94, 96, 101; morale, 85, 88, 94, 97; production speed, 83, 84, 85, 88; strike (1976), 96; strike (1987), 44, 93–100; union in, 90, 92, 93, 95, 99–101; workforce and wages, 36, 92–93, 102, 194(n22); working conditions, 83–89, 93
Potter, Wes, 55, 56
PrairieFire Rural Action, 200–201(n17)
Price leadership, 135, 136
PrimeTime Live (ABC), 51

Racism, 12, 13, 14, 102, 108, 129–30, 141; as management tool, 99, 107, 149, 151
Ranching. *See* Farming
REAP. *See* Research, Education, Advocacy, People
Recession, economic, ix, 34, 38, 160
Red meat. *See* Meat consumption
Repetitive motion disorders, 3, 83, 109, 111, 114–19, 174
Research, Education, Advocacy, People (REAP), 77–78
Research methods, ix–x, 7, 167
Retail Clerks International Union, 72, 143
Return to the Jungle, 155
Rifkin, Jeremy, 52
Right-to-work legislation, 37, 72, 126
Rocky Mountain Fuel Company, 12
Rocky Mountain Service Employment and Redevelopment (SER), 23, 41
Rodriguez, Joaquina, 16, 17, 18, 25
Rodriguez, Pedro, 16, 25, 38
Rodriquez, Roberto, 112
Romer, Roy, 50, 98, 204(n59)

Safety and health: additive regulation violations, 34, 194(n15); additive regulations, 38; additives, 197(n68); ambulance service, 196(n47); backhaul trucking, 34; consumers, 50, 136,

157–59; deaths, work-related, 110, 112, 208(n16); equipment controls and maintenance, 93, 97, 110, 175–76; Food and Drug Administration standards, 56; hazard claims, unsupported, 50; hearing problems, 65–66, 118; illnesses, work-related, 3, 66, 85, 89, 156; injuries, work-related, 3, 4, 16, 65–67, 88–89, 93, 97, 110–13, 156; inspection of meat (*see* Streamlined Inspection System-Cattle); knife condition, 66, 83, 84, 173; liability and releases, 112; medical staff, company, 85–87, 89, 105; medical treatment, private, 85, 113, 118; monitors, 85; OSHA and (*see* Occupational Safety and Health Administration); repetitive motion disorders, 3, 83, 109, 111, 114–19, 174; statistics at Monfort plant, 6, 31, 53, 117–18, 202(n31); statistics generally, 3–4, 114, 155; studies, 117, 118, 203(n39); under-reporting, 40, 115, 117, 159; workers' compensation (*see* Workers' compensation); workplace violations, 31, 110, 112, 117, 174–77
Safety Training Observation Program, 182
Safe Workplace Colorado!, 159, 208(n18)
St. Peter's Church (Greeley), 25, 92
Salazar, Secundino (Sal), ix, 13, 14, 20, 25; Chicano groups, work with, 17–18; history, 10, 11; as union steward, 37
Sanctions, legal, 23. *See also* Monfort, Inc./Monfort of Colorado, legal sanctions against
San Joaquin Valley (California), 27
Scabs, 164; Portion Foods plant strike, 95, 96, 98, 101
Schmidt, Elaine, ix
SER. *See* Rocky Mountain Service Employment and Redevelopment Sexism, 99, 106, 107, 151
Sexual harassment, 98–99
Sinclair, Upton, 3, 7, 136, 205(n14)
SIPCO. *See* Swift Independent Packing Corporation
SIS-C. *See* Streamlined Inspection System-Cattle
SLC. *See* Stockyards Labor Council
Smith, Gary, 49
Smith, Jo Ann, 158
Smith, Marvin, 111, 120, 121, 122
Social assistance programs, 20–21, 124
Social Democrats-USA, 146
Socialism, 148, 150–51, 153, 164

Spanish-American Citizens Association, 13
Spohr, Jim, 60, 61, 63, 66, 69, 70
Stander, Patty, 110–11
State Grievance Committee, 118
Steig, Dr. Richard, 203(n38)
Stein, Dan, 23
Stockyards Labor Council (SLC), 141
Streamlined Inspection System-Cattle (USDA), 155–58, 172, 173, 182; purposes of, 50–52, 136; violations, 51–52, 155–56, 157
Strikes, 140, 142, 206(n30); coal miners, 12; Greeley slaughterhouse (*see* Greeley slaughterhouse [Monfort]); meatpacking plants, 77, 143; Portion Foods plant (*see* Portion foods plant); public support for, 44; union support for, 77, 143; worker support for, 77, 143
Sugar beet industry, 10, 12, 13, 14, 15
Sunrise Medical Clinic, 113, 203(n39)
Swift & Company, 5, 38, 39, 43, 135, 142, 206(n25); master contract with, 73, 143; size, 75
Swift Independent Packing Corporation (SIPCO), 74, 75
Sykes, Charlie, 101, 103, 164, 199–200(n37); labor law violation charges, 79, 200–201(n17); Portion Foods plant negotiating, 93–94

Taft-Hartley Act, 142
Taxes, 28
Teamsters union, 76, 104, 143, 144
Third World, vii, 130, 204(n60)
Thomas, Steve, 40, 62, 65, 67; union representation prestrike, 61, 68, 69, 70; union representation poststrike, 78, 80–81
Tointon, Robert, 196(n45)
Torres, Viviano, ix, xi, 19, 108, 120
Trade, international, viii
Transitional House, 21
Trout Unlimited, 56
Truman, Harry S., 142
Tungate, Sue, ix

UFCW. *See* United Food and Commercial Workers Union
UFWA. *See* United Farm Workers of America
UNC. *See* University of Northern Colorado
Unemployment benefits, 70
Union Colony, 9–10

Union Hall Lounge, 71
Union Pacific Railroad, 10, 11
Unions. *See also* individual unions: alliances outside unions, 146–47, 152; backdoor deals, 76, 203(n33); community opposition to, 59–60, 67, 70; conflict among workers, 12, 141, 148; conflict with workers, 7, 40, 73–74, 80, 99, 139, 141, 144, 165; Coors Company, relations with, 49; corporate opposition to, viii, 37, 75, 76, 139; foreign policy and, 144–47; government opposition to, 145–46, 165; in Grand Island plant, 39, 68, 195(n28); in Greeley slaughterhouse (*see* Greeley slaughterhouse [Monfort]); history of efforts, 140–44; immigrant workers and, 12, 147, 148–49; international efforts, 144–47, 148; labor force restructuring and, 75, 99; lawsuits, 80–81, 95, 143–44, 153; locals, 74, 143; master contracts, 73, 143; Monfort anti-union efforts, 59–60, 69, 70, 73, 93, 99, 117, 143, 169; Monfort notice to employees regarding, 185–89; NLRB suit, 198(n3); nonmeat industries, 12, 72–73, 149, 196(n45); organization, obstacles to, 15, 40, 59–60, 76, 139; in Portion Foods plant (*see* Portion Foods plant); power, 143, 151; purpose, 7, 100–101, 144, 152; salaries of officials, 77, 199(n36); scabs (*see* Scabs); strikes (*see* Strikes); structure, 72, 74, 81, 152; sweetheart deals, 68, 143, 203(n33); in Weld County, 27, 126; worker representation by, 78, 108, 149, 165–66
United Agri Products, 196(n63)
United Farm Workers of America (UFWA), 148, 207(n36)
United Food and Commercial Workers Union (UFCW), x, 72, 117, 185; conflicts with workers, 68, 73, 77, 80, 99–100, 144; in Grand Island plant, 110, 162; in Greeley slaughterhouse (*see* Greeley slaughterhouse [Monfort]); internal power struggles, 73, 74, 99, 144; leadership, 74, 80, 99, 144; in Marshalltown plant, 104; membership, 74, 76, 147; in Portion Foods plant (*see* Portion Foods plant); power, 76, 77, 143; structure, 74, 78 United Labor Party, 140
United Packinghouse Workers, 142, 143, 206(n26)

United States Department of Agriculture: Packers and Stockyards Administration, 134–35; SIS-C program (*see* Streamlined Inspection System-Cattle) United States Department of Labor, 41
United Way, 44
University of Northern Colorado (UNC) (Greeley), ix, 32, 196(n45); Greeley community, relations with, 48–49; ConAgra, patronage relationship with, 48–50, 196(n63); journalism at, 48–49; language classes, 193(n35); professorships, 48, 49
University of Northern Colorado Foundation, 97
University of Southern Colorado (Pueblo), 49
Urban, Father Leonard, 92
Urban, Father Peter, 25, 92
USDA. *See* United States Department of Agriculture

Val-Agri, 47, 75
Valdez, Guadalupe, 113
Valencia, Martha, 101
Ventilation, inadequate, 175. *See also* Safety and health Villa, George, ix, 111–12, 201(n9)

Wages: adequacy, 28; competition with other employers, 26, 193(n37); contracts, avoiding, 75; employer suppression, 27, 28; improvement opportunities, 33; increases, 67; labor availability, 27, 28; overtime and cutbacks, 120, 203(n43); reduction, 3, 5, 39, 40, 60, 74–75, 195(n31); regulation, 13–14; two-tier system, 68, 75, 93, 103–104
Walker, Arden, 195(n34)
Water: pollution (*see* Pollution); rights, sale of, 37; use, viii, 193(n37); wastewater treatment, 56, 104
Weld County: Economic Development Action Partnership, 27; economy of, x, 27–28; Health Department, 55, 56, 102; immigrant *colonias,* 11; Information and Referral Service, 41; labor force, 43; land ownership, 47; political representation of, 126, 160; prisoner of war camps in, 14–15; wage scale, 27; waste treatment, 37, 54; water pollution in, 53–54

Weld County Medical Society, 118
Whelan, Elizabeth M., 158
Whistleblower protection, 51, 177–183
Wilson Foods Corporation, 38, 73, 74, 142, 143
Windsor (Colorado), 27, 126
Wobblies. *See* Industrial Workers of the World
Women, 14, 15, 207(n35); family responsibilities, 106–107; job capabilities, 201–202(n16); job competition by, vii, 107; leadership by, 149–50, 152; Portion Foods plant (*see* Portion Foods plant); sexual harassment, 98–99; single mothers, 76, 152; workforce presence, 3, 14, 41, 76, 78, 104, 140, 160
Women's Place, 20–21
Workday, length of, 140–41
Worker health and safety. *See* Safety and health
Workers' compensation: claim process, effectiveness and abuses, 124–25, 204(n49); company avoidance of claims, 85, 88, 90, 105, 111, 113, 118, 123; costs, 156, 159–60; releases of liability, 112; state advisory committee, 118
Workers' Compensation Coalition, 125
Workforce (U.S.): composition of, vii, 3, 75–76, 78, 149; "de-skilled," 36, 42, 109; ethnic antagonism in, 14, 102, 105, 149; immigrants (*see* Immigrant workers); nonunion groups, 159, 209(n41); turnover, 5, 76; unity, need for, 102–103, 108, 131, 139, 145, 149, 150–54, 165
Working conditions, 1–2, 3–4, 16–17; benefits (*see* Benefits); Greeley slaughterhouse (*see* Greeley slaughterhouse [Monfort]); Portion Foods plant (*see* Portion Foods plant); safety (*see* Safety and health); speed required, 4, 20, 66, 83, 84, 105, 114–19; stress, 3, 4, 66, 72, 83
Work Injured Citizens Coalition of Colorado, x, 19, 159
Workplace Fairness Act, 165
Workplace safety. *See* Safety and health
World economy, 130, 153; free production zones, vii, 146, 206–207(n32); effect on rural areas, x, 133, 137, 160–61; effect on national economies, vii, 34, 131; labor competition in, vii, 144, 146
Wynn, William, 68, 74